COMPUTER
BOOK SERIES
FROM IDG

Perl 5 For Dummies

W9-CTK-113

Cheat Sheet

The Most Useful File Tests

Test	Description
-e	File exists
-r	File can be read
-w	File can be written to
-z	File is exactly zero bytes long
-d	Named item is a directory, not a file
-T	File is a text file (the first hunk of a file is examined, and it's a text file if fewer than 30 percent or so of the characters are non-printable)
-B	File is a binary file (this is the exact opposite of the -T test)
-s	Size of the file in bytes
-C	Creation age of file
-A	Access age of file
-M	Modification age of file

Special Characters

Character	Meaning
\n	Newline
\r	Carriage return
\t	Tab character
\f	Formfeed character
\b	Backspace character
\v	Vertical tab
\a	Bell or beep
\e	Escape character

Common List Functions

Function	splice Equivalent	What It Does
push(@r, @s)	splice(@r, $#r+1, 0, @s)	Adds to the right of the list
pop(@r)	splice(@r, $#r, 1)	Removes from the right of the list
shift(@r)	splice(@r, 0, 1)	Removes from the left of the list
unshift(@r, @s)	splice(@r, 0, 0, @s)	Adds to the left of the list

IDG
BOOKS
WORLDWIDE

...For Dummies: #1 Computer Book Series for Beginners

Perl 5 For Dummies®

True-False Comparison Operators

Comparison	Math	String
Equal to	==	eq
Not equal to	!=	ne
Less than	<	lt
Greater than	>	gt
Less than or equal to	<=	le
Greater than or equal to	>=	ge

Pattern-Matching Quantifiers in Regular Expressions

Symbol	Meaning
+	Match 1 or more times
*	Match 0 or more times
?	Match 0 or 1 time
{n}	Match exactly n times
{n,}	Match at least n times
{n,m}	Match at least n but not more than m times (these values must be less than 65,536)

Shortcuts for Character Ranges in Regular Expressions

Code	Replaces	Description
\d	[0..9]	Any digit
\w	[a-zA-Z_0-9]	Any alphanumeric character
\s	[\t\n\r\f]	A whitespace character
\D	^[0..9]	Any non-digit
\W	^[a-zA-Z_0-9]	Any non-alpha-numeric character
\S	^[\t\n\r\f]	A non-whitespace character

...For Dummies: #1 Computer Book Series for Beginners

PERL 5 FOR DUMMIES®

by Paul E. Hoffman

IDG Books Worldwide, Inc.
An International Data Group Company

Foster City, CA ♦ Chicago, IL ♦ Indianapolis, IN ♦ New York, NY

Perl 5 For Dummies ®

Published by
IDG Books Worldwide, Inc.
An International Data Group Company
919 E. Hillsdale Blvd.
Suite 400
Foster City, CA 94404
www.idgbooks.com (IDG Books Worldwide Web site)
www.dummies.com (Dummies Press Web site)

Library of Congress Catalog Card No.: 96-77278

ISBN: 0-7645-0044-9

Printed in the United States of America

10 9 8 7 6 5 4 3 2

1DD/RS/QV/ZY/IN

Distributed in the United States by IDG Books Worldwide, Inc.

Distributed by Macmillan Canada for Canada; by Transworld Publishers Limited in the United Kingdom; by IDG Norge Books for Norway; by IDG Sweden Books for Sweden; by Woodslane Pty. Ltd. for Australia; by Woodslane Enterprises Ltd. for New Zealand; by Longman Singapore Publishers Ltd. for Singapore, Malaysia, Thailand, and Indonesia; by Simron Pty. Ltd. for South Africa; by Toppan Company Ltd. for Japan; by Distribuidora Cuspide for Argentina; by Livraria Cultura for Brazil; by Ediciencia S.A. for Ecuador; by Addison-Wesley Publishing Company for Korea; by Ediciones ZETA S.C.R. Ltda. for Peru; by WS Computer Publishing Corporation, Inc., for the Philippines; by Unalis Corporation for Taiwan; by Contemporanea de Ediciones for Venezuela; by Computer Book & Magazine Store for Puerto Rico; by Express Computer Distributors for the Caribbean and West Indies. Authorized Sales Agent: Anthony Rudkin Associates for the Middle East and North Africa.

For general information on IDG Books Worldwide's books in the U.S., please call our Consumer Customer Service department at 800-762-2974. For reseller information, including discounts and premium sales, please call our Reseller Customer Service department at 800-434-3422.

For information on where to purchase IDG Books Worldwide's books outside the U.S., please contact our International Sales department at 650-655-3200 or fax 650-655-3295.

For information on foreign language translations, please contact our Foreign & Subsidiary Rights department at 650-655-3021 or fax 650-655-3281.

For sales inquiries and special prices for bulk quantities, please contact our Sales department at 650-655-3200 or write to the address above.

For information on using IDG Books Worldwide's books in the classroom or for ordering examination copies, please contact our Educational Sales department at 800-434-2086 or fax 817-251-8174.

For press review copies, author interviews, or other publicity information, please contact our Public Relations department at 650-655-3000 or fax 650-655-3299.

For authorization to photocopy items for corporate, personal, or educational use, please contact Copyright Clearance Center, 222 Rosewood Drive, Danvers, MA 01923, or fax 978-750-4470.

is a trademark under exclusive license to IDG Books Worldwide, Inc., from International Data Group, Inc.

About the Author

Paul E. Hoffman has written more than a dozen computer books, many of them about the Internet (including *Netscape and the World Wide Web For Dummies* and *The Internet*, the official book of the Public Television presentation "The Internet Show," both from IDG Books Worldwide, Inc.); in fact, he's been active on the Internet for more than 15 years. As a founder of the Internet Mail Consortium, he is responsible for the popular Web service there as well as the mail response system. He also organized the Internet Computer Index. Since 1987, he has been the News Editor at *MicroTimes,* the largest regional computer magazine in the United States.

ABOUT IDG BOOKS WORLDWIDE

Welcome to the world of IDG Books Worldwide.

IDG Books Worldwide, Inc., is a subsidiary of International Data Group, the world's largest publisher of computer-related information and the leading global provider of information services on information technology. IDG was founded more than 25 years ago and now employs more than 8,500 people worldwide. IDG publishes more than 275 computer publications in over 75 countries (see listing below). More than 60 million people read one or more IDG publications each month.

Launched in 1990, IDG Books Worldwide is today the #1 publisher of best-selling computer books in the United States. We are proud to have received eight awards from the Computer Press Association in recognition of editorial excellence and three from *Computer Currents'* First Annual Readers' Choice Awards. Our best-selling *...For Dummies*® series has more than 30 million copies in print with translations in 30 languages. IDG Books Worldwide, through a joint venture with IDG's Hi-Tech Beijing, became the first U.S. publisher to publish a computer book in the People's Republic of China. In record time, IDG Books Worldwide has become the first choice for millions of readers around the world who want to learn how to better manage their businesses.

Our mission is simple: Every one of our books is designed to bring extra value and skill-building instructions to the reader. Our books are written by experts who understand and care about our readers. The knowledge base of our editorial staff comes from years of experience in publishing, education, and journalism — experience we use to produce books for the '90s. In short, we care about books, so we attract the best people. We devote special attention to details such as audience, interior design, use of icons, and illustrations. And because we use an efficient process of authoring, editing, and desktop publishing our books electronically, we can spend more time ensuring superior content and spend less time on the technicalities of making books.

You can count on our commitment to deliver high-quality books at competitive prices on topics you want to read about. At IDG Books Worldwide, we continue in the IDG tradition of delivering quality for more than 25 years. You'll find no better book on a subject than one from IDG Books Worldwide.

John Kilcullen
CEO
IDG Books Worldwide, Inc.

Steven Berkowitz
President and Publisher
IDG Books Worldwide, Inc.

Eighth Annual
Computer Press
Awards ≥1992

Ninth Annual
Computer Press
Awards ≥1993

Tenth Annual
Computer Press
Awards ≥1994

Eleventh Annual
Computer Press
Awards ≥1995

IDG Books Worldwide, Inc., is a subsidiary of International Data Group, the world's largest publisher of computer-related information and the leading global provider of information services on information technology. International Data Group publishes over 275 computer publications in over 75 countries. Sixty million people read one or more International Data Group publications each month. International Data Group's publications include: **ARGENTINA:** Buyer's Guide, Computerworld Argentina, PC World Argentina; **AUSTRALIA:** Australian Macworld, Australian PC World, Australian Reseller News, Computerworld, IT Casebook, Network World, Publish, Webmaster; **AUSTRIA:** Computerwelt Osterreich, Networks Austria, PC Tip Austria; **BANGLADESH:** PC World Bangladesh; **BELARUS:** PC World Belarus; **BELGIUM:** Data News; **BRAZIL:** Annuário de Informática, Computerworld, Connections, Macworld, PC Player, PC World, Publish, Reseller News, Supergamepower; **BULGARIA:** Computerworld Bulgaria, Network World Bulgaria, PC & MacWorld Bulgaria; **CANADA:** CIO Canada, Client/Server World, ComputerWorld Canada, InfoWorld Canada, NetworkWorld Canada, WebWorld; **CHILE:** Computerworld Chile, PC World Chile; **COLOMBIA:** Computerworld Colombia, PC World Colombia; **COSTA RICA:** PC World Centro America; **THE CZECH AND SLOVAK REPUBLICS:** Computerworld Czechoslovakia, Macworld Czech Republic, PC World Czechoslovakia; **DENMARK:** Communications World Danmark, Computerworld Danmark, Macworld Danmark, PC World Danmark, Techworld Denmark; **DOMINICAN REPUBLIC:** PC World Republica Dominicana; **ECUADOR:** PC World Ecuador; **EGYPT:** Computerworld Middle East, PC World Middle East; **EL SALVADOR:** PC World Centro America; **FINLAND:** MikroPC, Tietoverkko, Tietoviikko; **FRANCE:** Distributique, Hebdo, Info PC, Le Monde Informatique, Macworld, Reseaux & Telecoms, WebMaster France; **GERMANY:** Computer Partner, Computerwoche, Computerwoche Extra, Computerwoche FOCUS, Global Online, Macwelt, PC Welt; **GREECE:** Amiga Computing, GamePro Greece, Multimedia World; **GUATEMALA:** PC World Centro America; **HONDURAS:** PC World Centro America; **HONG KONG:** Computerworld Hong Kong, PC World Hong Kong, Publish in Asia; **HUNGARY:** ABCD CD-ROM, Computerworld Szamitastechnika, Internetto online Magazine, PC World Hungary, PC-X Magazin Hungary; **ICELAND:** Tolvuheimur PC World Island; **INDIA:** Information Communications World, Information Systems Computerworld, PC World India, Publish in Asia; **INDONESIA:** InfoKomputer PC World, Komputek Computerworld, Publish in Asia; **IRELAND:** ComputerScope, PC Live!; **ISRAEL:** Macworld Israel, People & Computers/Computerworld; **ITALY:** Computerworld Italia, Macworld Italia, Networking Italia, PC World Italia; **JAPAN:** DTP World, Macworld Japan, Nikkei Personal Computing, OS/2 World Japan, SunWorld Japan, Windows NT World, Windows World Japan; **KENYA:** PC World East African; **KOREA:** Hi-Tech Information, Macworld Korea, PC World Korea; **MACEDONIA:** PC World Macedonia; **MALAYSIA:** Computerworld Malaysia, PC World Malaysia, Publish in Asia; **MALTA:** PC World Malta; **MEXICO:** Computerworld Mexico, PC World Mexico; **MYANMAR:** PC World Myanmar; **NETHERLANDS:** Computer! Totaal, LAN Internetworking Magazine, LAN World Buyers Guide, Macworld Netherlands, Net, WebWereld; **NEW ZEALAND:** Absolute Beginners Guide and Plain & Simple Series, Computer Buyer, Computer Industry Directory, Computerworld New Zealand, MTB, Network World, PC World New Zealand; **NICARAGUA:** PC World Centro America; **NORWAY:** Computerworld Norge, CW Rapport, Datamagasinet, Financial Rapport, Kursguide Norge, Macworld Norge, Multimediaworld Norge, PC World Ekspress Norge, PC World Nettverk, PC World Norge, PC World ProduktGuide Norge; **PAKISTAN:** Computerworld Pakistan; **PANAMA:** PC World Panama; **PEOPLE'S REPUBLIC OF CHINA:** China Computer Users, China Computerworld, China InfoWorld, China Telecom World Weekly, Computer & Communication, Electronic Design China, Electronics Today, Electronics Weekly, Game Software, PC World China, Popular Computer Week, Software Weekly, Software World, Telecom World; **PERU:** Computerworld Peru, PC World Profesional Peru, PC World SoHo Peru; **PHILIPPINES:** Click!, Computerworld Philippines, PC World Philippines, Publish in Asia; **POLAND:** Computerworld Poland, Computerworld Special Report Poland, Cyber, Macworld Poland, Networld Poland, PC World Komputer; **PORTUGAL:** Cerebro/PC World, Computerworld/Correio Informático, Dealer World Portugal, Mac*In/PC*In Portugal, Multimedia World; **PUERTO RICO:** PC World Puerto Rico; **ROMANIA:** Computerworld Romania, PC World Romania, Telecom Romania; **RUSSIA:** Computerworld Russia, Mir PK, Publish, Seti; **SINGAPORE:** Computerworld Singapore, PC World Singapore, Publish in Asia; **SLOVENIA:** Monitor; **SOUTH AFRICA:** Computing SA, Network World SA, Software World SA; **SPAIN:** Communicaciones World España, Computerworld España, Dealer World España, Macworld España, PC World España; **SRI LANKA:** Infolink PC World; **SWEDEN:** CAP&Design, Computer Sweden, Corporate Computing Sweden, Internetworld Sweden, it branschen, Macworld Sweden, MaxiData Sweden, MikroDatorn, Nätverk & Kommunikation, PC World Sweden, PCaktiv, Windows World Sweden; **SWITZERLAND:** Computerworld Schweiz, Macworld Schweiz, PCtip; **TAIWAN:** Computerworld Taiwan, Macworld Taiwan, NEW ViSiON/Publish, PC World Taiwan, Windows World Taiwan; **THAILAND:** Publish in Asia, Thai Computerworld; **TURKEY:** Computerworld Turkiye, Macworld Turkiye, Network World Turkiye, PC World Turkiye; **UKRAINE:** Computerworld Kiev, Multimedia World Ukraine, PC World Ukraine; **UNITED KINGDOM:** Acorn User UK, Amiga Action UK, Amiga Computing UK, Apple Talk UK, Computing, Macworld, Parents and Computers UK, PC Advisor, PC Home, PSX Pro, The WEB; **UNITED STATES:** Cable in the Classroom, CIO Magazine, Computerworld, DOS World, Federal Computer Week, GamePro Magazine, InfoWorld, I-Way, Macworld, Network World, PC Games, PC World, Publish, Video Event, THE WEB Magazine, and WebMaster; online webzines: JavaWorld, NetscapeWorld, and SunWorld Online; **URUGUAY:** InfoWorld Uruguay; **VENEZUELA:** Computerworld Venezuela, PC World Venezuela; and **VIETNAM:** PC World Vietnam.   3/24/97

Author's Acknowledgments

The Perl world is full of very helpful people who will answer questions for just about anyone. Perl's main developer, Larry Wall, started this trend when he released Perl, and there are now hundreds of people on various Usenet news groups and mailing lists who are keeping alive the spirit of cooperation. Many of my ideas in this book have come from things these people have said in different forums over the past few years. Tens of thousands of hours have been spent on making Perl free and useful, and I'm grateful for all this effort by Perl enthusiasts all over the world (and you should be too!).

This is my second book in the ...*For Dummies* series, and I'd like to repeat what I said in my first book. Writing for computer novices is always easier if you have a few of them around asking you questions. My close circle of novices and ex-novices keeps me on my toes and reminds me what is not obvious, how frustrating it can be when the system is designed by know-it-all dweebs, and what parts are fun. I am indebted to my friends, my family, and my family-by-choice.

All the folks at IDG Books Worldwide, Inc., who worked on this book, have helped in many ways. I am thankful for their efforts and patience.

Publisher's Acknowledgments

We're proud of this book; please register your comments through our IDG Books Worldwide Online Registration Form located at: http://my2cents.dummies.com.

Some of the people who helped bring this book to market include the following:

Acquisitions, Development, and Editorial

Project Editor: Bill Helling

Acquisitions Editor: Gareth Hancock

Product Development Director: Mary Bednarek

Media Development Manager: Joyce Pepple

Associate Permissions Editor: Heather H. Dismore

Copy Editor: Michael Simsic

Technical Editor: Publication Services, Inc.

Editorial Manager: Mary C. Corder

Editorial Assistant: Chris H. Collins

Production

Project Coordinators: Debbie Stailey, Valery Bourke

Layout and Graphics: Theresa Ball, Brett Black, Cameron Booker, Linda M. Boyer, Elizabeth Cárdenas-Nelson, J. Tyler Connor, Dominique DeFelice, Angela F. Hunckler, Todd Klemme, Ruth Loiacano, Jane Martin, Drew R. Moore, Mark C. Owens, Anna Rohrer, Brent Savage, Michael Sullivan

Proofreaders: Melissa D. Buddendeck, Nancy Reinhardt, Rachel Garvey, Nancy Price, Robert Springer, Ethel Winslow, Karen York

Indexer: Steve Rath

Special Help: Kevin Spencer, Associate Technical Editor; Access Technology, Inc.

General and Administrative

IDG Books Worldwide, Inc.: John Kilcullen, CEO; Steven Berkowitz, President and Publisher

IDG Books Technology Publishing: Brenda McLaughlin, Senior Vice President and Group Publisher

Dummies Technology Press and Dummies Editorial: Diane Graves Steele, Vice President and Associate Publisher; Mary Bednarek, Director of Acquisitions and Product Development; Kristin A. Cocks, Editorial Director

Dummies Trade Press: Kathleen A. Welton, Vice President and Publisher; Kevin Thornton, Acquisitions Manager

IDG Books Production for Dummies Press: Beth Jenkins Roberts, Production Director; Cindy L. Phipps, Manager of Project Coordination, Production Proofreading, and Indexing; Kathie S. Schutte, Supervisor of Page Layout; Shelley Lea, Supervisor of Graphics and Design; Debbie J. Gates, Production Systems Specialist; Robert Springer, Supervisor of Proofreading; Debbie Stailey, Special Projects Coordinator; Tony Augsburger, Supervisor of Reprints and Bluelines; Leslie Popplewell, Media Archive Coordinator

Dummies Packaging and Book Design: Patti Crane, Packaging Specialist; Kavish + Kavish, Cover Design

◆

The publisher would like to give special thanks to Patrick J. McGovern, without whom this book would not have been possible.

◆

Contents at a Glance

Cartoons at a Glance

By Rich Tennant

Fax: 978-546-7747 • *E-mail:* the5wave@tiac.net

Table of Contents

Introduction

· ·

*W*elcome to *Perl 5 For Dummies*! You should know that you are not a
dummy. On the other hand, you are probably not a full-time programmer or computer science professor, either. If you were, you'd probably be
looking at the more "professional-looking" Perl books on the shelf near this
one. More than 90 percent of the people you meet do not know anything
about programming, so it would be silly to call *everyone* a dummy: Who else
would be left? So, because you're probably neither a dummy nor a nerd, this
book will be the right one for you.

This book's title comes from the name of the very popular book that started
the entire series: *DOS For Dummies.* The book and the . . .*For Dummies* series
are quite popular — . . .*For Dummies* books exist on every possible computer topic, and also on many noncomputer topics like sex and investing.

With computer technology advancing so rapidly, it's no wonder that many
people feel left behind, and thus may label themselves a "dummy." But
you're not alone in feeling left behind. When you finish this book, you'll
know more about how to program than most people do. As it turns out, Perl
is one of the easiest programming languages to learn and use, so you made
the right decision in choosing both the Perl programming language *and* this
book!

About This Book

If you're interested in discovering how to program, *Perl 5 For Dummies* is for
you. If you already know something about programming (but not about
Perl), this book is also for you. If you are already an expert programmer,
you're welcome to read this book, but it isn't really intended for folks
like you.

No programming experience required!

Many computer novices think, "I can never learn to program, it's too hard." So, they don't even start. If that were the case, there would be no programmers: Everyone was a novice at one time. This book shows you how to program, even if you've never done any programming before.

Many people forget that we all have to start somewhere and that we often end up in different places when we're done. After learning how to program Perl with this book, you may decide to go on and become someone who makes his or her living programming Perl. You may also decide that, although programming is interesting, a career in programming isn't something that you want to do. Millions of people have learned how to program, but don't do it on a regular basis.

There is a chance (but I think it is a slight chance) that you will learn to program in Perl and decide that, although you like programming, you don't like Perl. Fortunately, most of the Perl programming skills that you learn in this book can also be useful if you want to learn a different programming language later. Perl is easier than most programming languages to learn and use — Perl uses many of the same concepts as other languages, making it an excellent first programming language to learn.

What You Should Know Before You Read This Book

There are a few things that you should know before you read this book. I'm assuming that you have a computer, or have access to a computer, and you know a little bit about how to use it. By a "little bit," I mean things like how to turn on the computer, how to move around in the directories, and how to run basic programs.

This book covers how to use Perl under four different operating systems: Unix, Windows 95, Windows NT, and Macintosh. To use this book to learn Perl programming, you need to know how to use at least one of these operating systems. Note that you do *not* need to know more than one operating system, and only a few people know how to use all four. If you are one of those people who's familiar with all four of these operating systems, you can enjoy the title of Computer Dweeb and know that very few of the rest of the world has these skills.

So, you don't need to know anything about programming, or even what Perl is, to get lots of value from this book. However, you do need to know the very basics of using your computer so that you can follow the directions in this book on how to load Perl and create text files that Perl can use as programs. In most cases, if you've used your computer for more than a week or two, you'll be just fine.

What You'll Find In This Book

Because this book is meant for both programming novices and folks who already know a little about programming (but not Perl), I've arranged the book so that both groups of people can quickly find what they want. Most people will read the book straight through, but if you're one of those folks who skips around, you may find it useful to know how the book is arranged.

Part I: Getting Going with Perl

Part I tells you what programming is, what Perl is, and what it means "to program." This part contains some example programs so that you can see what programs look like and how they are put together.

Part II: Most of What You Need

By the time you finish Part I, you'll know most of the raw facts that you need in order to write your own Perl programs. Part II contains lots of additional facts and lots of programming examples. When you're done with this part, you will probably have written a few of your own short programs.

Part III: The Nuts and Bolts on the Perl

After all these facts, you may want to know some of the nuts and bolts of Perl, which is the topic of Part III. This part shows you how to structure Perl programs, how you can put together larger programs, and how you tell Perl to read and write files on your computer.

Part IV: Advanced Perl Is Still Somewhat Easy

This part covers many of the more advanced topics in Perl. Novice programmers aren't really expected to use these features immediately, but if you are one of those novices who zooms ahead (and you may surprise yourself if you think, "Nah, that's not me"), you'll find lots of useful information in these chapters.

Part V: The Part of Tens

The last major part of this book has an odd title, doesn't it? All ...*For Dummies* books have a "Part of Tens" at the end. This part contains a nice, lightweight group of lists of interesting information about Perl.

Appendixes

This book has two appendixes: information about the contents of that CD-ROM at the back of the book, and a complete Perl reference that you can use as you create your programs.

Typestyles in This Book

It seems like all computer books and manuals must have a section talking about the typestyles used in the book, and this book is no different. I find this to be a quaint habit, but I've been doing it for my 18 years of writing, so why stop now?

Throughout the book, you will find lines that show examples of Perl programs that look like this:

```
print "Hello, world!\n";
```

Those lines are in a distinctive, not-terribly-attractive typestyle so you can tell the difference between lines of programming code and the regular text.

You will also see examples of this kind of same typestyle in the body text `like this` to indicate that `this text` is a part of a Perl program.

Icons Used in This Book

One of the fun things about writing books in the ...*For Dummies* series is that you get to use these stylized icons in the text. I tried not to go overboard with the icons, so you won't find them on every page, but you will find them sprinkled around the book.

A note that you may find useful. Of course, you will hopefully find everything in the book useful, but these tips are especially useful.

Something that you should look out for. A couple of important *gotchas* are buried in Perl, and these warnings can help steer you clear of them.

A sidenote about something particularly dweeby. Mind you, learning a programming language is, in and of itself, sort of dweeby, but these icons point out technical information that isn't particularly necessary to know, but handy nonetheless.

This book covers two versions of Perl: Perl 4 and Perl 5. The two versions are quite similar, and you can still get great value out of the book even if you're using version 4. This icon highlights features that are specific to the new version, Perl 5.

Perl Awaits You

Okay, enough of this gentle introductory stuff. It's time to plunge right in and learn about programming and Perl. Within a few chapters, you'll be writing your own programs. So settle in, turn on the learning part of your brain, and enjoy!

Part I
Getting Going with Perl

The 5th Wave

By Rich Tennant

"Great goulash, Stan. That reminds me, are you still scripting your own Web page in Perl?"

In this part . . .

You've got to start somewhere, and the beginning is the best place, is it not? In these first few chapters, you find out what a programming language is, what Perl is, and what Perl programs look like. You may also discover how much fun it is to program in Perl!

Some people think that if they learn to program, they can write any kind of program for their computer. "I have this great idea for a word processor that's different than the ones I've seen." "I'll create an Internet program that makes Netscape look like a kid's toy!" "There are no good programs that convert English into ancient Greek: I'll create one and make a fortune." And on and on.

The problem is that, although all these programs are possible, each would take months or years to create. When you learn to program, you learn to create simple programs. To create complex ones, you have to practice, practice, practice, usually full time. After you finish this book, you'll certainly be able to create lots of simple programs, but not a word processor, Internet browser, or English-to-ancient-Greek translator (although the latter is certainly possible with Perl).

Yet, people still want to learn to program. There are probably many reasons for this, including the following:

- ✔ Some people still think that all computer professionals are programmers. If they want to get into the computer business, they think they have to become programmers. This is certainly not the case, but it is a common misconception held by people outside the industry.

- ✔ Learning programming is a good way to understand how computer programs work. Because everything that happens on your computer is controlled by one program or another, learning what it takes to create programs is a good way to learn what makes your computer tick.

- ✔ Programming is fun, at least to some people. If you like computers and like to create things, programs are great things to create. Programming is also great for tinkerers, because once you create a program, you can change it a bit here, add a few features there, and so on.

- ✔ Professional programmers get paid big bucks, and there are jobs for them all over the world. Note, however, most of the programmer jobs you see advertised in the Sunday paper are for experienced programmers, and there is an absurdly low number of entry-level jobs in the field. Still, with a bit of patience and a bit of luck, you can teach yourself programming and turn it into a profession within a few years.

So, Why Perl?

Computer scientists can argue ad nauseam about which programming language is "best" or "easiest" and so on. The fact is, no one language is perfect for all tasks, and the top three or four languages for most tasks are equally well suited. For a novice or intermediate programmer, then, the question is not really what is best, but what is easiest to learn and use.

Perl scores high on both of these scales. If you want to write a really small Perl program to do something simple, you can do so after reading just a few chapters of this book. In fact, you'll understand enough about Perl by the end of Chapter 3 to be reading programs; by the middle of Chapter 4, you'll be modifying programs to your heart's content.

There are certainly other languages that are easy to learn and use, but they do not have the features of Perl that make it a great all-around language. BASIC has the "easy" parts of Perl, but is not very good for modern programming due to its lack of flexibility. Microsoft's Visual Basic is not nearly as easy to learn as good old BASIC, and although it is very powerful, many novices find it pretty confusing.

Some people think C is easy to learn, but it is difficult to use unless you are very careful. C is also pretty difficult for handling text data, one of the areas in which Perl shines.

Perl is also particularly good at a few common tasks that most other programming languages are poor at. In Perl, it is quite trivial to open a file on your computer, read it, and perform tasks based on what you find in the file. Perl can handle text files with aplomb, but has no problems with binary files. Perl is also good at handling text in ways that you as a human would do.

As the Perl online documentation describes it

> Perl is an interpreted language optimized for scanning arbitrary text files, extracting information from those text files, and printing reports based on that information. It's also a good language for many system management tasks. The language is intended to be practical (easy to use, efficient, complete) rather than beautiful (tiny, elegant, minimal).

Another great reason for using Perl is because it is free. There are versions of Perl for many operating systems on the CD-ROM in the back of this book, and they are all freeware. This no-cost policy has caused many people to try to help the Perl development effort and has caused Perl to be widely spread in a very short period of time.

Perl's History

Programming languages have been around for many decades. Perl is probably the youngest of the popular programming languages, having been started in the mid-1980s. It pretty much sprang from the head of one person, Larry Wall, who had a bunch of system-administration tasks to do and no good language to use.

Interpreters and compilers

Not all programming languages run their programs the same way. There are two main types of programming languages: compiled and interpreted. There are advantages and disadvantages to each type. Probably the best-known language that is compiled is C. Perl, on the other hand, is interpreted.

The difference is only important in that compiled languages often run faster. Many people, particularly C programmers, contend that compiled programs are better because they are faster. In our faster-is-better society, this might be a compelling argument.

However, the speed difference between a compiler and an interpreter can sometimes be only infinitesimally faster, often unnoticeable by mere mortals. For instance, even for large and complex Perl programs, an equivalent C program might take one-half of a second shorter to run. Another difference is that interpreted languages are a bit easier to debug, because there is no compiling step involved with creating the program.

System administrators are demigods who know how to run computers in ways that mere mortals can only imagine. Most sysadmins love challenges, and networked computers are always a challenge. The more important a particular computer on a network is, the more important its system administrator becomes. There is lots of geek macho involved with chasing down system-level bugs and making systems run more smoothly and faster. System administrators love their software tools even more than auto mechanics love theirs, and Perl has become one of the premier system-administration tools.

Basically, Perl sprung out of necessity. Larry needed a language that could open a bunch of text files, read them in a fairly general way, and create new files that were reports about the original files. Sure, he could have used C, the popular language at the time, but C is ornery when dealing with text and is prone to making odd errors if you are not careful.

So, Larry created Perl. The name comes from Practical Extraction And Report Language. Rumor has it that Larry was going to name it "pearl," but he found another language named "pearl," so he chose the shorter version. For a long time, Perl was mostly a Unix-only language. Perl has been extended to do much more than extract text and reporting on it, and there are thousands of very useful system-administration and Internet tools that rely on Perl. In fact, there are a few Web servers written completely in Perl.

Today, Perl comes bundled with almost every copy of every flavor of Unix. Until recently, virtually all work on Perl was done on Unix systems (and other workstation operating systems). It hasn't become as popular on PCs and Macintoshes yet, but the interest in Perl by users of small computers is growing by leaps and bounds. Perl is the only popular, free programming language available for Windows 95 and Macs, and as these computers need more and more system administration, Perl will certainly become even more popular on them.

Two Versions, One Perl

Throughout this book, I talk about Perl as if it were just one programming language. Well, like all software, Perl has gone through many changes since it first sprung out of Larry Wall's fingers. Fortunately, there are only two versions of Perl you need to think about: Perl 4 and Perl 5.

Perl version 4 was the stable version of Perl for many years. In fact, many people still use Perl 4 instead of Perl 5 because they just got so used to it. The last subversion of Perl 4 is "patchlevel 36," but most people just refer to it as version 4.036. Whenever this book talks about Perl 4, it means Perl version 4.036.

Starting in early 1996, many people have been switching to Perl 5. There are many reasons for this, all of them good ones. Perl 5 is not a huge change from Perl 4, but the changes that are there make it so that there will probably never be a Perl 6. Perl 5 is pretty stable (although not completely bug free, of course) and can certainly be used for almost any application.

This book is almost exclusively about Perl 5. This is not to say that a Perl 4 user can't use the programs in the book. In fact, about 95 percent of what's in this book works exactly the same under Perl 4 as it does under Perl 5. This is a testament to how carefully the folks working on the Perl project were to be sure that there was a smooth transition from Perl 4 to Perl 5.

There are, however, a few things in Perl 5 that just plain didn't exist in Perl 4, and they of course are covered in this book. For example, Chapter 19 covers object-oriented Perl, a feature that doesn't exist in Perl 4. There are also a few smaller, but still handy, new features in version 5 that are sprinkled throughout the book. Wherever possible, I try to point out when a feature is specific to Perl 5 so that Perl 4 users won't try things and wonder why they don't work. The icon you see next to this paragraph indicates that the paragraph covers material that only exists in Perl 5.

Having said that, however, I urge everyone using Perl 4 to upgrade to Perl 5. It is much easier for people to write programs for each other using Perl 5 than using Perl 4. In fact, the vast majority of the programs you'll find on the CD-ROM that comes with this book are for Perl 5 because it is so much easier to share programs this way.

Chapter 2

Running Perl on Your Computer

In This Chapter . . .

▶ Installing Perl on Unix, Windows 95, Windows NT, and Macintosh

▶ Running Perl programs

▶ Getting the latest version of Perl

▶ Learning about Perl on other systems

*E*ach programming language that runs on a particular kind of computer has to know a fair amount about the computer in order to run programs. For instance, each type of computer and operating system has its own way of reading and writing files on disk. In order to read and write files, a programming language must know how the computer on which it is running reads and writes files.

To be absolutely correct, one must say that a programming language like Perl runs on an operating system, not a computer. Virtually every computer today comes with its own operating system, and some computers have many possible operating systems. For instance, IBM-compatible PCs can run MS-DOS, Windows 95, Windows NT, Linux, other flavors of Unix, QNX, and on and on. Perl doesn't really care much about the actual computer it is running on, only the operating system.

Perl Isn't Just For Unix

Perl was written first and foremost for Unix and similar operating systems. Many of Perl's advanced features only make sense on Unix. One of the wonderful things about Perl (or, should I say, "yet another of the wonderful") is that it tries valiantly to hide any differences between operating systems. The vast majority of the interesting stuff in Perl works the same on any kind of operating system. You open files the same way, you do math the same way, and so on.

However, you should be aware of a few important differences between Perl running on Unix and Perl running on other operating systems. Well, you don't need to know about them right now, but they'll become important in other parts of the book. These differences will be pointed out in warnings such as this, because ignoring them can lead to programs that don't work the way you expect.

Most of this book is about the parts of Perl that work the same on all kinds of computers. Before you can start running Perl programs, however, you need to install Perl on your computer; of course, this takes different steps for each kind of computer.

Perl for Windows 95 and Perl for the Macintosh have a few features not found on Perl for Unix. These features are described in different parts of the book as they become appropriate. Because there are only a few of them, don't worry about them for now.

The name game

This book describes how to run Perl on four different operating systems: Unix, Windows 95, Windows NT, and Macintosh (MacOS). Note that there is no supported Perl for Windows 3.1.

Perl for Windows 95 and Perl for Windows NT are actually the same program. In this book, I call the program Perl-Win32 because that's what the authors call it. Perl on the Macintosh is called MacPerl, and Perl on Unix is called, well, just plain Perl.

Getting the latest from the Internet

If for some reason you don't want to use the version from the CD-ROM, you can get the latest version of Perl from many sites on the Internet. The files on the CD-ROM were the very latest available in December 1996. The Perl installations as of this date are all stable and run great, so don't feel like you have to go off and get the latest version in order to get going.

However, there are some people who need the up-to-the-second newest programs. All the Perl installations on the CD-ROM are available from dozens of Internet sites in the CPAN (Comprehensive Perl Archive Network) library. See Chapter 23 for more information on where to look on the Internet for the latest CPAN library and other Perl resources.

Unix: Perl's Home

Because Perl started as a Unix application, Perl's integration with Unix is much tighter than with Windows or the Mac. However, this does not always mean that installing and using Perl on Unix is a trivial task. The following two sections should help any Unix users get going with Perl on their system.

Unix installation, or hopefully you don't have to

If you have used Unix very long, you know that there are a million different Unix variants. For some folks, the differences are not of much concern. If you're trying to install a program, however, the differences can sometimes make installing a complex program such as Perl agony. In my personal experience, installing Perl can be anywhere from trivial to mind-bending.

Fortunately, Perl is so popular among Unix folks that almost every implementation of Unix now comes with Perl fully installed. A good way to find out whether or not you already have Perl on your system is to use the following simple Unix command:

```
perl -v
```

If Perl is installed and in your Unix search path, you will see something that looks like this:

```
This is perl, version 5.001
        Unofficial patchlevel 1m.
+ suidperl security patch

Copyright 1987-1994, Larry Wall

Perl may be copied only under the terms of either the
Artistic License or the GNU General Public License, which
may be found in the Perl 5.0 source kit.
```

Note the version number in the first line. You want it to say `This is perl, version 5.001` or `This is perl, version 5.002`. That means you're running Perl 5, the latest major version of Perl. If instead the line says something like `This is perl, version 4.0`, you are running Perl 4, which is okay but not great. As explained in Chapter 1, a few of the features described in this book are only present in Perl 5.

Many Unix systems have both Perl 4 and Perl 5 running at the same time. Usually, one is invoked as **perl** and the other as **perl4** or **perl5**. In the example, **perl** is Perl 5, and there may be a program called **perl4** which will run Perl 4. If running **perl** gives you Perl 4, you should definitely check whether or not **perl5 -v** results in the version message for Perl 5.

If you don't have Perl in your Unix search path, when you give the perl -v command you will see

```
perl: command not found
```

Not to worry: You may still have Perl on your system. You should have Unix do a bit of searching for you using the whereis command:

```
whereis perl
```

If Perl is in any of the standard places where one might expect to find it, you will probably see something like

```
/usr/bin/perl
/usr/contrib/bin/perl
```

(whereis sometimes puts the responses on a single line.)

If you get a blank response from the whereis program, it means that you most likely don't have Perl on your system. You must then resort to the thing that many of us hate to do: asking someone else. Your best bet is to ask a system administrator about where Perl might be. He or she might have installed a copy but not made it publicly available or might need just one more person (you!) to bug him or her about installing Perl.

Unix installation if you really have to

If you are a Unix system administrator (welcome, oh wizard!), you can often install Perl with a minimum of muss or fuss if your flavor of Unix is supported in the Perl build. However, usually it isn't. I've had times where installing Perl consisted of two commands, and I've had other times where I had to get on the phone with the tech support people at my Unix vendor to figure out what went wrong.

You can only install Perl for other people to use if you are a system administrator. You can, however, install it for yourself without having system administrator privileges. Perl requires access to some privileged files in order to install correctly for general use, and you must therefore be the root user when doing the installation. If you aren't a system administrator with root privileges, you need to ask the person who is to do the Perl installation for you.

The first thing you need to do is to get the latest version of the Perl program. The easiest way get it is from the CD-ROM that came with this book. The Perl distribution files for Unix on the CD-ROM are located in the directory called Unix. The Perl 5 distribution file is called perl5.tar.gz, and it is about 1.5 megabytes. (If you instead want to install Perl 4, you will use the file called perl4.tar.gz, which is about 650K. This section only describes installing Perl 5.)

You can install Perl 5 by following seven basic steps:

1. **Use gunzip and tar to uncompress and unpack the .tar.gz file.**

   Of course, you should probably put the sources in the same area you put your other program sources (usually in /usr/src).

2. **Read the file called INSTALL.**

   This gives you much more information about what you need to install Perl than the minilist you are reading. The file isn't all that long, and it lists some of the picky details you need to know for different Unixes.

3. **Remove any config.sh file that you may have in the installation directory.**

   There may be one there if you previously tried to install Perl, for instance.

4. **Give the command**

   ```
   sh Configure
   ```

   This is a shell script that will figure out lots of information about your system. It creates the config.sh file, which contains dozens of variable definitions for your system.

5. **Give the command**

   ```
   make
   ```

   This compiles and links everything using the parameters that were determined from the previous step.

6. **Give the command**

   ```
   make test
   ```

   This performs regression tests on the Perl that was made in the previous step. This command should reply `All tests successful`; if it doesn't, the other messages that come out will (hopefully) help you figure out which part of the compilation or linking failed.

7. Last, but certainly not least, give the command

```
make install
```

This installs all the parts of Perl in the various system directories on your computer.

There are many parts of Perl, and the installer program will put different files in different places, possibly wiping out previous versions of some system files. Just to be sure, look through the Makefile to be sure things are going to go where you want them.

Running Perl programs under Unix

Assuming that you have Perl on your system, you can easily run Perl programs using the `perl` command. Perl programs are just text files, and you can create your Perl programs with any text editor such as vi, emacs, and so on.

For example, if you have a Perl program in the file called proc-invoices, you can run that program with the command

```
perl proc-invoices
```

Perl has a myriad of command line options, many of which you can find at the end of this chapter, as well as in Appendix B. For example, one of the most useful command line options is `-c`, which tells Perl not to run the program but to just check it for any syntax errors. Thus, to check your proc-invoices program, you would give the command

```
perl -c proc-invoices
```

Under Unix, Perl acts like a shell interpreter. If that makes no sense to you, that's okay: it's an advanced subject, known by more Unix-savvy readers. To you and me, the fact that Perl acts a shell interpreter means that you can write Perl programs that you can invoke from the Unix command line without starting the command with **perl**. For instance, you can run your proc-invoices program with the command

```
proc-invoices
```

However, in order to make the above command work, the very first line of your Perl program must look something like

```
#!/usr/bin/perl
```

The text to the right of the #! must be the location of Perl on your system. Most Unix systems have Perl at /usr/bin/perl. If your system has it at a location such as /usr/contrib/lang/perl, the first line of your Perl programs would be

```
#!/usr/contrib/lang/perl
```

 If you are both a Unix and MS-DOS user, you might fall into a common trap. Under MS-DOS (or the DOS window in Windows 95), you don't type the program's extension when you run a program. For example, if you have a program called PROCINV.EXE, you would give the command

```
procinv
```

Under Unix, however, there are no real "extensions." Thus, if your program is called proc-invoices.pl (.pl being the common way of indicating that a file is a Perl program), you have to give the command

```
proc-invoices.pl
```

not just **proc-invoices**.

Perl-Win32 on Windows 95 and Windows NT

Okay, enough of that Unix stuff. Installing Perl 5 on Windows 95 or Windows NT is much easier. You just need to get a copy of the file, use WinZip from the CD-ROM or some other similar Windows-based utility to unpack the file, run the installer, and go.

Installing Perl-Win32 under Windows 95 and Windows NT

If you are running under Windows 95 or Windows NT, you will find the Perl-Win32 files on the CD-ROM in the directory called Windows. To Install Perl 5, open the Perl-W32 folder and extract the contents of 4intel.zip archive.

Windows 95 only runs on Intel-based PCs, but Windows NT can run on computers that have three different kinds of CPUs: Intel, PowerPC, and Alpha. Thus, there are three different programs that Windows NT users can choose from: 4intel.zip for Intel-based systems, 4PPC.zip for PowerPC-based systems, and 4alpha.zip for Alpha-based systems.

Whether you are using Windows 95 or Windows NT, it is important that you unzip the .zip file into the directory you intend to run Perl from. For example, I always have Perl on my system running in C:\Perl5. The Perl for Windows 95 installer is a bit primitive, and it won't let you install into a different directory.

To unzip the distribution file, you must use a Windows-based unzipping program. You cannot use the popular PKZIP program for MS-DOS because it doesn't know anything about long file names. A copy of the shareware program WinZip is included in the Windows directory of the CD-ROM. WinZip is a great program, and works well under Windows 95 and Windows NT. If you use it for longer than the trial period (and I'm sure you will), remember to register it and send in your shareware fee.

After you have unzipped whichever of the files you are using, you must then run the install.bat program. This program will extract some additional files, update your registries, and do other housekeeping so that Perl will run smoothly. The result is a group of files shown in Figure 2-1.

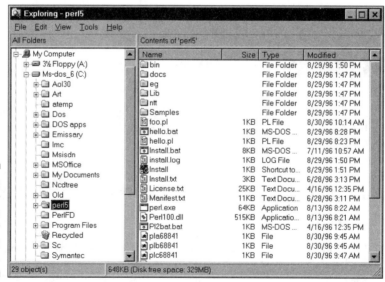

Figure 2-1:
Explorer
view of the
file list after
installing
Perl-Win32.

Running Perl-Win32 in a (yuck!) DOS window

Okay, here's the sad part. Perl-Win32 isn't a Windows program: You run it from the command line in a DOS window. Yes, you read that correctly. No menus, no dialog boxes, and lots of typing. When I first started using Perl-Win32, I could barely believe that this was true, but I have learned to live with it.

So, yes, you have to open a DOS window manually. Go to the Start menu, and choose MS-DOS Prompt from the Programs item. An MS-DOS window that is probably not in the directory where you put Perl-Win32 appears. Use the (ouch!) MS-DOS CD command to get to your Perl directory. The MS-DOS Prompt window, which you will see many times in this book, is shown in Figure 2-2.

Figure 2-2:
MS-DOS
Prompt
window
ready to run
Perl
programs.

Now you can see why I use C:\Perl5 as my Perl directory: I can get there with very little typing. However, you can go one step better than that. You can create a shortcut so you don't have to give the CD command each time you start an MS-DOS window.

1. **With the mouse's right button, click on the desktop until the right button menu appears.**

2. **In the New choice, select Shortcut.**

   A window appears asking for the command line of the shortcut you are creating.

3. **Type** C:\Command.com **in the text area for the command line and then choose the** N̲ext **button.**

4. **For the shortcut name, type** Perl5.

5. **Choose the** F̲inish **button.**

   You now have a new icon on your desktop.

6. **With the mouse's right button, click on the new icon until the right button menu appears.**

7. **Select the** P̲roperties **choice.**

8. **In the Properties window, select the Program tab.**

9. **In the Working option, enter the directory that you have Perl-Win32 in, such as** C:\Perl5.

   You can make any other choices you want in the other tabs of the Properties window.

10. **Select the** O̲K **button in the Properties window to make these new settings stick.**

Now when you double-click the icon that was created in the last step, the MS-DOS prompt window will start in your Perl directory. Easy, huh?

You can easily run Perl programs using the `perl` command. Perl programs are just text files, and you can create your programs with any text editor such as the Windows Notepad program or the MS-DOS `edit` command.

For example, if you have a Perl program in the procinv.pl file , you can run that program with the command

```
perl procinv.pl
```

Perl has a myriad of command line options, many of which are described at the end of this chapter and in Appendix B. For example, one of the most useful command line options is `-c`, which tells Perl not to run the program but to just check it for any syntax errors. Thus, to check your proc-invoices program, you would give this command:

```
perl -c procinv.pl
```

It gets a bit cumbersome to have to type **perl** for each command and to have to remember the file extension each time. Perl-Win32 has a program, charmingly called pl2bat, that will turn a Perl program into a batch file that can be run by name. For example, to change the procinv.pl program into a batch file, you would use this command:

```
pl2bat procinv.pl
```

This command creates the procinv.bat file, and you can run this program as

```
procinv
```

MacPerl: The Mac Interface You Expect

The Macintosh fans in the audience are probably bored silly with all the Unix and Windows command lines and typing and so on (you may have even decided not to read it!). Fear not, it's your turn. Compared to Unix, Windows 95, and Windows NT, installing Perl for the Mac is a breeze.

Installing MacPerl

In the Macintosh folder on the CD-ROM, you will find the MacPerl Installer, which does all the work of installing MacPerl on your hard drive. When you run MacPerl Installer by double-clicking on it, it asks you where you want the MacPerl folder and then installs about 450 files that are associated with Perl, including all the online documentation. The result is a folder shown in Figure 2-3.

Figure 2-3:
The
MacPerl
folder.

Running MacPerl programs

MacPerl is a program that runs Perl programs. This means that you run MacPerl, and from within that program, you tell it which Perl programs you want to run. The MacPerl program itself has very little of a user interface. In fact, when you start MacPerl, it doesn't even open up any windows.

MacPerl programs are plain text files, and you can create them with any text editor such as SimpleText or BBEdit. MacPerl also has a very minimalist text editor built into it.

To create a new text file in MacPerl, select the New command from the File menu. Enter and edit your program, and then save the file with the Save command. Yes, you can also use the Open, Close, Print, Cut, Copy, and Paste commands in the MacPerl editor just like you would in any other Mac program.

To run a Perl program in MacPerl, choose one of the two Run commands from the Script menu. The first Run command runs a program that you have on disk, while the second Run command runs the program that you are editing in MacPerl. If you want to use some editor other than MacPerl's internal editor, you should use the first command.

When you run a Perl program, MacPerl opens an empty window for input and output. This is where you will read messages from MacPerl, and also where you will type in your text responses to prompts. Chapter 3 covers reading and typing in Perl programs.

You can also use MacPerl to check for errors in your programs before you run them. Instead of using one of the Run commands, use one of the Syntax Check commands in the Script menu.

Perl on the Command Line

When you run Perl from the Unix or MS-DOS command line, you can include command line options that change the way Perl behaves; these options are also available for MacPerl. There are over a dozen command line options for Perl (Unix dweebs love their command line options!), but only a few are interesting to most programmers. These few are covered here. Appendix B contains the entire list of command line options.

You can give command line options in either of two ways. The first, of course, is on the command line. As an alternative, you could include a line at the beginning of your program that looks like the command line but starts with #!. For example, you can indicate that you always want to use the -w command line option by inserting

```
#!perl -w
```

as the first line of your program.

Mac users, who don't have a command line, will be especially thankful for this option. Unix users should note that, as described earlier in this chapter, they must put the full path to the Perl program in the command line in their programs. Thus, instead of the line above, a Unix user might have

```
#!/usr/bin/perl -w
```

as the first line of the program.

The most common Perl option you will use is -c, which causes Perl to check the syntax of a program without running it. For you Mac users, the Syntax Check command in MacPerl does the same thing as the -c command line option.

Similar to the -c option is the -w option that causes Perl to look carefully through your program for common programming errors. If it finds any of these errors, it prints them so that you can edit your program and fix them. Using the -w option before you really start to use a Perl program is a great way to avoid embarrassing problems. Chapter 20 explains the list of things that -w warns you about.

As the Unix readers saw earlier in this chapter, the -v option tells you what version of Perl you are running. The -v option works on Perl-Win32 and MacPerl as well. For instance, if you include the line

```
#!perl -v
```

at the beginning of a MacPerl file, MacPerl will print

```
This is perl, version 5.001

Copyright 1987-1994, Larry Wall
Macintosh port Copyright 1991-1995, Matthias Neeracher
Perl may be copied only under the terms of either the
Artistic License or the GNU General Public License, which
may be found in the Perl 5.0 source kit.
```

Perl has a funny mode in which you can run one-line programs without having to enter them into a text file. If you use the -e option, Perl assumes that the rest of the command line is a one-line Perl program, not the name of a text file that has a program in it. For instance, to find the product of two numbers, you could use

```
perl -e 'print 27.35 * .0825;'
```

The -i option allows you to use Perl programs to edit files. Chapter 13 covers this option in the section discussing how to read and write files.

After you get more advanced with Perl, you may want to use Perl's internal debugging system. The debugger is a program that allows you to find errors in your Perl program by moving through them step by step. The debugger is an advanced topic well beyond the scope of this book, however. Just in case you want to experiment with it, you turn on the debugger with the -d command line option:

```
perl -d proc-invoices
```

Other Perls

The CD-ROM included with this book contains the Perl language for many operating systems other than just Unix, Windows NT, Windows 95, and MacOS. Perl has been made to run on a wide variety of systems, and implementations of Perl for all the following operating systems are available:

- Acorn
- Atari
- MVS
- OS/2
- RiscOS
- Windows 3.1
- Amiga
- MS-DOS
- Novell NetWare
- QNX
- VMS
- Xenix

Note, however, that some of these versions of Perl are old and unsupported. Most notably, the Windows 3.1 version is for Perl 4 and hasn't been updated in almost two years.

Some of the other versions are up to date and well-supported and you can use them with impunity. If you want to run Perl on one of these other operating systems, take a look at the program files on the CD-ROM, see if there is any documentation, and if so, see if there is any e-mail contact information for the program. If so, you might be in luck.

Again, this book only covers Perl running on Unix, Windows NT, Windows 95, and MacOS. It is likely that if you are using Perl on a different operating system, at least 95 percent of what is in this book will work just fine on your system, but I make no guarantees.

Chapter 3

Into the Guts of Perl

*O*kay, so are you ready to start? It's time to get your hands dirty. Many introductory programming books go on for chapters and chapters with explanations of what each part of a language is before letting you see a real program. Yawn. I think you'll find that, although the first programs you see won't make complete sense, you'll understand much of what's going on in them and be able to start writing your own programs very quickly.

This isn't to say that anyone will be able to learn how to program just by reading the sample program in this chapter. Some people prefer a step-by-step approach; however, it's almost impossible to teach programming this way because so many parts of programming are interrelated. Even for these kinds of people, seeing what a program looks like and what Perl does with a program should make the process of learning Perl much easier. This chapter gives you an overview of some of the basic concepts in Perl, and Chapter 4 lets you walk through two sample Perl programs. By the time you get to Chapter 5, you'll be familiar with lots of Perl so that learning the specifics will go smoothly.

How You Enter Programs

Perl programs are plain text files. You can write these files using any old text editor. Unix folk will probably use vi and emacs, two popular editors that come with most Unix systems. Windows folk might use the Notepad or WordPad programs that come with Windows, or even the EDIT program that's part of MS-DOS, but there are lots of other better editors available. Macintosh users can use the SimpleText program that comes on the Mac, but, again, there are many better editors available from a variety of sources.

The freeware BBEdit Lite and commercial BBEdit Pro editors are particularly useful for Mac programmers.

Feel free to use whatever text-editing program you like to create and edit your Perl programs. However, if you end up doing lots of programming in Perl, you should definitely consider getting an editor that has extra features for programmers. For now, though, you can use any old text editor because the programs you will enter will be reasonably short and easy to type.

What a Program Looks Like

So, without further ado, I present to you Listing 3-1, the program called counter1.pl. It's typical of the kinds of Perl programs you will write: about 50 lines long.

Listing 3-1: counter1.pl, a typical Perl program.

```
#!/usr/bin/perl -w

# counter1.pl: one way to count the characters, words, and
#     lines in a text file.

# The name of the file that will be counted
$TheFile = "sample.txt";

# Open the file but quit if it doesn't exist
open(INFILE, $TheFile) or die "The file $TheFile could " .
    "not be found.\n";

# Initialize the counters
$CharCount = 0;
$WordCount = 0;
$LineCount = 0;

while(<INFILE>) {
    $TheLine = $_;  # Save the line's contents
    chomp($TheLine);  # Get rid of the line break
    $LineCount = $LineCount + 1;  # This is the easy part!
    $LineLen = length($TheLine);
    # We now know how many characters (minus the line
    #     break) are on this line
    $CharCount = $CharCount + $LineLen;

    # Do the tricky stuff for counting words on the line
```

```
    # The line is empty, so we're done
    if($TheLine eq "") { next };
    # The line has at least one word on it
    $WordCount = $WordCount + 1;
    # Now loop through each character on this line
    #     to look for words
    $CharPos = 0;  # Position we are in the line
    # Check for line end; if not, check for a space
    until($CharPos == $LineLen) {
        if(substr($TheLine, $CharPos, 1) eq " ")
            { $WordCount = $WordCount + 1 }
        $CharPos = $CharPos + 1;
    }  # End of until
}  # End of while(<INFILE>) loop

# All finished, so print out the results

print "For the file $TheFile:\n";
print "Number of characters   $CharCount\n";
print "Number of words        $WordCount\n";
print "Number of lines        $LineCount\n";
```

For now, don't worry about what the program actually does. Trust me, it does something, but that's not the point of this chapter. In fact, you'll see exactly what it does at the beginning of the next chapter.

Incidentally, you don't have to type this program in by hand (I can hear a collective "Whew!" from the audience). All the programs in the book are on the CD-ROM.

When Perl runs a program, it starts at the top and reads down. It executes each statement it comes to. A *statement* in Perl is like a command in English: It tells Perl what to do. Thus, in the line

```
print "For the file $TheFile:\n";
```

print is the statement, and the rest of the line tells Perl what to print. There are dozens of kinds of statements in Perl. Learning which statements do what is the essence of learning Perl. It's not hard to follow what's going on in a Perl program. Just start reading from the top and go down. Perl doesn't always follow only a straight line, however. Some statements define *loops,* which are sets of lines that Perl repeats over and over until told not to. In the counter1.pl program, there is one loop, which starts with the while statement. The loop is all the lines between

```
while(<INFILE>) {
```

and

```
}  # End of while(<INFILE>) loop
```

You'll see later what happens in loops and how to tell Perl when it should stop looping. For now, all you need to know is that when you leave a loop, Perl starts executing statements right after the loop one at a time, just as it did before the loop. In this program, when Perl leaves the loop, it starts again at

```
# All finished, so print out the results
```

Comments

Of the 50 lines in the sample program, only about half really do anything. The other half are *comments,* stuff that Perl ignores. You may be thinking, "What!? Half of my program is going to be ignored by Perl!? Why bother writing it then?" I'll give you two very good reasons, ones that are true for every programming language:

- ✔ Comments help you read your program later so you can fix things or use the program for new purposes.
- ✔ Comments let other people who might have to read your program figure out what the heck you meant when you wrote it.

Writing programs is a bit like the organization of the junk in your garage: It all makes perfect sense when you're putting the stuff in the first time, but six months later, you can't remember why you did it that particular way. Comments are notes to yourself about what is going on in a program so that if you later look at the program, you can make some sense of what you meant when you wrote it.

Having comments in your program may be even more important if someone else has to read your program. You may think (probably incorrectly) that you will remember forever why you wrote something in a particular way, but you certainly shouldn't think that someone else will be a mind reader if they have to look at what you wrote. When you leave comments in your program, you provide notes to other people so that they can hopefully understand your program.

How to comment

Now that you hopefully feel a bit better about what comments are and why they take up half your program, take a look again at Listing 3-1. Every line that starts with a # character is a comment. (By the way, there is no universally accepted name for this character. In the U.S., it's generally called the "pound" character, but in other countries it is often called the "hash" character.)

A comment tells Perl to ignore everything from the # character all the way to the end of the line. Thus, the first couple of lines are all comments:

```
#!/usr/bin/perl -w
# counter1.pl: one way to count the characters, words, and
#    lines in a text file.
```

You can also start a comment on the same line with other Perl statements. When Perl sees a # in the middle of a line, it again assumes that everything from the # character all the way to the end of the line is a comment and ignores it. Thus, in the line

```
    $TheLine = $_;  # Save the line's contents
```

Perl only pays attention to the text up to the ; and ignores the comment.

By the way, you may have noticed that there are many blank lines in the program. Blank lines are also comments, in a way. Perl ignores blank lines, so you can have as many or as few of them as you want. You can use blank lines wherever you want in your programs to make the program easier to read. I usually put blank lines between each major section of the program so that when I glance at the program as a whole, I can see where each section starts. For most programmers, blank lines are like part separators. Blank lines and spaces are described again later in this chapter.

Statements, the Stuff Perl Programs Are Made Of

You saw earlier in this chapter that Perl knows what you want to do through *statements*. Each statement is like a sentence that tells Perl what to do next. Like in English, some of these "sentences" are very short, others are long, and some just go on and on and on.

I'm going to avoid going into any detail here about what is a statement. Suffice it to say that every Perl statement falls into one of three categories:

  ✔ A verblike action, such as "display this text" or "add these numbers"

  ✔ A *conditional* test, such as "if such-and-so is true, then do this"

  ✔ A loop, such as "keep doing this set of things until I tell you to stop"

Listing 3-1 contains all three kinds of statements. In fact, almost every Perl program has verblike actions and conditionals, and many have loops. You'll become comfortable with all of these in a short time.

The majority of statements that you see in Perl programs are verblike actions. Three of the action statements from the Listing 3-1 include

```
open(INFILE, $TheFile) or die "The file $TheFile could " .
   "not be found.\n";
   $LineCount = $LineCount + 1;  # This is the easy part!
```

In these cases, the actions are open, die, and =. As you probably guessed, the = statement is used a great deal in Perl. It's called the *assignment statement,* and you use it to set variables. Assignment statements and variables are covered a little later in this chapter.

Perl has an easy way to know where one statement ends and the next one starts: the semicolon (;). That's why you see so many semicolons in the listing above, and in almost every listing you see in this book. Thus,

```
$CharCount = 0;
```

is a single statement.

You do not need to put a whole statement on a single line. In fact, it is often impossible. Perl keeps reading until it finds a semicolon and then goes back and sees if that whole glob looks like a single statement.

Perl allows you to have more than one statement on a line. For instance, Listing 3-1 contains the three statements:

```
$CharCount = 0;
$WordCount = 0;
$LineCount = 0;
```

You could just as easily put all three of these on the same line:

```
$CharCount = 0; $WordCount = 0; $LineCount = 0;
```

Again, what's important is the semicolons, not the line breaks.

By the way, the reason I put these three statements on three different lines in the listing is that it is easier to see each one when you scan the listing. The purpose here is clarity, not saving a few lines on the page.

Blocks

Conditional and loop statements are special in that they allow you to include lots of other statements in them. This set of additional statements is called a *block* and is enclosed in curly braces ({ and }). You can think of blocks as a single set of statements that always hangs together, like a mini-program.

Naming punctuation marks is always a bit of a pain. Some people call the different marks different things. You already saw the two names for the # mark: "pound sign" and "hash." Names are important for the four pairs of marks that enclose things. The names used in this book for these are "parentheses" for (and); "curly braces" or just "braces" for { and }; "angle brackets" for < and >; and "square brackets" for [and].

Conditional statements use blocks to say what to do if a conditional state-ment is true. For example, think of the English sentence, "Unless you phone me before 4:00, I will pick up Chris from the day care center and start dinner." The conditional in the sentence is "Unless you phone me before 4:00," and the block of statements that follows is "I will pick up Chris from the day care center and start dinner." The block is just like a block in Perl: The two things will happen in order, and they won't happen unless the conditional is true.

Loops also use blocks. A loop in English might be, "Until the tree is covered with leaves, I'll water and fertilize it every week." The loop statement is "Until the tree is covered with leaves," and the block is "I'll water and fertilize it every week."

Blocks have one feature that often confuses beginning Perl users: You don't need to have a semicolon after the closing brace of a block. For instance, notice the lines

```
if(substr($TheLine, $CharPos, 1) eq " ")
    { $WordCount = $WordCount + 1 }
```

There is no semicolon after the } because Perl knows that a block is the end of the conditional. You can put the semicolon there if you want:

```
if(substr($TheLine, $CharPos, 1) eq " ")
    { $WordCount = $WordCount + 1 };
```

Give yourself a gold star if you noticed something else odd in this example: There's no semicolon *before* the closing brace! That's another option in Perl that, although a bit confusing, lets you get a tad lazy with your typing. Perl knows that if you're ending a block with a }, you're also ending the last statement in the block, and therefore it lets you skip the semicolon on the last statement in the block. Feel free to add it if you want:

```
    if(substr($TheLine, $CharPos, 1) eq " ")
        { $WordCount = $WordCount + 1; }
```

Blocks within blocks

A block is a set of statements. Some statements have blocks in them. Thus, a block can have blocks in it. In fact, the majority of the example program is a block, and you can see another block inside.

The first block is the one associated with the `while` statement. Within that, there is an `until` statement that has a block, and within the `until`, there's another block in the `if` statement. Here's an excerpt from Listing 3-1:

```
while(<INFILE>) {
    $TheLine = $_;  # Save the line's contents
    . . .
    until($CharPos == $LineLen) {
        if(substr($TheLine, $CharPos, 1) eq " ")
            { $WordCount = $WordCount + 1 }
        $CharPos = $CharPos + 1;
    }  # End of until
}  # End of while(<INFILE>) loop
```

It is often tricky for even advanced programmers to keep lots of nested blocks straight in their minds. As you will see soon, you can keep blocks straight by indenting those blocks that fall under another block (see "Indentation and Spacing" later in this chapter).

Even if indentation fails you, however, you can always determine which brace goes with which block in the same way that Perl does. You can find the right brace that matches a particular left brace by counting left and right braces; each left brace counts +1, and each right brace -1. When you get to zero again after counting the first left brace, you found the match.

In the preceding example, if you were trying to find which of the many right braces matches the left brace on the `while` line, you would go through the rest of the program, adding 1 for each left brace and subtracting 1 for each right brace. Here's the same code, with extra comments added:

```
while(<INFILE>) {  ###Start at 1
    $TheLine = $_;
    . . .
    if($TheLine eq "") { next };  ###+1, -1: total is 1
    . . .
    until($CharPos == $LineLen) {  ### +1: total is 2
```

```
         if(substr($TheLine, $CharPos, 1) eq " ")
            { $WordCount = $WordCount + 1 }
         ###+1, -1: total is 2
         $CharPos = $CharPos + 1;
   }  # End of until  ### -1: total is 1
}  # End of while(<INFILE>) loop  ### -1: total is 0
```

This means that the last brace, which took the count to 0, is the match of
the first one.

Operators and functions

You should know about two other kinds of Perl items before going further
into the language. *Operators* are symbols that let you perform actions on
data, such as adding two numbers together. Listing 3-1 contains lots of
statements that have operators, such as

```
    $LineCount = $LineCount + 1;  # This is the easy part!
```

Here, the + is an operator that tells Perl to add 1 to the value of
$LineCount.

Functions are statements that act like operators, but they have nonsymbolic
names like chomp:

```
    chomp($TheLine);  # Get rid of the line break
```

Functions have *arguments,* usually shown in parentheses, to tell Perl what
the function is operating on. Many functions have more than one argument;
if so, the arguments are separated by commas. For example, this excerpt
from the substr function in the listing has three arguments:

```
substr($TheLine, $CharPos, 1)
```

Throughout the book, I sometimes call functions "functions" and sometimes
call them "statements." In Perl programming, there is no important distinction between the two, so you can use either interchangeably.

Indentation and Spacing

Another thing you may (or may not) have noticed in the listing is that not all
the lines start at the left margin. Here is an example:

```
open(INFILE, $TheFile) or die "The file $TheFile could " .
    "not be found.\n";
```

The indentation here is completely optional. Like comments, Perl ignores spaces at the beginning of lines.

Indentation is another good way to make your Perl programs more readable. In the example above, the indentation is used to show that the die statement was not finished on the first line. If you continue a statement on the next line, indenting the continuation makes it easier to understand.

To see how indentation is useful, compare the following two lines to those in the previous example:

```
open(INFILE, $TheFile) or die "The file $TheFile could " .
"not be found.\n";
```

In the unindented case, if you were scanning down the page, you might think that the bit in quotation marks on the second line was another statement, when in fact it's part of the statement from the first line.

Indenting blocks

Indentation is also important in blocks. Most programmers like to indent all the lines in a block so that it is easy to see where Perl will go after the block finishes. In the program you've been looking at so far, there is a loop that starts with the while statement. Notice that all the lines in the loop's block are indented four spaces. This is a common way of using indentation to make your programs visually easier to follow.

The astute readers among you may have noticed that there is a set of lines within the while loop that is indented even further:

```
until($CharPos == $LineLen) {
    if(substr($TheLine, $CharPos, 1) eq " ")
        { $WordCount = $WordCount + 1 }
    $CharPos = $CharPos + 1;
}
```

This example shows another place where indentation helps. The until statement has a block as its argument, and that block is indented four spaces further than the until statement. Inside the until block is an if statement, and that too has a block, which is indented another four spaces.

This last example also shows one of the nice features of Perl: Indenting is optional. You can use it however you like, and if you do it "wrong," you'll still have a perfectly functional (but possibly hard to read) program. Perl goes even further in its lenience: You can also put the block and end it where you want. For instance, you could choose to have the if block look like it does in the listing:

```
if(substr($TheLine, $CharPos, 1) eq " ")
    { $WordCount = $WordCount + 1 }
```

Or you could choose to have the braces looking like they do in the until loop:

```
if(substr($TheLine, $CharPos, 1) eq " ") {
    $WordCount = $WordCount + 1;
    } # End of if(substr
```

Some programmers insist that the second way is better than the first because then all your blocks look the same. To me, the first way is better because it saves lines in your program and is easier to read. If a block is one statement long, I usually put it on one line with its braces on the same line. As you program more, you'll probably gravitate toward one style or the other.

In fact, you could even put the whole if statement and its block on one line. The main reason I didn't do that here is that this book isn't wide enough to show the whole line. In fact, my screen is not wide enough to show the whole thing: The line would be more than 80 characters. This is why it's nice that Perl lets you break up the lines where you want for such nonprogramming reasons as "it won't fit in the book" or "it won't fit on my screen" or "I just feel that way right now, so there."

Indenting for the fun of it

By the way, Perl also ignores extra spacing between each part of a statement. For instance, Perl sees the following three statements exactly the same:

```
$CharCount = 0;
$CharCount=0;
$CharCount    =        0        ;
```

Five-Minute Guide to Numbers and Text

One of the topics that I have glossed over a bit in this discussion is how Perl deals with data. Your programs can have many different kinds of data, such as numbers, text, lists, files, and so on. For now, the two most important types of data are numbers and text.

Ah, numbers. Math. Remember how much *fun* math was when you were a kid? To this day, I'm still not sure how they made it so miserable, even for those of us who wanted to enjoy it. Probably 80 percent of all adults still have a mild (or heavy) dislike for math, even though we all use numbers all the time. Well, Perl loves numbers. It handles them just fine, and makes using numbers a breeze. Perl can handle all sorts of numbers, but the two that you will care about most are *integers* and *real numbers*. In case you've forgotten your high school math, integers are numbers that do not have a fractional part, while real numbers are numbers that, well, have a fractional part. Therefore, 3 is an integer, and 3.5 is a real number.

But the world is much more than numbers. There's also text. Heck, you're reading this book, and it's mostly text. Text is made up of individual *characters,* such as the letter a, the letter b, the hyphen (-), and so on.

In Perl, text is called *strings*. A string is a gang of characters. Thus, a string of five characters might be abcde; another one would be ae-@c. Perl is great with text. You can ask Perl to do things like "tell me the fifth character in this string" or "find the first place in this string that has the letter 'j', and tell me everything that comes after it" or "split this string into two strings: the stuff before the first space, and the stuff after it" or even "split this string into a bunch of little strings, each one being the stuff that is between the tab characters."

Variables and Literals

One of the parts of the listing that you probably noticed (and also probably noticed I hadn't talked about before now) is all those words with the dollar sign ($) in front of them. Those are Perl *variables*. If you are familiar with any other programming language, you already know what variables are because every language has variables or something just like them. If Perl is your first language, don't worry; variables are fairly easy to understand, and they will help make everything else make sense.

A *variable* is place to store a value. Think of a variable as a box with a name on it. The box can hold exactly one thing (the variable's value), and it has exactly one name on it (the variable's name). You can put anything you want in the box, but it is important to remember that the box can only have one thing in it. You can have as many boxes (variables) in your program as you want.

A *literal,* on the other hand, is something that is just a value. The number 47 is a literal: It means 47 and can never change. It doesn't have a name; it's just the value 47. The string "Cedar" is a literal: It can never be anything other than the set of characters "C", "e", "d", "a", and "r" in exactly that order with no other characters involved.

In Perl, you can tell what is and isn't a variable by looking for the $. Anything with a $ at the beginning is a variable name. Thus, in the listing, $TheFile and $TheLine are variables. Literals don't have names: They're just values.

Variable names can be long or short, but they cannot have any spaces in them. They can have uppercase and lowercase letters in them, as well as digits, but they cannot start with a digit. You can also use the underscore (_) character in your variable names. Here are some more examples of variable names:

- ✔ $Bill
- ✔ $BoyIsThisALongVariableName
- ✔ $I_BET_this_IS_hard_TO_type

Perl variable names are *case sensitive,* meaning that uppercase and lowercase letters in variable names are different. Thus, the name *$FirstCar* and the name *$firstcar* are different and name two different variables. When you edit programs, be very careful when you use uppercase and lowercase letters.

There are two things you can do with a variable: Look at its value or change its value. The first time you use a variable, you assign a value to it, usually with a literal. For instance, the first statement in the program (ignoring all the introductory comments) is

```
$TheFile = "sample.txt";
```

This says to Perl

Give the variable called $TheFile a value of "sample.txt"

When you make an assignment statement like this, Perl ignores whatever was in the variable before. If you have not used the variable before, Perl creates it; if you *have* used the variable before, Perl wipes out its old value (and inserts the new value.)

Going back to the box analogy, making an assignment is like telling Perl,

If there isn't already a box with the name $TheFile on it, create the box and put the literal sample.txt into it. If there is a box with the name $TheFile on it, dump out its contents and put the literal sample.txt into it.

In addition to changing the value of variables, you can look at their values. For instance, look at the following statement:

```
if($TheLine eq "") { next };
```

This statement means

> Look at the value that is in the variable named $TheLine, and see if that value equals "". If so, do what's inside the block.

Here's another statement that looks at the value of a variable:

```
print "For the file $TheFile:\n";
```

This statement means

> Print the literal For the file (including the space after file), then look at the value that is inside the variable named $TheFile, then print that value, then print the character :, and then go to a new line.

Here's an example in which Perl both looks at one variable, $TheLine, and changes another ($LineLen):

```
$LineLen = length($TheLine);
```

This line means

> Look at the variable called $TheLine, find its length, and put the value of its length in the variable called $LineLen.

Your statements can have a combination of assignments, commands to have Perl look at the current value of a variable, and literals, all in the same statement. Here is a very typical example of such a statement:

```
$WordCount = $WordCount + 1;
```

At first, this may be a tad confusing, but it can make good sense. It means

> First, look at the value of the variable named $WordCount. Next, take that value, add 1, and then place that new value into the variable called $WordCount.

Here that is again, this time with the relevant parts underlined.

> First, look at the value of the variable named $WordCount.

```
$WordCount = $WordCount + 1;
```

> Next, take that value, add 1,

```
$WordCount = $WordCount + 1;
```

and then place that new value into the variable called $WordCount.

```
$WordCount = $WordCount + 1;
```

I guess this is a long-winded way of saying, "Make the $WordCount variable 1 higher than it already was."

Why you always assign variables first

Even though you have yet to write your first program, you're ready to see the number one, classic, top, supreme mistake that most programmers make. The technical term is "using an unassigned variable," and it's one of the most difficult things to find in a program.

Basically, the problem occurs when you either look at or change a variable that you have not already given a value to. For instance, consider the statement

```
$LineLen = length($TheLine);
```

That's all fine and good if you assume that $TheLine has been assigned. However, if you have not already had a statement like

```
$TheLine = $_;   # Save the line's contents
```

Perl doesn't know what it is taking the length of. Perl will silently make a guess about what you wanted in $TheLine, and that guess is almost always wrong.

How can you avoid this all-too-common mistake? Always check your Perl programs with the -w command line option (discussed in Chapter 2). One of the greatest blessings of using -w is that it will find almost every instance in which you look at or change a variable without having first given it a value. Perl is one of the few languages that has this kind of feature built in, and the result is that it is much harder to write a program that uses unassigned variables.

Perl's special variables

Okay, so you have literals, whose values never change, and your own variables, whose values change when you tell Perl to change them. And you've just received a strict warning about how you should always assign your variables before you use them for anything. However, there is a class of variables that comes with values already assigned.

Perl's *special* variables are ones that Perl starts off with values assigned. You can treat these like any other variable in a Perl program: You can look at them and assign them values. For example, the variable called $0 contains the name of the program you are running. Perl contains dozens of special variables, most of which are of little interest to novices (or even advanced users). The few that are important are mentioned in this book where needed, and the entire list is given in the grand Perl reference in Appendix B.

Default arguments

Many Perl functions allow you not to specify some of their arguments. If you don't specify an argument, the function uses its *default* value. This makes typing the program go faster. However, it also makes the program harder to read, because you have to remember what the defaults for each function are. Thus, I rarely use the default arguments. However, you should probably know a bit about default arguments because lots of other programmers use them all the time, and you'll see them in Perl programs you come across.

Almost all the functions that let you skip arguments fill in what would have been that argument with the Perl special variable $_. Many things set this special variable, such as reading from a file line by line, or doing a pattern search. Functions that often follow these kinds of actions assume that you want the argument of the function to be $_, so they let you skip including it as an argument.

For example, the lc function, which changes text to lowercase, normally takes one argument: the text to change to lowercase. If you have no arguments to lc, the function returns the lowercase of $_ instead. Thus, the following three lines are equivalent:

```
lc($_);
lc();
lc;
```

Although it's faster to type the second or third, I think that the first is much clearer.

What's Next?

You now know the framework for what Perl does, and you're probably interested in seeing how it processes a real program. The next chapter goes one step better: It shows you how Perl handles two real programs: the one you've been working with in this chapter, and a second program that has additional common Perl features.

Chapter 4
Your First Program, Times Two

• •

In This Chapter

▶ Looking at two sample Perl programs

▶ Processing text files

▶ Accepting user prompts

• •

*B*elieve it or not, you probably are ready to hop into some programming. The best way to start, in my opinion, is to look at a model program, one which has lots of the kinds of things that you will use when you write your own programs. But why stop at one? This chapter shows you two real, working programs to get you familiar with Perl programming.

So What Does the counter1.pl Program Do?

You spent most of Chapter 3 looking at bits of the counter1.pl program. It's time to look through the program as a whole, instead of a line here and a line there, and determine what it does. After you've seen what is in the program, you'll see what it looks like when it runs. The program in full is listed in Listing 4-1.

Listing 4-1: counter1.pl, a program that counts characters, words, and lines in a text file.

```
#!/usr/bin/perl -w

# counter1.pl: one way to count the characters, words, and
#    lines in a text file.

# The name of the file that will be counted
$TheFile = "sample.txt";

# Open the file but quit if it doesn't exist
open(INFILE, $TheFile) or die "The file $TheFile could " .
```

(continued)

(continued)

```
       "not be found.\n";

# Initialize the counters
$CharCount = 0;
$WordCount = 0;
$LineCount = 0;

while(<INFILE>) {
    $TheLine = $_;  # Save the line's contents
    chomp($TheLine);  # Get rid of the line break
    $LineCount = $LineCount + 1;  # This is the easy part!
    $LineLen = length($TheLine);
    # We now know how many characters (minus the line
    #    break) are on this line
    $CharCount = $CharCount + $LineLen;

    # Do the tricky stuff for counting words on the line

    # The line is empty, so we're done
    if($TheLine eq "") { next };
    # The line has at least one word on it
    $WordCount = $WordCount + 1;
    # Now loop through each character on this line
    #    to look for words
    $CharPos = 0;  # Position we are in the line
    # Check for line end; if not, check for a space
    until($CharPos == $LineLen) {
        if(substr($TheLine, $CharPos, 1) eq " ")
            { $WordCount = $WordCount + 1 }
        $CharPos = $CharPos + 1;
    }  # End of until
}  # End of while(<INFILE>) loop

# All finished, so print out the results

print "For the file $TheFile:\n";
print "Number of characters   $CharCount\n";
print "Number of words        $WordCount\n";
print "Number of lines        $LineCount\n";
```

```
#!/usr/bin/perl -w
```

The first line tells Unix Perl where to find the Perl language. It's an optional comment. The special comment on the first line was described in Chapter 2.

```
# counter1.pl: one way to count the characters, words, and
#    lines in a text file.
```

The next set of lines is a comment to ourselves about ìàat the program is and why we wrote it. As silly as this might seem, ten years from now when you're trying to figure out what the heck counter1.pl does, having an explanation right at the top of the program will be a great time-saver.

```
# The name of the file that will be counted
$TheFile = "sample.txt";
```

These lines initialize the $TheFile variable. Because the counter1.pl looks in a file, you need to tell it the name of the file it will look in. This variable gets used at the end of the program as well.

```
# Open the file but quit if it doesn't exist
open(INFILE, $TheFile) or die "The file $TheFile could " .
    "not be found.\n";
```

The first real action is to open the file. Opening a file means to make the file available to Perl. In this case, opening the file means making it readable to the program. Chapters 12 and 13 describe opening files in intimate detail.

The open function takes two arguments: a "handle" that you'll use for the rest of the program and the name of the file. The second part of the statement is a die statement. In essence, the lines mean "Try to open the file or die if you can't." The die statement tells the program to stop running and to put the message on the screen just before it stops.

This use of or may seem a bit peculiar because there is no semicolon after the open statement. You'll see in Chapter 8 how or works. For now, assume that being able to say "Try to open the file or die if you can't" is exactly what you want to do when you open files.

```
# Initialize the counters
$CharCount = 0;
$WordCount = 0;
$LineCount = 0;
```

Hopefully, you learned your lesson about initializing all your variables before using them. These lines contain some counters that we will use to (you guessed it!) count characters, words, and lines. They will keep a running total for the whole file.

```
while(<INFILE>) {
```

The next long section is the `while` loop. A `while` statement takes an argument that is evaluated to be true or false. If it is true, Perl goes through the steps in the loop and then tests the argument again. The very first time the argument is false, Perl skips to the first statement after the loop's block.

This is the beginning of the loop. In this case, the argument is `<INFILE>`, which to Perl means "Read a line from the file that was opened with the handle called `INFILE`. If you've read to the end of the file, return false." Thus, the loop will keep going as long as there are lines in the file, and skip to the end of the block when there are no more lines.

```
$TheLine = $_;   # Save the line's contents
```

`$_` is a special variable that means "the stuff you just read." This statement says "Take the line you just read from INFILE and put it in the variable called `$TheLine`."

```
chomp($TheLine);   # Get rid of the line break
```

When you read a line, you also get the *line terminator,* which is the character or characters that tell your computer "this is the end of a line." The `chomp` function removes that from the end of the variable so all you have left is the text that was on the line, not the end bit.

`chomp` is one of the new functions in Perl version 5, so Perl 4 users can't use this statement. The `chop` function in Perl 4 does pretty much the same thing, however.

```
$LineCount = $LineCount + 1;   # This is the easy part!
```

Because `$LineCount` is keeping track of how many lines are in the file, add 1 to the count because Perl just read another line. The first time through, Perl assigns `$LineCount` to the sum of 0 (the value set before the loop) and 1; this sum is 1. The next time through the loop, Perls sets `$LineCount` to the sum of 1 (the value from the last time through the loop) and 1, which is 2. This is like those little counters that people use to count the number of people going into a museum or other events: It just keeps adding 1 to the previous value.

```
$LineLen = length($TheLine);
```

The `length` function looks in a text variable and tells how many characters are in it.

```
# We now know how many characters (minus the line
#     break) are on this line
$CharCount = $CharCount + $LineLen;
```

Because $CharCount keeps track of the total number of characters, you want to add the length of this line (minus the line terminator) to the total count. This is another kind of counter. Instead of adding 1 each time, you add the length of the line.

```
# Do the tricky stuff for counting words on the line
```

Remember, the more comments in your programs, the better!

```
# The line is empty, so we're done
if($TheLine eq "") { next };
```

This statement tests whether the line has any text in it. Like the while statement, the if statement takes one argument, a test that will evaluate to true or false. Here, we're testing if $TheLine equals no text at all; if so, the block is executed. In that block, the next statement tells Perl to "skip all the rest of the lines in the current enclosing block," meaning that it should go back and try the while test again.

```
# The line has at least one word on it
$WordCount = $WordCount + 1;
```

If Perl gets this far, it means that the line has something on it (otherwise, the previous if test would have prevented Perl from getting to here). Therefore, there is at least one word, so this statement updates the variable.

```
# Now loop through each character on this line
#     to look for words
$CharPos = 0;  # Position we are in the line
```

The preceding line initializes the variable $CharPos, which you use to remember which character *on this line* you are on. The next statement will walk through the line one character at a time, looking for spaces.

```
# Check for line end; if not, check for a space
until($CharPos == $LineLen) {
```

until is the exact opposite of while: It causes Perl to execute the block in a loop only if its argument is false. Here, the test is "Am I at the end of the line yet?" If not, do the block again; otherwise, skip to the end of the block, which is also the end of the while loop.

```
        if(substr($TheLine, $CharPos, 1) eq " ")
            { $WordCount = $WordCount + 1 }
```

Inside the `until` loop, this statement tells Perl to use the `substr` function to see if the character it is looking at is a space character. The three arguments to `substr` mean "look in `$TheLine`, starting at the position `$CharPos` from the left side of the string, and look at 1 character." So if this character is a space character, Perl would add 1 to `$WordCount` because there is a space after each word.

Note that the word count is being based on the number of spaces that the program sees. At first glance, this process makes good sense, but it can lead to very bad word counts. What if you have two spaces after some words? What if you have space characters at the end of some lines? What if you indent some lines with spaces? All of these situations would tend to make the word count reported much higher than what actually appears in the text file.

```
        $CharPos = $CharPos + 1;
```

This tells Perl to add 1 to the variable holding the line's character position.

```
    }  # End of until
```

This is the closing brace for the `until` loop.

```
    }  # End of while(<INFILE>) loop
```

And this is the closing brace of the `while` loop, way up above.

```
# All finished, so print out the results
```

Well, okay, maybe this isn't the most useful comment, but it at least tells us that we're almost done with the program.

```
print "For the file $TheFile:\n";
```

`print` statements cause Perl to display text on your screen. (Actually, `print` can do much more than that, as you will see in the chapter on reading and writing files.) Here, `print` displays the text `For the file`, followed by a space, followed by the value of the variable `$TheFile`, followed by a colon. The `\n` indicates that after printing this, Perl will display the next text on the next line of your screen. Printing `\n` is like pressing the Enter key in a word-processing program.

```
print "Number of characters    $CharCount\n";
print "Number of words         $WordCount\n";
print "Number of lines         $LineCount\n";
```

These three lines are similar to the first `print` statement: They print some text, the value of a variable, and go to the next line.

And, you're done! Wait, you say you want to actually *do* something with this program now, like run it? Of course! We don't write programs just for the fun of writing them: We want to do real work with them.

Running counter1.pl

Because the program counts characters, words, and lines in a text file, you need a text file for it to work on. Create a file called sample.txt with the following text (which, incidentally, is lifted from the first chapter of my other . . . *For Dummies* book, *Netscape and the World Wide Web For Dummies,* from IDG Books Worldwide, Inc.):

```
The Internet is a collection of thousands of computers that
communicate through certain methods that have been agreed on
for many years. The Internet started about 25 years ago with
a small handful of computers run by a few people as an
experiment. The initial results were successful; the network
was useful, so it grew.
In fact, the Internet was partially intended to be an
experiment for how to design a network that could grow
easily, with very little central control. That concept is
still considered radical today, and you find few networks as
loose as the Internet.
```

Okay, I admit it's not the most breathtaking prose in the world; still, you'd be surprised how many people don't know how or when the Internet began. Anyhow, that's not the point here. You just needed a short text file to measure.

Because there are three kinds of readers, I have to take a brief digression to explain how to run Perl programs on Unix, Windows 95 or Windows NT, and MacOS. After that, we'll regroup and show what the program prints. By the way, if Perl find errors when it checks your program, you should skip to the end of this chapter where I describe how to understand Perl's error messages.

Running a program on Unix

First thing, be sure that the first line of counter1.pl actually points to the location of Perl on your system. If it doesn't, edit that line, or else you will get a confusing error message from Unix. If you're not sure about Perl's location on your system, reread the section in Chapter 2 about installing Perl on Unix.

To check the program for errors (such as if you forgot one of the semicolons or quotation marks), give this command:

```
perl -c counter1.pl
```

To run the program, give this command:

```
./counter1.pl
```

This tells Unix to "run the program called counter1.pl from the current directory."

Running a program under Windows 95 and Windows NT

Be sure that you have opened an MS-DOS window and are in the Perl directory, as described in Chapter 2. To check the program for errors (such as if you forgot one of the semicolons or quotation marks), give the command

```
perl -c counter1.pl
```

To run the program, give this command:

```
perl counter1.pl
```

Running a program on the Macintosh

Launch MacPerl like you do any other Mac program by double-clicking on its icon in the Finder. To check the program for errors (such as if you forgot one of the semicolons or quotation marks), choose Syntax Check from the Script menu. To run the program, choose Run Script from the Script menu.

What counter1.pl Displays

Assuming that you've copied the sample.txt program correctly from the CD-ROM (or, if you typed it by hand, that you typed everything correctly), you should see the following after you run the counter1.pl program:

```
For the file sample.txt:
Number of characters  562
Number of words        98
Number of lines        12
```

The program then exits. On Unix or Windows 95 or Windows NT, you will be back at the operating system prompt, as shown for Windows 95 in Figure 4-1. On the Macintosh, MacPerl is still running, waiting for you to give a command from one of the menus.

Note that the numbers above may not match exactly what Perl reports to you. If you added extra spaces, or extra lines, or possibly spelled things differently than in the example, the numbers will be slightly different.

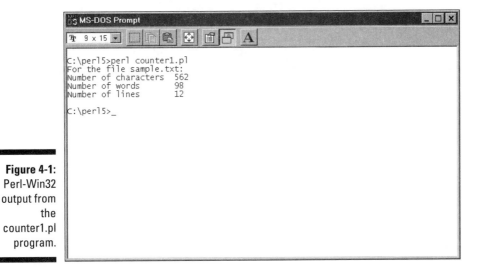

Figure 4-1:
Perl-Win32
output from
the
counter1.pl
program.

Your Second Program, with More Features

The second example program, empdata1.pl, is shown in Listing 4-2. The structure is somewhat similar to counter1.pl, but the program has a different purpose: It lets you look through a small text database and search for records.

Listing 4-2:
empdata1.pl,
a program
that lets
you query
an
employee
database.

```perl
#!/usr/bin/perl -w


# empdata1.pl: a very simple employee database application.
#    This program reads a text file that is an employee
#    database and lets you query it by ID number.
#
#    Each record is on a single line. Each field in the
#    record is separated by a single tab character
#    ("\t"). The database has four fields:
```

(continued)

(continued)

```perl
#    - Last name
#    - First name
#    - ID number
#    - Telephone extension

# The name of the database file
$TheDB = 'edata.txt';

# Open the database file but quit if it doesn't exist
open(INDB, $TheDB) or die "The database $TheDB could " .
    "not be found.\n";

while(1) {  # Loop forever
    print "\nDo you want to search by employee ID (I), " .
        " or quit (Q): ";
    $DoSearch = <STDIN>;
    chomp($DoSearch);
    $DoSearch =~ tr/A-Z/a-z/;
    # Check if they want to quit
    if($DoSearch eq 'q') { last }
    # Check if they did *not* say i or I
    unless($DoSearch eq 'i') {
        print "You must enter either I or Q.\n";
        next;  # Go out to the while loop
    }

    # Ask them what ID they want to search for
    print "Search for ID number: ";
    $SearchFor = <STDIN>;
    chomp($SearchFor);
    # Go to the top of the database in case this isn't
    #    the first time they are searching
    seek(INDB, 0, 0);
    # Reset the count of successes
    $SuccessCount = 0;
    # Loop through the records in the file
    while(<INDB>) {
        $TheRec = $_;
        chomp($TheRec);
        ($LastName, $FirstName, $ID, $Tel) =
            split(/\t/, $TheRec);
        if($ID eq $SearchFor) {
            $SuccessCount = $SuccessCount + 1;
            print "$ID: $FirstName $LastName, ext. ".
```

```
            "$Tel\n";
       }   # End of if
    }  # End of while(<INDB>)
    if($SuccessCount == 0) { print "No records found.\n" }
    else { print "$SuccessCount records found.\n" }
}  # End of while(1)

print "Program finished.\n";
```

The database used in the program, edata.txt, is a simple text file shown here:

```
Anastasio      Trey       12   143
Manzanera      Phil       15   156
Stewart        Dave       17   154
Thompson       Richard    20   112
```

The four columns in the data file are for last name, first name, ID number, and telephone extension.

You should probably copy this file from the CD-ROM if you can, even though it is short. If you type it in, be sure to use a single tab between each column. Don't use spaces, and don't use more than one tab, or the empdata1.pl program won't work.

The gist of the program is that it prompts you for employee numbers and then prints out the information on that employee from the database. It lets you go through this loop as many times as you want. When you are finished, you type **q** or **Q** and the program exits.

What's going on in empdata1.pl

```
#!/usr/bin/perl -w
```

This is the same preamble as you saw before.

```
# empdata1.pl: a very simple employee database application.
#    This program reads a text file that is an employee
#    database and lets you query it by ID number.
#
#    Each record is on a single line. Each field in the
#    record is separated by a single tab character
#    ("\t"). The database has four fields:
```

(continued)

(continued)

```
#      - Last name
#      - First name
#      - ID number
#      - Telephone extension
```

These lines contain more description of what the program does. Whenever you have a program that needs a data file in a particular format (such as four columns with tabs between them), you really, truly should say that in the comments right at the top of your Perl program.

```
# The name of the database file
$TheDB = 'edata.txt';
```

Like in the previous program, I named the file with its own variable so that it is easy to later change it. Astute readers will notice that the file name in this program is in single quotation marks (more properly called *apostrophes*) instead of the double quotation marks in the previous program. You'll find out the difference between single quotation marks and double quotation marks in Chapter 5.

```
# Open the database file but quit if it doesn't exist
open(INDB, $TheDB) or die "The database $TheDB could " .
    "not be found.\n";
```

Yup, just like the previous program. These lines tell Perl to open the file and to quit the program with a helpful message if it can't find the program.

```
while(1) {  # Loop forever
```

Now this may seem a bit strange, but there are times when you want Perl to run a loop forever because the value 1 always means "true." Of course, it won't really go forever, but you don't want to put the test for when it should stop in the `while` statement. Instead, you'll see how you'll get out of the loop a few lines down.

```
print "\nDo you want to search by employee ID (I), " .
    " or quit (Q): ";
```

These lines tell Perl to print a prompt on your screen. Notice that the prompt does *not* end with "\n"; this way, you'll get to type on the same line as the prompt.

```
$DoSearch = <STDIN>;
```

Perl waits for you to type a line at the keyboard and puts whatever you type into the variable $DoSearch.

```
chomp($DoSearch);
```

Same as the previous program: This line tells Perl to remove the end-of-line character(s) from $DoSearch.

```
$DoSearch =~ tr/A-Z/a-z/;
```

This little bit of obscurity does a very neat trick: It translates any uppercase characters in $DoSearch into lowercase. Thus, if you typed **HOWDY**, it would be changed into "howdy." Even though you told the users to type **I** or **Q**, they might have used lowercase letters. Instead of telling them that they did something wrong, it's nicer to just let them enter either upper- or lowercase characters and not complain.

```
# Check if they want to quit
if($DoSearch eq 'q') { last }
```

If the users type **q** or **Q**, the loop will stop. The last statement tells Perl "Jump out the bottom of the block you're in." It's different from the next statement you saw in the previous program, which caused Perl to start the block again at the top. last is the best way to break out of an infinite while loop.

```
# Check if they did *not* say i or I
unless($DoSearch eq 'i') {
    print "You must enter either I or Q.\n";
    next;  # Go out to the while loop
}
```

Well, if the users didn't say **q** or **Q** or **i** or **I**, they must have typed something wrong. The next instruction will restart the loop.

```
# Ask them what ID they want to search for
print "Search for ID number: ";
```

The users are here if they entered an **i** or **I**, so ask them which ID number they want.

```
$SearchFor = <STDIN>;
chomp($SearchFor);
```

Like before, Perl waits for them to type something on the keyboard but this time puts the results in $SearchFor. Don't forget to munch off the end-of-line stuff.

```
# Go to the top of the database in case this isn't
#     the first time they are searching
seek(INDB, 0, 0);
```

In the previous program, you went through the text file from the top to bottom, just once. In this one, you want to look through the file each time they type an ID number. Thus, you have to tell Perl "stop reading the file where you are and start at the top again." The seek statement lets you tell Perl where in the file to start; in this case, the instruction is to start at the top.

```
# Reset the count of successes
$SuccessCount = 0;
```

You want to know how many records are found for each request. The database being used right now has one person per ID. Because you might later have more than one person per ID, counting the number of successes may be useful.

```
# Loop through the records in the file
while(<INDB>) {
    $TheRec = $_;
    chomp($TheRec);
```

This while loop reads each record of the database. As before, the program reads a record, assigns it to a variable, and chomps the end-of-line from it. After Perl has read the last record, it will jump outside this while's block.

```
($LastName, $FirstName, $ID, $Tel) =
    split(/\t/, $TheRec);
```

Here's something new. The split function splits a string into many other strings, based on a separator string. The /\t/ tells Perl to look for tab characters. This statement then fills in the four variables $LastName, $FirstName, $ID, and $Tel with the four fields from the record.

```
if($ID eq $SearchFor) {
    $SuccessCount = $SuccessCount + 1;
    print "$ID: $FirstName $LastName, ext. ".
```

```
            "$Tel\n";
    }  # End of if
```

The if statement compares the field from the record with the field the user was looking for. If they match, the block is executed. These statements add 1 to the $SuccessCount and print out the record.

```
    }  # End of while(<INDB>)
```

This is the end of the inner while block, meaning that there are no more records in the database.

```
    if($SuccessCount == 0) { print "No records found.\n" }
    else { print "$SuccessCount records found.\n" }
```

Print the number of records found. The else is part of the if, and only is executed if the if is false.

```
}  # End of while(1)
```

Users will end up here after they enter **q** or **Q**.

```
print "Program finished.\n";
```

You know, it's always polite to say goodbye when you leave.

Running empdata1.pl

Because this is an interactive program, it's not quite as easy to show how it runs. You start the program the same way you started the previous one (which is the same way you'll start the rest of them). If you've forgotten how to run programs, it's all covered earlier in this chpater. Figure 4-2 shows what the screen looks like when Perl is waiting for the first input.

Type **I** or **i** and press Enter or Return.

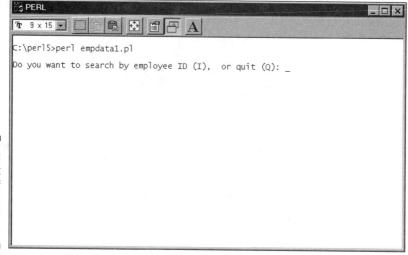

Figure 4-2:
The first
prompt of
the
empdata1.pl
program.

A side note: The key above the right Shift key on your keyboard may be labeled one of two things: Enter or Return. In this book, whenever I say "press Enter," I mean to press the key above the right Shift key, not the key on the extreme right of the keyboard on the numeric keypad. This is a frightfully confusing problem for many novice computer users, and even advanced folks get it wrong from time to time as well.

The program now prompts you

```
Search for ID number:
```

and waits for you to type something. For this example, type **15** and press Enter. The program finds the record and gives you the original prompt again, as shown in Figure 4-3.

You can keep playing around with the program, entering different things for the various prompts and watching the result. As you know, to leave the program, just type **q** or **Q** when the program prompts you.

What to Do If Perl Finds a Problem

If you type in a program for this book or start writing your own programs, it is easy to mistype. When you run a program with an error that causes Perl to not understand what is going on, Perl will report an error. The natural reaction for most people, even those of us with years of programming, is to get worried or angry or both.

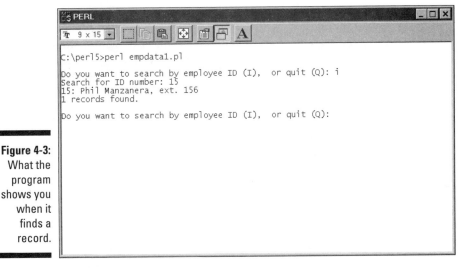

Figure 4-3:
What the
program
shows you
when it
finds a
record.

Don't panic. Take a deep breath. Take another slow, deep breath. Seriously, you won't be able to fix the problem effectively if you're tense and bothered and not breathing. Trust me, no matter how long you program, you'll always find errors when you enter programs. I've been doing this for years, and I still often get Perl errors when I first type in a new program. Breathing is good, and a silly computer error shouldn't get in the way of your life.

So, now that you are (hopefully!) a bit calmer, you can start to appreciate that Perl has more helpful error messages than almost any other programming language. The messages aren't always exactly right, but they get you pretty close to where the problem is with the least searching on your part.

Perl has a myriad of error messages, but a few of them come up over and over when you have typing errors in your programs. The following errors were produced by slightly mistyping parts of counter1.pl.

The forgotten semicolon

Probably the most common error message you might see looks something like this:

```
# syntax error, near "open"
File 'counter1.pl'; Line 10
# Execution aborted due to compilation errors.
```

You look and you look at line 10, the one with the open statement, and you don't see anything wrong with it. The trick here is to look one statement *before* the open statement and see if it ends with a semicolon. Remember that Perl only knows when you end a statement when it sees a semicolon. If you leave one out, Perl gets confused when it sees what you thought was the next statement of the program. In this case, the error was caused by a missing semicolon at the end of line 7:

```
$TheFile = "sample.txt"
```

The forgotten quotation mark

This is also one of the most frustrating errors:

```
# Bare word found where operator expected, near
# "open(INFILE, $TheFile) or die "The"
# (Might be a runaway multi-line "" string starting on
#        line 7)
File 'counter1.pl'; Line 10
```

This error is similar to forgetting a semicolon: forgetting a quotation mark.

```
$TheFile = "sample.txt;
```

In this case, Perl did a good job of guessing what I had done wrong, suggesting that I might have created a "runaway multi-line "" string" on line 7, which is precisely right.

Having one parenthesis too many or too few

When you have lots of left and right parentheses, it's easy to slip an extra one in by accident. In that case, you'll see something like this:

```
# syntax error, near ") eq"
File 'counter1.pl'; Line 38
# syntax error, near "}"
File 'counter1.pl'; Line 42
```

Here, Perl can't really decide where I made the error, but it actually got it right on the first guess: I added a second right parenthesis on line 38:

```
if(substr($TheLine, $CharPos, 1)) eq " ")
```

Having one parenthesis too few can cause harder-to-find problems:

```
# Can't use constant item as left arg of implicit ->,
# near "1 )"
File 'counter1.pl'; Line 39
# Scalar found where operator expected, near "$CharPos"
File 'counter1.pl'; Line 40
# (Missing semicolon on previous line?)
# syntax error, near "$CharPos "
File 'counter1.pl'; Line 40
```

Yarp! All this because I forgot the last parenthesis on line 38:

```
if(substr($TheLine, $CharPos, 1) eq " "
```

This is another good lesson in hunting down typing errors: start where Perl says it found an error. If you don't find the error there, go up a line or two and see if the problem started there.

Onward into Perldom!

Enough of worrying about what to do in case of errors. Trust Perl to find the simple typos for you (where it can), and remember that it's giving you all the help it can, which is more than you can say for many programming languages. The next five chapters tell you how to really get into Perl, how to do some pretty nifty things with text and numbers, how to make lists (which are much more useful than they sound right now), and how to get the most out of loops and conditional statements.

These following chapters have their own short programs, but they also use parts of the two programs from this chapter. You'll see how to change some of the lines in these two sample programs to extend the programs to do more things and to make them more flexible and friendly.

Perl awaits you.

Part II
Most of What You Need

THE GREAT THING ABOUT OBJECT-ORIENTED PROGRAMMING IS, IT'S MADE SOFTWARE DEVELOPMENT AS EASY AS PUTTING ONE FOOT IN FRONT OF THE OTHER.

In this part . . .

Perl is a fairly easy programming language to learn. By the time you finish the five chapters in Part II, you'll know much of what you need to know to program in Perl. This part contains information about text, about numbers, and about some programming features that only Perl has. Discovering these programming features will get you well on the way to being a Perl programmer.

Chapter 5
Terrific Text

. . . .

. . . .

So far, you've only seen a smattering of what Perl can do. The two examples in Chapter 4 had about two dozen different Perl statements, functions, and operators, but there's much more to Perl. This chapter and the next four chapters introduce you to the way Perl works by looking at the major types of data Perl works on, showing you the ways you can use Perl to handle the data. This chapter starts the series by describing one of Perl's strongest features, text handling.

Some of the examples in these chapters are based on the two programs you saw in Chapter 4. You'll see some examples in which one or the other of the programs is changed to do something different or more interesting. I have included many other examples to show you a small sample of how to use new Perl features.

Seeing Your Text: The print Statement

By far, one of the most common Perl statements that you will use over and over is the print statement. You saw it in both examples in Chapter 4, and you'll see it all over this book because it is the best way for you to try out new features and experiment with them yourself.

The `print` statement has many forms, but the one you'll use for now has the statement followed by one argument. The argument for `print` can be a string or a number, such as

```
print "This is a string!";
print 72;
```

(When you learn about lists in Chapter 7, you'll see that `print` can take a list as an argument. When you learn about files in Chapter 12, you'll see how to use `print` to write to a file.)

As you go through the rest of the book, feel free to experiment with what you're learning by writing short Perl programs and running them on your computer. You can always use the `print` statement to see the results of what you're doing. For example, if you just learned how to add two numbers together with the + operator (as you will in Chapter 6), you can test your addition capabilities with a one-line program like

```
print 2+3;
```

Just as you would expect, the program will display

```
5
```

You can also do the same thing with a two-line program:

```
$a = 2 + 3;
print $a;
```

The result is the same: Perl prints 5 on your screen.

The Basics of Text

Even the dweebiest of us use text much more than numbers in our daily lives. We talk, we read, we jot down notes, and so on all day long. Even slow readers know how to do interesting things with text, such as quickly skimming through a book or down a list of names when looking for a particular person.

Thinking in computer terms, there are four basic things that you would want a program to do: read text, write text, search through text, and change text. Perl can do all of these and more.

Text items in Perl are called *strings*. A string is zero or more characters put together in a single chunk. The characters can be any character that you can type, and many that you can't. An example of a one-character string is the letter *d*. An example of a five-character string literal is *vbn59*. Perl variables can hold either strings or numbers. This chapter talks about strings; Chapter 6 talks about numbers.

There is no practical limit to the length of a Perl string: Go ahead and make them as long as you want. The shortest string you can create has zero characters; this is also called a *null string*. This may at first seem odd to you: How can a string with "some text" have no text in it?

A null string makes sense because Perl knows how to remove things from strings. If you have a string called `$Short` that has one character and you remove that character from the string, you would expect the string to be smaller, not to disappear. In a similar vein, if you want to build a string character by character, you would want to start with no characters and go from there.

What is a Character?

Strings consist of zero or more characters. That's fine and good, but most people don't know what computers think characters are. You may think that characters are the things you see on the screen of your computer or on the page of this book, but computers have a much more liberal view of what characters are.

Certainly, the letters, digits, and punctuation you see are characters. The following line contains seven characters:

```
Yy18*#.
```

But many other kinds of characters exist that don't appear on the screen or paper, or that appear differently on different computers.

For the purposes of Perl, a character is an eight-bit byte. Not a very interesting definition, is it? However, this kind of generality is needed because there are many characters that cannot be represented on the screen or in print.

So, how does this bits and bytes definition fit in with what you often think of as characters? Each byte can have a value in it. The values range from 0 to 255, inclusive. International standards exist for how some of the values correspond to letters, digits, and punctuation. The standards say things like

- ✔ The value 65 means A
- ✔ The value 66 means B
- ✔ The value 97 means a
- ✔ The value 48 means 0

and so on. If a computer thinks it is supposed to display a byte, and that byte has the value 65, the computer knows that it should display a capital A.

One of the problems with this scheme is that there are some character values that cannot be displayed. A simple one is the value 20, which means the character "space." Maybe you type so much you don't think that when you press the spacebar on your keyboard you are entering a character, but you are.

A more problematic example is the value 13, which means "carriage return." On a typewriter (remember those?), this means "stay on the same line but go to the far left." On a computer screen, it can mean something similar, but usually not. Other examples of nonprinting characters are the value 7 ("beep"), value 12 ("form feed"), and value 24 ("cancel"). A slew of these values represents valid characters even though they do not result in anything being displayed.

And why stop there? The original standard for characters, ASCII, is now a relic even though it is the basis for all other character standards. ASCII only defined equivalents for the values 0 to 127, and as you've just seen, not all the equivalents can be seen. Because characters can have values from 0 to 255, ASCII leaves 128 to 255 undefined.

Well, computer geeks hate to leave anything undefined, so they have specified what the other values should signify. Unfortunately, computer geeks often aren't all that strong on communication skills, so different groups define the values differently. Every group thinks that its set of value-to-character mappings is best and tries to force other people to go along. So far no one has been successful.

For instance, when the IBM PC came out in 1981, IBM decided to make its own set of definitions. It decreed that the value 128 meant a capital C with a cedilla underneath it (Ç), 129 meant a lowercase u with an umlaut over it (ü), and on and on. Apple, on the other hand, defined 128 as a capital A with an umlaut over it (Ä), 129 as a capital A with a circle over it (Å), and so on.

What a pandemonium. The thing to learn here is that in computers, characters are really just numeric values between 0 and 255 and that there are standard representations for 93 of them. The 93 visible characters are

```
ABCDEFGHIJKLMNOPQRSTUVWXYZ
abcdefghijklmnopqrstuvwxyz
0123456789
!"#$%&'()*+,-./:;<=>?@[\]^_'{|}~
```

Note that these are not shown in order by value.

Listing 5-1 shows a program that displays all 93 of the standard visible characters. It uses math that is explained in Chapter 6 (the % operator), the `for` loop statement that is described in Chapter 8, and the `sprintf` function that is shown in Chapter 9. In other words, don't be surprised if you don't understand what's going on in the program. However, the results are two handy tables that show the correspondence between characters and their values, as shown in Figure 5-1.

Listing 5-1: chartab1.pl, a program that displays a table of characters and their values.

```perl
# chartab1.pl: A program to display character tables

$Column = 1;
$Out = '';
for ($i = 33; $i<=126; $i++) {
    $Out .= sprintf("%3s", $i) . "=" . chr($i) . "  ";
    if(($Column % 10) == 0) { $Out .= "\n" }
    $Column += 1;
}

$Out .= "\n\n";
$Column = 1;
for ($i = 33; $i<=126; $i++) {
    $Out .= chr($i). "=" . sprintf("%3s", $i) . "   ";
    if(($Column % 10) == 0) { $Out .= "\n" }
    $Column += 1;
}
print $Out;
```

Quoting Text

When you want to tell Perl to use a literal string, you use quoted text. There are two main ways that you enter quoted text: with single and double quotes. For example, you can assign the characters "Help me!" to the variable `$Shout` with the statement

```
MS-DOS Prompt                                                          _ □ ✕
T  9 x 15 ▾    □ ⬚ 🗐   🗐 🗗  A

C:\perl5>perl chartab1.pl
33=!    34="    35=#    36=$    37=%    38=&    39='    40=(    41=)    42=*
43=+    44=,    45=-    46=.    47=/    48=0    49=1    50=2    51=3    52=4
53=5    54=6    55=7    56=8    57=9    58=:    59=;    60=<    61==    62=>
63=?    64=@    65=A    66=B    67=C    68=D    69=E    70=F    71=G    72=H
73=I    74=J    75=K    76=L    77=M    78=N    79=O    80=P    81=Q    82=R
83=S    84=T    85=U    86=V    87=W    88=X    89=Y    90=Z    91=[    92=\
93=]    94=^    95=_    96=`    97=a    98=b    99=c    100=d   101=e   102=f
103=g   104=h   105=i   106=j   107=k   108=l   109=m   110=n   111=o   112=p
113=q   114=r   115=s   116=t   117=u   118=v   119=w   120=x   121=y   122=z
123={   124=|   125=}   126=~

!= 33   "= 34   #= 35   $= 36   %= 37   &= 38   '= 39   (= 40   )= 41   *= 42
+= 43   ,= 44   -= 45   .= 46   /= 47   0= 48   1= 49   2= 50   3= 51   4= 52
5= 53   6= 54   7= 55   8= 56   9= 57   := 58   ;= 59   <= 60   == 61   >= 62
?= 63   @= 64   A= 65   B= 66   C= 67   D= 68   E= 69   F= 70   G= 71   H= 72
I= 73   J= 74   K= 75   L= 76   M= 77   N= 78   O= 79   P= 80   Q= 81   R= 82
S= 83   T= 84   U= 85   V= 86   W= 87   X= 88   Y= 89   Z= 90   [= 91   \= 92
]= 93   ^= 94   _= 95   `= 96   a= 97   b= 98   c= 99   d=100   e=101   f=102
g=103   h=104   i=105   j=106   k=107   l=108   m=109   n=110   o=111   p=112
q=113   r=114   s=115   t=116   u=117   v=118   w=119   x=120   y=121   z=122
{=123   |=124   }=125   ~=126
C:\perl5>
```

Figure 5-1:
Character-
value tables
output by
the
chartab1.pl
program.

```
$Shout = 'Help me!';
```

or

```
$Shout = "Help me!";
```

In this case, the two different methods of quoting have the same result.
However, in other cases they have very different meanings. In order to
understand how to use text in Perl, you must understand how to use
quotation marks.

Single versus double quotes

The difference between single and double quotation marks can be summa-
rized as "single quotation marks do not interpret, but double quotation
marks do." That is, if you put something in single quotation marks, Perl
assumes that you want the exact characters you see between the marks. If
you place text inside double quotation marks, however, Perl interprets
variable names. As you will see later, Perl also interprets special characters
inside double-quoted literals.

To see this clearly, note that the following short program uses single quotes
in the print statement:

```
$Book = 'Perl For Dummies';
print 'The title is $Book.';
```

When you run this program, Perl displays

```
The title is $Book.
```

Now change the single quotes to double quotes in the `print` statement:

```
$Book = 'Perl For Dummies';
print "The title is $Book.";
```

When you run this revised program, Perl displays

```
The title is Perl For Dummies.
```

In the first program, the single quotes tell Perl not to interpret anything inside the quotation marks. In the second program, Perl sees the double quotes, interprets the variable `$Book`, and then inserts that into the text.

Note that the period at the end of the `print` statement appears immediately after the value of `$Book`. After interpreting the variable `$Book`, **Perl starts** looking for text again, sees the period, and therefore prints it.

You can have as many variables as you want inside double-quoted strings:

```
$Word1 = "thank";
$Word2 = "you";
$Sentence = "I just wanted to say $Word1 $Word2.";
print $Sentence;
```

These lines print

```
I just wanted to say thank you.
```

Perl interprets each variable and places it directly in the variable `$Sentence`. Notice that when `print` displays the contents of `$Sentence`, it has a space between the two words, just as it should, as well as the period at the end. Perl knows how to pick out just the variables and substitute for them, leaving other characters, such as spaces, as you enter them.

Special characters in text

There are many characters that you cannot type in regular text. Perl defines a few of these characters to make entering strings easy. (See Table 5-1.)

Table 5-1	Special Characters in Strings
Character	*Meaning*
\n	Newline
\r	Carriage return
\t	Tab character
\f	Formfeed character
\b	Backspace character
\v	Vertical tab
\a	Bell or beep
\e	Escape character

Note, however, that the actions that the `print` statement takes when displaying these characters changes from operating system to operating system. The only character that is sure to work everywhere is \n, which always (as far as I can tell) causes the `print` statement to go to the left end of a new line.

MacPerl users should be aware that \n means the same thing as chr(10). This is different than what Unix Perl users are familiar with. On Unix, \n is the same thing as chr(13). There are good technical reasons for this difference, but it can be a real puzzler when you convert programs from one operating system to the other.

The \v character only exists in Perl 5.

For example, the statement

```
print "This is on line one.\nThis is on line two.\n";
```

displays

```
This is on line one.
This is on line two.
```

Here is another example:

```
$Blue1 = "Sapphire";
$Blue2 = "Azure";
print "$Blue1\n$Blue2\n";
```

This statement displays

```
Sapphire
Azure
```

For those of you out there who like to count in hexadecimal or octal, you can also use special backslash formats to indicate characters in these number systems. You can use \x followed by two characters that are the hex value you want, or just \ with an octal value. For instance, the letter B could be represented as \x42 or \102. (Who the heck counts in octal anymore?)

Note that these special characters do *not* work in strings with single quotation marks. Note that the following statement uses single instead of double quotes:

```
print 'This is on line one.\nThis is on line two.\n';
```

Executing this statement displays

```
This is on line one.\nThis is on line two.\n
```

This is not to say that everything inside of single quotation marks appears exactly as it is entered. There are two exceptions: \' and \\. A \' inside either single or double quotation marks will be converted to a single quotation mark, and a \\ inside either single or double quotation marks will be converted to a backslash. This makes sense: You want some way to indicate an apostrophe (') or a backslash (\) inside single quotation marks. Here is an example:

```
print 'Here\'s a backslash: \\.';
```

This program displays

```
Here's a backslash: \.
```

There are two more tricks when using double quotation marks. If you want to put a double quotation mark inside your text, use \".

```
$Shout = "Help me!";
print "And then he shouted \"$Shout\" very loudly.\n";
```

When you run this program, Perl displays

```
And then he shouted "Help me!" very loudly.
```

To prevent Perl from trying to interpret a dollar sign inside double quotation marks, enter it as \$, as in

```
$Sweet = "sugar";
print "\$Sweet is $Sweet.";
```

This displays

```
$Sweet is sugar.
```

Perl also gives you a way to specify a character by its value. Earlier in this chapter, you saw that each character has a value from 0 to 255. If you know the value of the character you want to display, you can use the chr function, whose argument is the value:

```
$CapB = chr(66);
print "The letter after A is $CapB.\n";
```

This displays

```
The letter after A is B.
```

Functions for quoting text

Although quoting text with single and double quotation marks is easy, there are times when you want a function to do the same thing. Perl has two such functions, but they take their arguments in a different way than the functions you have seen. The q function quotes its argument like single quotation marks, and the qq function quotes its argument like double quotation marks. The first thing after the q or qq is the kind of quote you want to use. These functions allow you to use single and double quotation marks within the strings without using \', \\, and \".

For instance, you might want to use q if you have a string that has lots of apostrophes in it. Compare

```
$ISaid = 'This isn\'t Bill\'s shirt, I\'m sure.';
```

with

```
$ISaid = q/This isn't Bill's shirt, I'm sure./;
```

They both assign the same string to $ISaid, but the second one is much easier to read.

You can use any character for the beginning and ending quote. The slash (/) character is common, as is the vertical bar (|):

```
$ISaid = q|This isn't Bill's shirt, I'm sure.|;
```

You can also use parentheses, square brackets, angle brackets, and curly braces for the delimiters. Perl knows that if you use the left member of any of these, that the right member will be the closing one:

```
$ISaid = q(This isn't Bill's shirt, I'm sure.);
```

```
$ISaid = q<This isn't Bill's shirt, I'm sure.>;
```

When you have a lot to say

There's another way to quote text that is particularly useful if you have many lines that you want in your string. Instead of putting a quotation mark at the beginning and end, you can use a *here document*. A here document starts with << and a string that you will use to terminate the quote. At the end of the quote, you put the string by itself on a line. There must be no space between the << and the string.

Here is an example:

```
$TheLongString = <<'BLARG';
This is the first line,
And this is the second,
Which is followed by the third,
And so on, ad nauseum.
BLARG
```

The type of quote that you use for the string determines whether or not Perl interprets any variables. If you had instead used <<"BLARG", you could have put variable names in the long quote, and Perl would have substituted the variable values into $TheLongString.

Putting Strings Together

Okay, enough about quoting. You may have thought you'd never get to *do* anything with strings, just display them, but you're wrong. Perl has operators that let you do things to strings that are similar to addition and multiplication for math.

Think about it a bit: What would "string addition" do? It would take one string and add its text to the end of another string. The technical term for string addition is *concatenation;* Perl's concatenation operator is just a period:

```
print "win" . "dow";
```

displays

```
window
```

You use concatenation in string assignment as well:

```
$Name = "Susan";
$Sentence = "Ask ". $Name . " about the goldfish pond.";
print $Sentence;
```

This displays

```
Ask Susan about the goldfish pond.
```

You will find that you use string concatenation often in your Perl programs. It's a handy way to take information from different places and bring it all together into a single string. However, you often don't need to use it if you are using double-quoted strings. For example, the following two lines have the exact same result:

```
$Sentence = "Ask ". $Name . " about the goldfish pond.";
$Sentence = "Ask $Name about the goldfish pond.";
```

The first line here concatenates three strings; the second line uses substitution within a single string.

You can also use string concatenation for mundane things like making sure your program lines do not become too long. In the empdata1.pl program, you saw the statement

```
        print "$ID: $FirstName $LastName, ext. ".
            "$Tel\n";
```

I used concatenation to avoid running over the end of the line. Instead of printing just one string, Perl prints two concatenated together.

Perl even gives you a cute way of concatenating a string to the end of an existing string with less typing. Assume that you have the string $AllNames to which you keep adding names. You might have the statement

```
$AllNames = $AllNames . $CurrentName;
```

Perl lets you express this in a shorter fashion as

```
$AllNames .= $CurrentName;
```

The . = operator concatenates the string to the right at the end of the string to the left.

Just as you can add strings, you can multiply them. The not-so-technical term for this is *repetition*. Perl uses the x operator for repetition. You use a string on the left of the x and a number on the right, and Perl repeats the string that many times. For instance

```
print 'Q'x10;
```

displays:

```
QQQQQQQQQQ
```

A simple form of string subtraction is to hack the last character off the end of a string. The chop function does this. It is a bit tricky in that the function changes the string into the string minus its last character, but the function returns a value of what got chopped off. Here is an example:

```
$SixLet = "TUVWXY";
$A = chop($SixLet);
print "\$SixLet is now $SixLet and \$A is now $A.";
```

This displays

```
$SixLet is now TUVWX and $A is now Y.
```

chop is most commonly used to chop the newline character off the end of line-oriented input. For instance, the counter1.pl program read lines in from a file. These lines always end in the computers line-ending character. To get rid of that character, you can use chop.

The chomp function is similar to the chop function but with one important difference: chomp knows that some computers have two-character line endings and therefore chomps the right number of characters. You rarely need to worry about this difference, but if you're munching the ends of lines, it's safer to use chomp than chop. (chomp is new to Perl 5, so Perl 4 users can't take advantage of it.)

Simple string transformations

Perl lets you do more than just shove strings together. Many functions let you change the contents of a string. The basic ones are covered here.

When we think of text, we think mostly of letters, and letters come in two varieties: lowercase and uppercase. You can force letters in your text to be in one or the other case with the lc, lcfirst, uc, and ucfirst functions. lc and uc change the case of an entire string; lcfirst and ucfirst change just the first letter. Note that these four functions are new to Perl 5, so Perl 4 users do not have access to them.

For instance

```
$Name1 = "AbCdEf";
$Name2 = "GhIjKl";
print lc($Name1) . " - " . uc($Name2) . "\n";
print lcfirst($Name1) . " - " . ucfirst($Name2) . "\n";
```

The result is

```
abcdef - GHIJKL
abCdEf - GhIjKl
```

If you really like using backslash characters instead of functions, you can use special characters to achieve much the same effect as these four functions. \l and \u cause the next letter in the string to be put into lower- or uppercase. These serve the same purpose as lcfirst and ucfirst.

```
$Name1 = "AbCdEf";
print "\l$Name1\n";
```

displays

```
AbCdEf
```

The \L and \U special characters cause all of the following characters in the string to be put in lower- or uppercase until Perl sees the \E:

```
$Name1 = "AbCdEf";
print "\L$Name1 AND THEN\E \U$Name1\n";
```

displays

```
abcdef and then ABCDEF
```

Getting information from strings

The last two string functions covered here give you information about a string. The counter1.pl program contains the statement

```
$LineLen = length($TheLine);
```

The `length` function returns the number of characters in a string. Here is a simple example:

```
$TodaysWord = 'equilibrate';
print length($TodaysWord);
```

This displays

```
11
```

Earlier in this chapter, you saw the `chr` function, which converts a numeric value into a character. The `ord` function does the opposite: It tells you the numeric value of a character:

```
print ord('C');
```

displays

```
67
```

If the string you use as an argument to `ord` is longer than one character, Perl only looks at the first character in the string when determining the value.

There's More about Strings

This chapter has covered all the simple functions and operators that deal with strings. Chapter 9 covers more advanced string functions, which you'll get to after you've seen some of the great things Perl can do with other kinds of data like numbers and lists.

And, if you're really patient, Chapter 14 is all about a more advanced use of strings called *pattern matching*. I've put off that whole topic until later because Larry Wall, the author of Perl, chose to use a particularly dweeby and not-so-understandable system for letting you search in your strings for particular text. Mind you, it's not impossible to learn, but it definitely does not belong in Chapter 5 of an introductory book. Had he chosen a more sensible and easy way of looking for strings in other strings, I certainly would not have waited until halfway through the book to bring it up, because it is a very useful feature of Perl, one that you do not find in any other popular programming language.

And now, it's time to leave the world of text and go into the realm of numbers.

Chapter 6

Nifty Numbers

· ·

In This Chapter

▶ Understanding numbers

▶ Differentiating integers and reals

▶ Getting to the truth of the matter

▶ Doing all kinds of math, Perl style

▶ Exploring bits and bytes

· ·

So far, you've seen much more about how Perl handles text than you have about how it handles numbers. I don't want you to think, "Oh, Perl must not be very good with numbers." Part of the reason I haven't talked much about Perl's math capabilities is that pretty much every programming language is good with math, and Perl isn't much better or worse than any of them.

Part of the reason that computer programs are so good with math is that computers themselves are pretty darn good with math. No one has made a CPU in the last 20 years that *wasn't* good with math. So people who create programming languages have it pretty easy when it comes to adding a zillion math functions to their programs.

The other reason I haven't said much about math up to this point is that so few people really care. For the vast majority of us, if it adds, subtracts, multiplies, and divides, we're happy. Give us a hand-held calculator that costs $4.99 at the drugstore, and we can do 99 percent of what we need with numbers. I mean, how many of us remember even a teeny bit of what we learned in trigonometry?

Having said that, however, you'll be happy to know that Perl will do a whole lot for you in terms of math, and it does it with less muss and fuss than languages like C or Java. Unlike these other languages, you don't have to spend as much time rigidly defining your numeric variables and making sure that you are only combining two variables of the same type. You can just use a number and go.

Integers and Reals

Computers know how to handle two kinds of numbers: *integers* and *real numbers*. Real numbers are also known as *reals* and *floating-point* numbers. The basic difference is that integers have no decimal point or fractions, while real numbers have a fractional part.

If this were a book about almost any programming language other than Perl, the previous paragraph would be followed by pages and pages of description of how integers are stored in the CPU, how real numbers are handled, how the programming language handles them differently, and so on. It's enough to make most novice programmers run away screaming, or at least crying. Fortunately, you're reading a book about Perl.

Perl stores all of its numerical values internally as real numbers in a fashion that best suits whichever operating system and CPU it is on. When you perform math on numbers in Perl, it uses floating-point math. This fact simplifies things incredibly for you when you write programs because you can just forget about all those different number systems if you want.

Perl can even figure out when you probably want to be thinking in terms of integers instead of reals. When you specify a number without a decimal point and fractional part, Perl knows that it should try really hard to do things as though the number were an integer.

You specify integers as numbers without decimals, and reals as numbers with decimals.

```
$Count = 43;  # An integer
$Temperature = 43.955;  # A real
```

You can also use scientific notation to specify numbers. Scientific notation consists of a number on the left, the letter E, and a number on the right (the "E" can be in either upper- or lowercase). The value on the left is multiplied by 10 after 10 has been raised to the number on the right.

```
$Temperature = .43955E2  # A real in scientific notation
```

This means ".43955 times 10 raised to the power of 2," which is the same as ".43955 times 100."

In other words, don't sweat it with the different kinds of numbers (that is, unless you also are learning some other programming language!). In Perl, a number is a number is a number, and you'll see that they work just fine in all the math you do.

True and False Are Numbers Too

In Perl, as in most other programming languages, you can use mathematical logic to handle values of "true" and "false." For instance, the if statement takes one argument, something that is either true or false. If it's true, the if statement executes the statements in its block.

Logic is covered in Chapter 8, which describes all the statements that use logic. For now you should understand one essential part of logic: how Perl handles things that are true and false. As you might have guessed because you are in the chapter on numbers, Perl uses numbers for true and false values. A false value is the same as the number 0 (zero), and a true value is any other value.

Thus, when a statement checks if something is true, it is really checking if it equals absolutely anything other than the number 0 or the string "0". If it equals either of these, it's false, but if it equals anything else, it's true.

For you text fanatics, a false value can also be the null string (""), but this is rarely used in Perl programs. It is much easier to think of false as 0 and true as everything else. Also, Chapter 9 contains a section on how to do bit-level math using logical values. Bit-level logic is quite different than simple true and false in Perl and can be ignored by all but the most technical programmers.

Perl's Basic Math Operators

Well, first things first. The simple math operations that we all learned in elementary school are addition, subtraction, multiplication, and division. The Perl operators for these are +, -, *, and /.

```
$BigNum = 93 * 46;
print $BigNum;
```

As you can figure out with your calculator, this displays

```
4278
```

As you learned in Algebra I, you can use parentheses to force certain operations to happen first.

```
$a = (5 + 2) - (4 * 9) + (3 / 7); print $a;
```

That's five plus two, minus the product of four and nine, plus the division of three by seven. And that produces

```
-28.5714285714286
```

You should always use parentheses in your mathematical statements. Perl has a list of which operators take precedence over which other operators in case you don't use parentheses, but it's easy to forget which does what. I mean, 5 + 2 - 4 * 9 + 3 / 7 may mean exactly what you want, or it might not. Why tempt fate? Use parentheses so that you can easily see what kind of math you are doing to the numbers and variables in your statements.

You're certainly familiar with how to use a minus sign to make a positive number negative and a negative number positive. For instance, -3 means negative three, and -(-4) means positive four. Perl also lets you use the minus sign with variables to invert their sign:

```
$Count = -2;
$InverseCount = -$Count;
print $InverseCount;
```

This displays

```
2
```

Perl uses the ** operator to raise the number on its left to the power of the number on its right. Thus, to raise 2 to the power of 10, you would use

```
$b=2**10; print $b;
```

This shows

```
1024
```

Modulo arithmetic involves dividing one number by an integer and determining the remaining value. Perl uses the % operator for this. For example, the remainder of 8 divided by 3 is shown as

```
$c=8 % 3; print $c;
```

This statement displays

```
2
```

Note that modulo arithmetic is different than regular division:

```
$c=8 / 3; print $c;
```

This statement displays

```
2.66666666666667
```

Modulo arithmetic uses integer division and remainders. In this case, 3 goes into 8 twice, with a remainder of 2. The % operator reports the remainder.

Doing math and an assignment at the same time

A common task in Perl is to take a variable, do some arithmetic on it, and assign the result to the same variable. For instance, if you want to double the value in $d, you might use

```
$d = $d * 2;
```

Perl lets you compress this statement a bit by putting the desired operator before the = and then not using the variable on the right side of the equation. The previous example can be written as

```
$d *= 2;
```

Another example might be adding 1 to the variable $e:

```
$e += 1;
```

Autoincrementing and Autodecrementing

One of the most common things you do in Perl is add one to a counter each time you go through a loop. You saw this in empdata1.pl, with the statement

```
$SuccessCount = $SuccessCount + 1;
```

Counters like this are so common in Perl that Perl has a special construct that lets you shorten the line even more than using += 1. The previous example with $e could be written as

```
$e++;
```

You can decrement a number (that is, subtract 1 from it) using - - in a similar fashion.

This is one area in which advanced Perl programmers like to get fancy but instead sometimes get cryptic. The ++ and - - operators can be used in the middle of an assignment, and Perl will do something very different if the operator is before or after the variable name. Let's look at just the ++ operator now, but all the same rules apply to the - - operator.

If the operator appears before the variable name, Perl increments the variable and returns the incremented value. If the operator appears after the variable name, Perl returns the original value of the variable and increments the variable. Confusing, huh? The following example may or may not clear this up.

```
$f = 7; $g = $f++;
print "Using \$f++, \$g is $g and \$f is $f\n";
$f = 7; $g = ++$f;
print "Using ++\$f, \$g is $g and \$f is $f\n";
```

This displays

```
Using $f++, $g is 7 and $f is 8
Using ++$f, $g is 8 and $f is 8
```

In the first case, Perl increments $f after its value is assigned to $g; in the second case, Perl increments $f first because the operator appears before it. Yes, this is really cute, and yes, this is sometimes useful. It's also almost always confusing, and most Perl programmers have to look closely at a line of a program that has the ++ or - - operators in it to be sure they're sure what it's doing. Most of the time, += 1 and -= 1 are much clearer, but you are free to use whichever you are most comfortable with.

Simple Numeric Functions

Okay, ready for a few functions instead of operators? Perl has a few functions for simple math that are just as easy to use as operators. sqrt takes the square root of its argument, log takes the natural log (base e) of its argument, and exp raises e to the power of its argument. Here is an example:

```
print "The square root of 121 is " . sqrt(121);
```

The abs function takes the absolute value of its argument, meaning it returns a positive value regardless of whether or not the argument is negative. The int function returns the integer portion of the value. int can be a bit tricky because it rounds down for positive numbers and rounds up for negative numbers.

```
$h = 3.4; $i = int($h); print "$i\n";
```

```
$h = -3.4; $i = int($h); print "$i\n";
```

These statements display

```
3
-3
```

Converting Numbers Into Strings

Here's another place where Perl is much more convenient than other programming languages. You can convert a number into a string without doing anything special. Perl understands that when you do "stringish" things to a number you want that number to be represented as a string. For instance

```
$Ann = 5; $Ann += 1;
$Ann = $Ann . "bcd";
print $Ann;
```

displays

```
6bcd
```

From that point on, $Ann is a string, and you shouldn't treat it like a number.

You can do "numberish" things to strings, but the results are almost impossible to predict accurately. For instance, you can use * to multiply two strings together. Perl tries hard to find numbers in the strings and do the "right thing" with them, but you cannot always guess what that "right thing" is. Don't risk it: Always use math functions and operators just for numbers.

Counting in Other Numbering Systems

If you like to count in either hexadecimal or octal, you can use them easily in Perl. If you have no idea what I'm talking about, feel free to skip to the next chapter; this section is very short and only of interest to folks who have a need to do math with hexadecimal or octal numbers, which is less than 5 percent of the programming population.

To specify a number in hexadecimal (sometimes just called "hex"), you preface it with the characters 0x. To specify a number in octal, you use a leading 0 (zero):

```
$Mask = 0xFF00;
$SomeOctal = 0177;
```

Perl has two functions for converting numbers from those systems to decimal values. The hex and oct functions take strings that represent numbers in their respective formats and return decimal numbers:

```
$Address = 'FFFF';
$Location = hex($Address) + 12;
```

You usually don't need these functions because you can just express the number. For those of you who like hexadecimal, the following program shows how to create a decimal-to-hex conversion chart. It uses some of the math shown in this chapter, as well as some of the list processing you learn about in the next chapter.

```
# hexchart.pl: Prints a decimal-to-hex conversion chart.
@HexD = ('0', '1', '2', '3', '4', '5', '6', '7', '8',
    '9', 'A', 'B', 'C', 'D', 'E', 'F');
for($i = 0; $i <= 255; $i += 1) {
    printf("%3s=$HexD[int($i / 16)]$HexD[$i % 16]   ", $i);
    if(($i % 8) == 7) { print "\n" }
}
```

The output of this chart is 32 lines long, so it can't be shown in a standard 80-character by 24-line screen. The top of the output looks like this:

```
 0=00    1=01    2=02    3=03    4=04    5=05    6=06    7=07
 8=08    9=09   10=0A   11=0B   12=0C   13=0D   14=0E   15=0F
16=10   17=11   18=12   19=13   20=14   21=15   22=16   23=17
24=18   25=19   26=1A   27=1B   28=1C   29=1D   30=1E   31=1F
```

```
32=20  33=21  34=22  35=23  36=24  37=25  38=26  39=27
40=28  41=29  42=2A  43=2B  44=2C  45=2D  46=2E  47=2F
48=30  49=31  50=32  51=33  52=34  53=35  54=36  55=37
56=38  57=39  58=3A  59=3B  60=3C  61=3D  62=3E  63=3F
64=40  65=41  66=42  67=43  68=44  69=45  70=46  71=47
72=48  73=49  74=4A  75=4B  76=4C  77=4D  78=4E  79=4F
80=50  81=51  82=52  83=53  84=54  85=55  86=56  87=57
88=58  89=59  90=5A  91=5B  92=5C  93=5D  94=5E  95=5F
```

Chapter 7

Learning to Love Lists

• •

• •

So far, you've seen two basic kinds of data: text and numbers. Most programming languages don't have any inherent data types other than these two. Well, to be honest, most other programming languages have a bunch of picky different kinds of numbers that seem to exist for no other reason than to make programming difficult. A good example is *long integers,* which are integers that can be much bigger than regular integers. Fortunately, Perl keeps those kinds of numbers to a minimum.

What's On the List for Today?

But I digress. Perl has a third type of data, *lists,* that will help you work much better with any of your data that comes in groups. Understanding lists is also crucial to using Perl's best features. When a Perl function returns more than one value, it always returns them as a list. Perl also uses lists when aggregating its own internal data, so you need to understand lists to use Perl to its fullest.

Fortunately, simple lists are not that hard to understand. A *list* is an ordered gang of things. Nice, simple definition, eh? The things are called *elements* or *items*. An element is either a number or a string. A list has an order: The first element is always first, the second element is always second, and so on. A list has also has a definite length; you can always tell how long a list is.

I lied in the previous paragraph, I admit. Elements can be numbers, strings, or something called *references*. That's the last time you're going to see "references" mentioned in this chapter. References are an advanced topic not covered again until Chapter 16 and then again in Chapter 19. Pretend (for now) that I didn't even mention them.

Incidentally, Perl uses two terms for lists: *lists* and *arrays*. For all practical purposes, these two words mean the same thing and can be used interchangeably. This book mostly uses the term lists but will sometimes slip into using the more formal-sounding array.

Perl uses a special term for "all things that are strings or numbers": *scalars*. A scalar is either a string or a number, and never anything else. Specifically, a scalar is never a list, and a list is never a scalar. You'll see soon why Perl has this additional term: To keep saying "strings or numbers" all the time gets really tedious.

Perl's lists are very much like what you might think they would be with a name like that. Think of a typical (well, maybe not so typical) grocery list:

```
juice
bread
paper towels
asparagus
```

This list has elements, it has an order (juice is first on the list no matter how you look at it), and the list as a whole can be thought of as one item ("my shopping list").

If you keep track of your car's gas mileage, you might have a list that looks like this:

```
23.4
23.6
23.4
22.9
```

Both of these lists are perfectly valid lists for Perl.

The elements in a single list can be both data types. For example, you might have a list that looks like this:

```
juice
bread
9
juice
```

It would be hard to imagine what the logic of the order of the list is, but it is still a valid Perl list.

Naming Lists

A literal list in Perl is almost always shown as a bunch of elements with a comma (,) between each element. In general, you will also see Perl lists in parentheses. Like for math, the parentheses are not absolutely required, but you can sometimes have some very hard-to-diagnose problems if you leave them off, so you should always use them. For example, the grocery list would be

```
('juice', 'bread', 'paper towels', 'asparagus')
```

There are other ways to show lists in Perl, such as without the parentheses, but they are confusing to readers, and sometimes to Perl itself. I won't go into them here because they will just make things more opaque.

So far, all the variable names you have seen have started with $. Perl uses a different symbol for the variable names of lists: the at-sign (@). For instance, you might see the assignment

```
@Shop = ('juice', 'bread', 'paper towels', 'asparagus');
```

This means "the list called Shop is assigned to be four elements long; the first element is 'juice', the second element is 'bread', the third element is 'paper towels', and the fourth element is 'asparagus'."

Thus, list variable names start with @, and scalar variable names start with $. When you see a variable name like @Shop, you know it's a list; when you see a variable name like $Shop, you know it's a string or a number.

Not all lists have elements. There is also the *empty list,* also called the *null list,* that consists of no elements. You can set a list to have no values with an assignment like

```
@Shop = ();
```

Slices of Lists

But what happens if you want to talk about just one element of a list, not the whole list itself? Because lists are ordered, you can refer to each element by its place in the list. You might want to say "set the variable $Dub to the value of the third element of the list @Music."

Here's where Perl's background as a language for people who already know programming rears its ugly head. Perl counts list elements starting at 0, not at 1, as you might expect. Thus, the first element of a list is element number 0, the second element is element number 1, and so on.

If you've used other programming languages like C and Pascal, you're probably already used to this notation. You've also probably forgotten how hard it was to learn this the first time. If Perl is your first programming language, it is exceptionally important for you to drill this into your brain: "Perl counts things in lists beginning at 0."

You can talk about part of a list as a *slice*. You specify a slice by putting the element number(s) of the slice in square brackets ([and]). If you are talking about a slice with a single element, that slice is a scalar slice and must have a $ at the beginning of the list's variable name.

For instance, if you want to print the first element of the @Shop list, you would use

```
@Shop = ('juice', 'bread', 'paper towels', 'asparagus');
print $Shop[0];
```

This would display

```
juice
```

You can assign scalar slices to scalar variables, such as

```
$Third = $Shop[2];
```

This assigns the string paper towels to the variable $Third.

You may be wondering, why do you change the symbol for a slice from @ to $ when discussing a slice that is one element? This is a bit difficult, but it really does make sense deep down. Remember that the values in a list are always scalars, never lists. For instance, the value in Shop[0] is a scalar, not a list. Thus, its name should start with the symbol for a scalar variable, $.

Slices of lists can have more than one element in them. Multi-element slices are themselves lists, and thus their variable names start with @. For instance, a slice of the @Shop list that consists of the second and third elements would be assigned with something like

```
@TwoEls = @Shop[1,2];
```

You can use list slices on the left side of assignments as well. This is common if you want to change the value of one element but don't want to redefine the whole list. For example

```
@Shop = ('juice', 'bread', 'paper towels', 'asparagus');
$Shop[1] = 'muffins';
```

This turns the list in @Shop into

```
('juice', 'muffins', 'paper towels', 'asparagus')
```

Perl makes it easy to know how many elements are in a list. The variable $#listname is the number of the last element. Thus, for our four-element shopping list,

```
print $#Shop;
```

would display

```
3
```

Note that this is *not* the length of the list; it is the number of the last element. The length of the list is that number plus 1.

Perl has what I consider to be a nasty feature that is supposedly there out of friendliness. You can have a list variable and a scalar variable *with the same name* that are completely unrelated. For instance, you can have a program that has both @Shop and $Shop, and the two variables have nothing to do with each other.

This gets pretty confusing when you are first learning how to use single-element array slices. If you forget to put the square brackets and the element number in the variable name, you can easily miss the fact that you're now using a scalar variable that has nothing to do with the list variable.

To keep your sanity, never purposely use a scalar variable with the same name as a list variable. If you have a list called @Shop, do not use a scalar called $Shop; call it something else like $ShopNum.

Lists Are Surprisingly Useful

Don't feel bad if all the above has inundated you a bit. People have a much easier time learning about strings and numbers than they do lists because we often think in terms of text and numbers in our daily lives, and don't really think in terms of lists. We think of list elements, but not lists as a whole.

However, Perl's list handling makes some common tasks really easy. For instance, assume that you want to compare one string against a long set of strings to see if the test string matches any of them. Assume that your test string is in the variable $Test and you know whether any of the words in the string are in the dictionary:

```
. . .
interest
interested
interesting
interface
interfaith
interfere
interferon
intergenerational
. . .
```

Without using lists, your program would look something like

```
. . .
if($Test eq 'interest') { print "A match was found.\n" }
if($Test eq 'interested') { print "A match was found.\n" }
if($Test eq 'interesting') { print "A match was found.\n" }
. . .
```

Creating such a program would be tedious. Further, if you want to perform some different action if the test was successful, updating all the lines of the program would be prone to error.

Instead, the task is simple when using lists. You create a list whose elements are all the words to test against and then loop through the list. You learn about loops in the next chapter, but you can see here how they are useful.

```
. . .
@WordList = (
    'interest', 'interested', 'interesting', 'interface',
    'interfaith', 'interfere', 'interferon',
```

```
        'intergenerational');  # Line breaks are ignored
$ListPos = 0;  # Start at position 0
# Loop until you go off the end of the list
until($ListPos > $#WordList) {
    if($Test eq $WordList[$ListPos])
        { print "A match was found.\n" }
    $ListPos += 1;
}
. . .
```

You now have just one place where the action is given, meaning that updating the program would be much, much easier.

But using lists goes beyond just ease of updating. For example, what if you didn't know the list that you are testing against — until you run the program. This problem is common: The list is kept in a text file that is updated separately from the Perl program.

If you don't use lists, the problem will be impossible to deal with. With lists, it is trivial. Instead of assigning the list at the beginning of the program, you write two or three lines of Perl code (that you learn about in Chapter 12) that will read lines from the text file and add each line to the list @WordList. The loop in the program above remains identical; only the source of the list changes.

The `print` *Statement with Lists*

Until this chapter, you didn't know what lists were, so you wouldn't have known what the phrase "the such-and-so function takes a list as its argument" meant. Many functions take lists as arguments. The most notable example of a function that you have seen that takes a list is the `print` statement (which is also a function, but you can ignore this distinction for now). The `print` statement as you have seen it so far takes one argument: a list. If that list has one element, fine:

```
$Color = "mossy teal";
print $Color;
```

This displays

```
mossy teal
```

You can also print a list in exactly the same fashion:

```
@Color = ('mossy teal', 'burnt umber', 'bone white');
print @Color;
```

This displays

```
mossy tealburnt umberbone white
```

The `print` statement runs the elements together because the list is just a gang of items. You could print the elements one at a time, of course:

```
print $Color[0] . ' ' . $Color[1] . ' ' . $Color[2];
```

This statement shows

```
mossy teal  burnt umber  bone white
```

In this case, you are printing a list that consists of a single string. You can also print a list such as

```
print ($Color[0], ' ', $Color[1], ' ', $Color[2]);
```

This statement shows

```
mossy teal burnt umber  bone white
```

Note that this is a true list with five elements: the first slice, a string, the second slice, another string, and the third slice.

Basic List Functions

You do not have to construct your lists only using assignments. In fact, it's quite common to build up a list by starting with a null list and adding elements one by one.

The two functions you use to add elements to a list are `push` and `unshift`. `push` adds one or more elements to the end of the list, while `unshift` adds elements to the beginning of the list. Each takes two arguments: the name of the list you want to add to and the list of elements you want to add.

Here is an example:

```
@SomeList = (8, 'eight', 9, 'nine');
@TenList = (10, 'ten');
push(@SomeList, @TenList);
unshift(@SomeList, "The Big Seven");
```

@SomeList is now

```
('The Big Seven', 8, 'eight', 9, 'nine', 10, 'ten')
```

You can also remove an element from the beginning or end of a list with the shift and pop functions, respectively. These functions take one argument — the name of the list — and return the value that was removed. For instance,

```
@SomeList = (8, 'eight', 9, 'nine');
$Removed = shift(@SomeList);
print $Removed;
```

displays

```
8
```

and the list @SomeList now contains only three elements:

```
('eight', 9, 'nine')
```

These four functions let you manipulate the two ends of a list to make it grow and shrink as you want. Because the names are not easy to remember, the following may help.

- ✔ shift removes from left side of a list

- ✔ push adds to right side of a list

- ✔ unshift adds to left side of a list

- ✔ pop removes from right side of a list

Perl, being the lenient and flexible language that it is, also has a function that lets you add or remove elements from any part of a list. The splice function removes some elements and adds others in their place. It takes four arguments:

- ✔ The list to modify

- ✔ The element number where to start

- ✔ The number of elements to remove

- ✔ The list of elements to insert

Here is an example:

```
@Nums = (1, 2, 3, 4, 5);
splice(@Nums, 3, 1, ('dog', 'cow'));
```

These lines result in

```
(1, 2, 3, 'dog', 'cow', 5)
```

You don't have to remove any elements in order to add elements with splice. If you set the third argument (the number of elements to remove) to 0, then you'll be just adding to the list:

```
@Nums = (1, 2, 3, 4, 5);
splice(@Nums, 3, 0, ('dog', 'cow'));
```

The @Nums list now equals

```
(1, 2, 3, 'dog', 'cow', 4, 5)
```

Note that when you do not remove any elements, the new elements go *before* the element indicated by the second argument.

Similarly, you can use splice just to remove elements by using a null list:

```
@Nums = (1, 2, 3, 4, 5);
splice(@Nums, 3, 1, ());
```

This results in

```
(1, 2, 3, 5)
```

Perl allows you to leave off the fourth argument if it's a null list. The equivalent splice statement without a null list would be

```
splice(@Nums, 3, 1);
```

When you use splice to remove items, Perl returns those items. For example

```
@Nums = (1, 2, 3, 4, 5);
$GotOne = splice(@Nums, 3, 1);
print $GotOne;
```

displays

```
4
```

If you are removing more than one item, remember to return them into a list:

```
@Nums = (1, 2, 3, 4, 5);
@GotSome = splice(@Nums, 3, 2);
```

The @GotSome list now equals:

```
(4, 5)
```

You can see that the push, unshift, shift, and pop functions are just special cases of splice. You can use them interchangeably. Table 7-1 shows the equivalent functions:

Table 7-1	How splice **Relates to** push, unshift, shift, **and** pop
Function	*splice Equivalent*
push(@r, @s)	splice(@r, $#r+1, 0, @s)
unshift(@r, @s)	splice(@r, 0, 0, @s)
shift(@r)	splice(@r, 0, 1)
pop(@r)	splice(@r, $#r, 1)

Two Nifty List Operators

There's more to lists than functions. Perl has two useful operators that operate on lists to make list creation easier.

You saw in Chapter 5 that the x operator repeats strings. The same operator repeats lists:

```
@h = (883, 895) x 3;
```

@h now equals

```
(883, 895, 883, 895, 883, 895)
```

Perl also makes it easy to create lists that consist of sequential numbers using the range operator, which is two periods (".."), between the starting and ending values:

```
@n = (3 .. 8);
```

This results in the list

```
(3, 4, 5, 6, 7, 8)
```

Note that you have to put the smaller number first when using the range operator; you can't use it, for example, to make the list (8, 7, 6, 5, 4, 3).

You can also use the range operator with characters. For instance, to create the list ('a', 'b', 'c', 'd', 'e', 'f'), you could use

```
('a' .. 'f')
```

Doing the Splits

As I've said over and over throughout the book, Perl is a great text-handling language. The split function is one of the greatest text-handling tools in Perl. The reason that I didn't bring up split in Chapter 5 with the other simple text tools is that split returns a list, and you didn't know about lists then.

Now that you understand lists, you can see why split is the greatest thing since, um, split bread. split looks at a string and splits it apart, returning a list of strings. For example, you can use split to look at a sentence and return a list of each word in the sentence. Or if you have a tab-delimited text file that is a database (like you saw in the empdata1.pl program in Chapter 4), split can split the lines up into fields in a single function.

Unless you use the default arguments (and I recommend against it), split takes two or three arguments. If you want to create a list of all the split-out strings, you use two arguments: the pattern to use as the delimiter and the string to search.

String patterns are reasonably advanced and are not covered until Chapter 14. For now, I'm only going to show you very simple patterns. For the sake of this chapter, the patterns you will use start and end with a slash (/) character and have the exact character you want to split between the slashes.

For instance, to split a sentence into a list of words, you would use

```
$Sentence = "It is time for our tea, Sir.";
@Words = split(/ /, $Sentence);
```

The @Words list is now

```
('It' , 'is' , 'time' , 'for' , 'our' , 'tea,' , 'Sir.')
```

Splitting by tab characters is just as easy. The empdata1.pl program contains the following lines:

```
($LastName, $FirstName, $ID, $Tel) =
    split(/\t/, $TheRec);
```

The first argument in this split statement is the pattern for a tab character (remember from Chapter 5 that \t is a special character). Because you know that each record has four fields, instead of splitting into a named record, you could split directly into the list of variables. This process is somewhat akin to (but much shorter than) doing

```
@TempList = split(/\t/, $TheRec);
$LastName = $TempList[0];
$FirstName = $TempList[1];
$ID = $TempList[2];
$Tel = $TempList[3];
```

If you only want the first few items in a string and don't care about the rest of them, you can use a third argument in split to say how many elements should be in the resulting list. In the previous example, if all you wanted was the last name and first name, you could have used

```
($LastName, $FirstName, $RestOfLine) =
    split(/\t/, $TheRec, 3);
```

In this case, $RestOfLine might or might not have tab characters in it. Split stops looking after the second tab character and stuffs whatever is left into the last element of the array on the left side of the assignment.

You'll probably find many uses for split as you write your own Perl programs. For instance, you may have a text file that has lines like this:

```
Temperature=28.3
Size=large
Color=crimson
Texture=rough
```

For each line, you want to know what the thing on the left is, as well as the value on the right. In your line-by-line loop of your program, you could have

```
($Attribute, $Value) = split(/=/, $TheLine);
```

You would then do some testing based on $Attribute, and so on.

More on Creating Lists

The list-creation assignments you've seen so far all used literals for the values. Of course, Perl is not this limiting. You can use scalar variables in your lists' assignments just as easily:

```
$LakeName = "Mammoth";
$LakeLen = 1291.3;
@Lake[8,9] = ($LakeName, $LakeLen);
```

This causes $Lake[8] to become the string Mammoth and $Lake[9] to become the number 1291.3.

You can also use existing lists when defining new lists. When you name a list while assigning another list, Perl expands the inside list to all its elements. This is a quick way to insert the elements from one list into another:

```
@a = (12, 24, 36);
@b = ('Dozens', @a);
```

@b is now set to

```
('Dozens', 12, 24, 36)
```

Perl does this because list elements cannot be lists themselves. If you try this, Perl politely pulls out all the elements of the inner list and puts them in the list on the left side of the assignment.

Scalar Context Versus List Context

It's time to talk about one of Perl's big weaknesses. This is something that was built into Perl from the very early days, and no one has fixed it because advanced programmers don't have many problems with it, even though novice and intermediate programmers can trip over it without warning.

Perl has two *contexts:* scalar and array. (Remember that "array" and "list" are synonymous.) Perl uses the context of an expression to determine what kind of output a function or operator will have. Without getting into too much detail, you can determine which context you are in by looking at what kind of assignment is going on. Here is an example:

```
$a = somefunction($b);    # scalar context
@c = somefunction($d);    # array context
($e, $f) = somefunction($g);   # array context
```

The general rule is that if the thing on the left of the assignment is a scalar, you're in scalar context; if the thing on the left of the assignment is a list, you're in array context. Note in the third example, even though there are scalar variables, they are in a list, so it is in the array context.

Most of the time, you don't care which context a function is in because the function returns the same result in either case. However, some Perl functions have completely different results depending on the context. A few Perl operators also change their output depending on the context.

So far, you have only come across one function that had this dual personality: the split function. All the previous examples showed the split function in an array context: The left-hand side of the assignments were always lists. If the left-hand side was a scalar, however, split returns the number of elements that it found. For instance

```
$x = "This has exactly five words.";
@y = split(/ /, $x);
$z = split(/ /, $x);
```

In this case, @y is set to the list

```
('This', 'has', 'exactly', 'five', 'words.')
```

However, $z is set to

```
5
```

These two different results, coming from the same function call of split(/ /, $x), are due to the differences in the context.

And, here's a place where Perl gets really confusing. If you use the name of a list in a scalar context, Perl interprets it as the length of the list. This little bit of shorthand is terribly confusing to even advanced programmers unless they look at it carefully. You can say something like

```
@h = ('A', 'short', 'list', 'of', 'words');
$ListLen = @h;
print $ListLen;
```

and Perl will display

```
5
```

Using $#h+1 is always less confusing than using @h to get the list length.

There are times when you want to force Perl to evaluate things in a scalar context. You can use the scalar function to do this. If you must use @ to get the list length, you can use scalar to prevent your program from being as confusing. For instance

```
@h = ('A', 'short', 'list', 'of', 'words');
print scalar(@h);
```

This prints

```
5
```

Without the scalar function, Perl would have printed out all the elements of the list.

Chapter 8

Cool Conditionals and Lovely Loops

Almost every Perl program you will write has an `if` statement in it. The nature of programs is that you use them to make decisions and then act on those decisions. It's amazing what kind of logic you can use with just the `if` statement.

The `if` statement gives you two simple choices: If this is true, do A, otherwise do B. However, a very common thing to do in programs is to say "loop around while this is true." For example, "as long as there are more lines in the file, do this," or "while there are still elements in this list, do that." Perl's `while` statement makes looping quite easy because you are assured that the program will come back to check if the loop is done every time it goes through the block of statements.

A Little about Logic

The `if` statement takes one argument: a logical value. The simple format of the `if` statement is

```
if(LOGICAL) { BLOCK }
```

This means that, if the argument is true, execute the block of statements, otherwise, just go on to the next statement after the if statement. The slightly less simple form is

```
if(LOGICAL) { BLOCK1 } else { BLOCK2 }
```

This means that, if the argument is true, execute BLOCK1, otherwise execute BLOCK2.

But before you get too far into if, you need to know a bit more about Perl's logic. In Chapter 6, where you learned about math, you saw that Perl uses 0 (zero) for logical false and everything else for logical true. In order to generate a true or false value, you usually use Perl's comparison operators to compare two things. For example, you might test if one numeric variable is larger than another, or whether a certain variable equals 7, or whether a string variable is equal to 'y', or some such thing.

The true-false comparison operators you use in Perl are contained in Table 8-1.

Table 8-1	True-False Comparison Operators	
Comparison	*Math*	*String*
Equal to	==	eq
Not equal to	!=	ne
Less than	<	lt
Greater than	>	gt
Less than or equal to	<=	le
Greater than or equal to	>=	ge

It is a good idea to put comparisons in parentheses so that you can easily see what's going on in a statement. When you do a comparison, Perl returns a 0 if the comparison is false or some value other than 0 if the comparison is true. In fact, Perl often returns 1 if the comparison is true, but you should not rely on Perl to do this.

Here is an example:

```
$T1 = 5;
$T2 = 3;
if($T1 > $T2) { print "$T1 is greater than $T2\n" };
```

Perl displays

```
5 is greater than 3
```

If you change the values for $T1 and $T2 to 4 and 6, respectively, you get different results; namely Perl does not print anything.

One of the most common mistakes people use with numeric comparison operators is to compare two numbers with the = operator instead of the == operator (that's two equal signs with no space between them). You *must* use the == operator in comparisons because = almost always returns true — because it's not comparing anything:

```
$a=3;
if($a = 7) { print "It's true!\n" }
else { print "It's false!\n" }
```

This will always print

```
It's true!
```

Even though you can see that you want it to not be true. Of course, if you replace the if($a = 7) with if($a == 7), the program will work as you expect.

Note that to compare strings, you must use the comparison operators in the third column of Table 8-1. Thus, you might have

```
if($Time eq 'early') { print "It is early!\n" };
```

Most of the time, you use only the eq and ne string comparison operators. However, you can also use the others to determine which string would come first in a comparison of the values of the characters in the two strings. For instance, 'a' is less than 'b', 'ad' is less than 'ae', and so on. The order of which letter is higher or lower comes from the ASCII ordering you saw in Chapter 5.

Perl compares two strings until it finds a letter that is not equal in each, and bases its result on that letter. For example, in comparing 'abcd' to 'abxy', it would find that the first two letters were identical, and make the comparison based on 'c' versus 'x'.

Perl also has a comparison operator that returns three different values. This operator, sometimes called "three-value compare," is <=> for numbers and cmp for strings. They return -1, 0, or 1 if the value on the left is less than, equal to, or greater than, respectively, the value on the right. For example, if $a is set to 4, 3 <=> $a would return -1, 4 <=> $a would return 0, and 5 <=> $a would return 1. For strings, if $b is set to Frank, 'Bob' cmp $b would return -1 because 'B' is less than 'F', 'Bob' cmp $b would return 0, and 'Bonnie' cmp $b would return 1 because 'n' is greater than 'b' (the first two letters are the same).

You can link conditional tests together in Perl just like you would in an English sentence. For example, you might say, "If I am hungry and there are cashews in the cupboard, I will have a snack." This means that only if both statements "I am hungry" and "there are cashews in the cupboard" are true will you have a snack; if either statement is false, you won't. Another example is "If it is Mickey or Billy on the phone, I'll take the call." In this case, if either of the two statements "Mickey is on the phone" or "Billy is on the phone" is true, then you will take the call.

Perl can handle this kind of multipart logic with ease. The two most common operators you will use are and and or, just as you would expect. You put these operators between logical tests, and the result is another logical value. Again, you should always use parentheses to help keep your programs readable.

Here is an example that uses and:

```
if(($Hunger >= 8) and ($Cupboard[4] eq 'cashews'))
    { print "OK, OK, you can have a small snack.\n" }
```

Here is an example that uses or:

```
if(($Caller eq 'Billy') or ($Caller eq 'Mickey'))
    { print "Answer the phone already!\n" }
```

You can also use the not operator to reverse the sense of one of the tests. For example, you might say, "If it's Sunday and I'm not resting, something must be wrong." You could write this as

```
if(($Day eq 'Sunday') and not ($RestVal >= 7))
    { print "Time to get away from that computer...\n" }
```

You can use && instead of and, || instead of or, and ! instead of not, if you wish. In fact, if you're using Perl 4, you have to use &&, ||, and ! because the and, or, and not operators were introduced in Perl 5.

If you are a Perl 5 user, you can also use the xor operator. This operator returns true if the two things have different truth values but returns false if they have the same truth value. (See Table 8-2.)

Table 8-2	The Results of the xor Operator	
If A is	*And B is*	*Then A xor B is*
True	True	False
True	False	True
False	True	True
False	False	False

xor isn't all that useful in daily life, but some programs have a need for it, so it's nice that Perl 5 provides it.

If You Like Conditionals Like I Like Conditionals . . .

Okay, it's time to get out of operators and back into statements. As you saw earlier in this chapter, the if statement looks like

```
if(LOGICAL) { BLOCK }
```

or

```
if(LOGICAL) { BLOCK1 } else { BLOCK2 }
```

If you are using the second form, and your else block starts with another if, you can use the form

```
if(LOGICAL1) { BLOCK1 } elsif(LOGICAL2) { BLOCK2 }
    else { BLOCK3 }
```

This means that if the first comparison is true, Perl executes BLOCK1 and ignores the rest. If the first comparison is false but the second one is true, Perl executes BLOCK2 but not BLOCK1 and BLOCK3. If neither of the comparisons are true, Perl executes BLOCK3. It is important to realize that, in any form of the if statement, Perl executes only one of the blocks.

By the way, you can stack elsif clauses:

```
if(LOGICAL1) { BLOCK1 }
   elsif(LOGICAL2) { BLOCK2 }
   elsif(LOGICAL3) { BLOCK3 }
   elsif(LOGICAL4) { BLOCK4 }
   else { BLOCK5 }
```

Also, you don't *have* to use an else if you've used elsif, but most programs usually do. Note that elsif is not spelled with a second "e." Do not use elseif or else if; Perl will give you an error if you do.

If your conditional test in the if statement starts with not, you can use unless instead of if. unless is exactly the same as if not. For instance

```
if(not($Flavor eq 'banana'))
   { print "Excuse me, but I ordered banana.\n" }
```

is the same as

```
unless($Flavor eq 'banana')
   { print "Excuse me, but I ordered banana.\n" }
```

Using unless makes programs a bit clearer, particularly if the logic inside the argument is already convoluted enough without the not.

Looking at old ifs

If you didn't already, now you can understand the if statements in the two programs from Chapter 4. In counter1.pl, you saw

```
   if($TheLine eq "") { next };
```

and

```
      if(substr($TheLine, $CharPos, 1) eq " ")
         { $WordCount = $WordCount + 1 }
```

The first if tests whether or not the contents of the string $TheLine equals the null string; if it does, Perl executes the next statement (which is described later). In the second if, Perl sees whether the result of the substr function is equal to a string that consists of a single space; if it is, Perl increments $WordCount.

In empdata1.pl, you saw

```
if($DoSearch eq 'q') { last }
```

and

```
if($ID eq $SearchFor) {
    $SuccessCount = $SuccessCount + 1;
    print "$ID: $FirstName $LastName, ext. ".
        "$Tel\n";
} # End of if
```

and

```
if($SuccessCount == 0) { print "No records found.\n" }
else { print "$SuccessCount records found.\n" }
```

as well as

```
unless($DoSearch eq 'i') {
    print "You must enter either I or Q.\n";
    next;  # Go out to the while loop
}
```

The first and second if statements are simple string equivalence tests. The third if has a simple numerical equivalence and an else clause. As you can see, if $SuccessCount is equal to 0, Perl prints a negative message. If $SuccessCount equals anything else, Perl prints a positive message with the number found.

The unless statement is used instead of an if and a negative test because it's easier to read. This statement could also have been written as

```
if($DoSearch ne 'i') {
    print "You must enter either I or Q.\n";
    next;  # Go out to the while loop
}
```

Note that the unless and eq have changed to if and ne.

A conditional operator

If you have an if statement that is used to determine an assignment, you might want to use the ? operator as a shorthand. This operator has a test before it; if the test is true, it returns the result to the right of the ?; but if it is false, it returns the result that is to the right of the following : operator. That is, the ? operator returns the value before the " operator if the test is true and returns the value after the : operator if the test is false.

As you can see, this is not an easy operator to describe in words. For instance, if you have something like

```
if($Texture eq 'smooth') { $PaintVal = 'yes' }
else { $PaintVal = 'no' }
```

you can turn it into

```
$PaintVal = ($Texture eq 'smooth') ? 'yes' : 'no';
```

Although this is more compact, it's also more difficult to read. You might therefore avoid using it merely for general aesthetic principles.

Going Around in Loops

The if statement is useful if you want to do a test, then execute one block of code if the test was true, and then move on after executing that block. However, the if statement doesn't help you if you want to loop around and keep trying the test. For instance, you might want to do something like this:

```
Look for any corners that have dirt in them. If you find
one, clean it. Keep looking and cleaning until you don't
find any more dirty corners.
```

Here is a more computerlike example:

```
See if there are any characters left in the string; if so,
cut off a character, do some more processing, and then go
            back
and see if there is anything left in the string.
```

Perl lets you create these kinds of loops easily. The while statement looks like

```
while(LOGICAL) { BLOCK }
```

The first time Perl comes across a while statement, it sees if the argument is true. If it is, Perl executes the statements in the block. When it reaches the end of the block, Perl checks the while argument again; if the argument is true, Perl executes the block again, and so on.

Avoiding infinite loops

You might be thinking, "Er, why would I write a program that keeps looping around forever?" Good question, and the answer is, "You wouldn't." Perl terminates while loops whenever one of the following things occurs:

- ✔ Something inside the loop makes it so the logical test will change from true to false.
- ✔ A last statement in the loop is executed.

It is quite common to have something inside a while loop affect the test on which the while loop is based. Here is an example:

```
$Counter = 3;
while($Counter > 0) {
    print "$Counter   ";
    $Counter -= 1;
}
print "\nI made it to zero.\n";
```

This displays

```
3  2  1
I made it to zero.
```

As you can see, Perl changes the $Counter variable inside the loop and performs the test each time with a new value.

Incidentally, the until statement is exactly like a while followed by a not or a similar negative. The relationship of until and while is just like unless and if. The preceding program with an until (and with the > changed to <=) would look like this:

```
$Counter = 3;
until($Counter <= 0) {
    print "$Counter   ";
    $Counter -= 1;
}
print "\nI made it to zero.\n";
```

Loop hopping

The second method for getting out of a loop is the `last` statement. This statement is just like saying "jump to the end of the loop, right after the closing brace." You can use `last` instead of using the logical test in the `while`. Here is an example:

```
$Counter = 3;
while(1) {  # This is always true!
    print "$Counter  ";
    $Counter -= 1;
    unless($Counter > 0) { last }
}
print "\nI made it to zero.\n";
```

As before, this displays

```
3  2  1
I made it to zero.
```

You can use two other statements, `next` and `redo`, to do other things inside of loops. The `next` statement causes Perl to jump up to the top of the loop and do the test again. You often use `next` to avoid executing the rest of the lines in the block. The counter1.pl program's `while` loop contains the following line:

```
    if($TheLine eq "") { next };
```

This tests for the line being blank. If it is, you don't want Perl to do all the character and word counting in the rest of the block, but you also don't want Perl to exit from the loop because the file contains more lines. This is typical of what `next` is used for in many programs with `while` or `until` loops.

The `redo` statement is rarely used. It is similar to `next`, but it jumps to the top of the block and does not go through the test, while `next` always goes through the test. There usually isn't much point to this, so you're safe using `last` to get out of a loop at the end or `next` to jump back up to the top.

There is another form of the `while` loop that is rarely used:

```
while(LOGICAL) { BLOCK1 } continue { BLOCK2 }
```

In this case, BLOCK2 is executed after BLOCK1 but before the LOGICAL is tested a second time. The value of this is that BLOCK2 gets executed even if you use next. You can use this if you want some steps that are executed after a next or at the end of BLOCK1. Because this is fairly confusing, you don't see it very often.

Knowing What You're Looking For

Although while loops are pretty handy, they aren't the end-all-be-all loop mechanism. For example, if you have a counter that increments in your loop, and you use that counter for the test, it might be nice to put the test and the incrementing together. For that, Perl offers the for statement.

The format of a for loop is

```
for(INIT; LOGICAL; REINIT) { BLOCK }
```

Here, INIT is a statement that is executed once before the loop begins, LOGICAL is a test just like in the while loop, and REINIT is a statement that is executed just before LOGICAL is tested after each time through the loop (but not on the first round).

For example, you might have a for loop like

```
for($i = 0; $i <10; $i +=1) { print "$i " }
```

This displays

```
0 1 2 3 4 5 6 7 8 9
```

The for loop acts exactly like a while loop but is more compact. The format

```
for(INIT; LOGICAL; REINIT) { BLOCK }
```

is identical to

```
INIT;
while(LOGICAL)
     { BLOCK }
continue
     { REINIT }
```

If you read the last section of Chapter 6, you will (I hope) remember the program

```
# hexchart.pl: Prints a decimal-to-hex conversion chart.
@HexD = ('0', '1', '2', '3', '4', '5', '6', '7', '8',
    '9', 'A', 'B', 'C', 'D', 'E', 'F');
for($i = 0; $i <= 255; $i += 1) {
    printf("%3s=$HexD[int($i / 16)]$HexD[$i % 16]  ", $i);
    if(($i % 8) == 7) { print "\n" }
}
```

Here, the `for` loop is used to count from 0 to 255, and the block is used to display data. The `printf` statement in the block uses the value of the counter `$i` in its calculations, and the `if` statement uses `$i` to decide when to put in the line breaks.

Perl's `for` loops are really handy when you need to cycle through a limited set of values and execute a block on each. It is a compact way of defining a loop in a single argument and leaving the associated block to be just the processing steps you want to take.

Working on Each Element in a List

When you have a list, you often want to use the data in the list for element-by-element processing. For instance, if your list is a set of words from a sentence, you might want to look at each word to see if it matches some special value. If the list is a set of numbers that are measurements, you might want to see which members of the list are over a certain test value.

You can use the `while` and `for` statements to step through each element in a list, but Perl makes your life easier than that. The `foreach` statement has the format

```
foreach $VARIABLE (LIST) { BLOCK }
```

For each item in the list, Perl sets `$VARIABLE` to the value of the element and executes the `BLOCK`. Here is an example:

```
@StartTimes = (25.6, 34.0, 26.7, 30.8, 32.7);
@LowTimes = ();
foreach $i (@StartTimes) {
```

```
    if($i < 30 ) {
        print "$i is a low time.\n";
        push(@LowTimes, $i);
    }
}
```

This displays

```
25.6 is a low time.
26.7 is a low time.
```

and the list @LowTimes ends up with the value (25.6, 26.7).

If you need it, the foreach statement can have a continue statement:

```
foreach $VARIABLE (LIST) { BLOCK1 } continue { BLOCK2 }
```

Perl 5 has a new function, map, that goes even further than foreach in convenience in some circumstances. The map function returns a list based on executing either a Perl expression or an entire block on each element of a list. It has two formats that do similar things. Note that map does not change the list in its argument: It returns a different list.

If you have a single expression that you want to execute on each element of a list, use

```
map(EXPRESSION, LIST);
```

For example, if you want the lowercase equivalent of every string in a list, you might use

```
@LCWords = map(lc, @Input);
```

Or if you want a list that is the logarithm of all the numbers in a different list, you might use

```
@Logs = map(log, @Measurements);
```

If you have a block that you want to execute on each element of a list, you would use a different format for map:

```
map { BLOCK } LIST;
```

At the beginning of the BLOCK, the Perl special variable $_ is set to the value of the element being examined. (The $_ variable is described in more detail in Chapter 10.) For example, if you want to create a list that has only the elements that are all lowercase, you could use

```
@AllLC = map { if(lc($_) eq $_) { $_ } } @Input;
```

You can even make it a bit more interesting by returning the elements that are all lowercase and returning the string error for every element that isn't lowercase:

```
@AllLC = map
    { if(lc($_) eq $_) { $_ } else { 'error' } }
    @Input;
```

Using Expressions as Logical Values

So far, all the conditional and loop statements you've seen have used comparisons in their arguments. Perl does not require that you use comparisons, however. You can put anything in the function to if, while, and so on. Comparisons make the most sense to beginners, but Perl expressions can be used as well.

Every Perl expression returns some value. If you use an expression as an argument to a conditional or loop statement, and the expression returns a value that is 0 or the null string, it will be treated as "false," any other return value will be treated as "true."

Using expressions in these arguments is a good way to make your programs more compact, although it sometimes affects the readability of the program. For instance, if you had the conditional

```
if($Counter != 0) { ... some statements... }
```

you could replace it with

```
if($Counter) { ... some statements... }
```

Here, $Counter being not equal to 0 is the same as $Counter being true, and thus you can just use its value in the argument to if.

You will see in future chapters that some Perl functions return a true value if they are successful and a false value if they are not. You can use these functions in if, while, and so on, instead of comparisons. You'll learn in Chapter 10 how to write subroutines, which return values, so you can use subroutines as logical values as well.

The two programs in Chapter 4 use the open function to open text files. They return true if they successfully open the file and false if they don't (such as if the file could not be found). Thus, you could write a program like this:

```
$CheckOpen = open(DATA, "datafile.txt");
unless($CheckOpen)
    { die "The file datafile.txt could not be opened." }
```

The unless sees whether open returned a false value, and if so, causes the program to quit with the die statement. This can be shortened to

```
unless(open(DATA, "datafile.txt"))
    { die "The file datafile.txt could not be opened." }
```

Short-Circuit Logic

You may have noticed that the programs in Chapter 4 do not use either of these forms of the open command, however. Instead, they have statements like this:

```
open(INFILE, $TheFile) or die "The file $TheFile could " .
    "not be found.\n";
```

In Perl, the or and and operators (and their Perl 4 equivalents of || and &&) "short-circuit" the evaluation of a statement. Perl only evaluates statements that are strung together with or and and if it has to.

or and and are not exactly the same as || and &&, but they are close enough. Serious Perl dweebs will tell you that or and and have lower precedence than || and &&, and lower precedence than many other operators as well. This means that you shouldn't use or and and in places where you aren't using parentheses around your function arguments. However, as I said earlier in the book, you should always be using parentheses to prevent this kind of misunderstanding regardless of the operators and functions you use.

Remember that the or comparison is true if either the statement to the left is true or the statement to the right is true. Thus, the statement

```
STATEMENT1 or STATEMENT2
```

means "Evaluate STATEMENT1; if it is true, ignore STATEMENT2." In the preceding open statement, Perl first evaluates open(INFILE, $TheFile). If that returns true, Perl doesn't even evaluate the expression on the right side. Thus, a true value "short-circuits" Perl from looking at whatever is to the right of the or (in this case, the die statement).

Short-circuiting in the and operator is similar. Because an and comparison is only true if both sides are true, there's no reason for Perl to look at the right side if the left side was false. Thus, the statement

```
STATEMENT1 and STATEMENT2
```

means "Evaluate STATEMENT1; if it is false, ignore STATEMENT2." You can use this statement when you are sure you don't want Perl to execute the second statement unless the first one returned a true value.

Using Labels

Perl, like most programming languages, allows you to jump around a program. So far, you have seen how you can do that with conditionals and loops. You use logic to help steer Perl around blocks of statements you don't want to execute right now; in loops, you can also use next and last to cause Perl to jump around within the block. Labels let you jump to a named part of your program.

The reason I haven't brought up labels before now is that they are generally a bad idea. I'm not saying that you should never, ever use labels, but in general you are better off using other Perl mechanisms because labels make your program very hard to read.

In Perl, a label is indicated as a single word followed by a colon. By tradition, labels are shown in all uppercase, but you can use mixed case if you want. A label can appear before a loop statement (while, until, for, and foreach), or it can appear before a block by itself.

Perl programmers commonly use labels to avoid using a loop. The last or next statements inside the block redirect Perl to the beginning or end of the block, just as they do in the loop statements. These are useful for checking if a value is one of many different values and then doing something different based on each outcome.

For example, assume that the variable $CheckID holds the ID of a product. If that ID is one of three special values, you want to print one of three different messages; otherwise, you just want to put that ID into the end of a list for later searching. This kind of program uses the last statement. The program might be

```
ID1CHECK: {
  if($CheckID == 101) {
    print "Supervisor's signature required.\n";
    last ID1CHECK;
```

```
    }
    if($CheckID == 121) {
        print "Backordered.\n";
        last ID1CHECK;
    }
    if($CheckID == 131) {
        print "Import duties apply.\n";
        last ID1CHECK;
    }
    #  Here if everything is OK
    push(@OnHold, $CheckID);
}
```

Two bad ideas that you can ignore

You can also use Perl labels with the `goto` statement. The `goto` statement jumps from wherever the statement is to the label.

There are people who *would* say "never, ever use `goto`." About ten years ago, many professional programmers claimed that unsystematic jumping with `goto` (or its equivalent in other languages) was inherently evil and counterproductive, and they tried to get everyone to agree. Well, they're probably mostly right, but I'm not quite that absolutist about it.

You will almost never have a good reason for using `goto`, so I'm not even going to give an example for you. However, if you must use it, it looks like last with a label.

The second very bad idea is the `reset` statement, which can be used in loops to reset the values of variables to their initial state. I'm not even going to go into how to use it, because doing so would be inherently evil and counterproductive. If you see it in someone else's Perl program and really need to know what it does, you can find out in Appendix B. Don't even think of using it yourself. Really.

Chapter 9

More Easy Operators and Functions

*W*elcome to the catch-all chapter. Here you'll find the somewhat more advanced string, numeric, and list operators and statements not covered in Chapters 5 through 8. My thinking was to try not to burden you with too many things in the earlier chapters and to give you a chance to breathe before getting into these intermediate-level Perl features. Some people will complain that I should have put these in their respective chapters, that they're not too advanced, but I think others will be glad that I held off a bit so that their brains didn't explode with too much too soon.

Either way, this chapter closes out Part II, and when you're done here, you'll be well on your way to Perl programmerhood.

Undefined Variables

In Chapter 3, you learned that you should always define your variables before using them on the right side of an assignment. Doing so prevents Perl from using default values for undefined variables.

You may, however, have a few good reasons for using undefined variables. Some functions return the undefined value if they fail. For instance, the pop function you learned about in Chapter 7 returns the undefined value if you are trying to pop from an empty list. You don't want it to return false because false is a perfectly reasonable value for an item in a list.

Of course, because some functions return the undefined value, you want to be able to determine if it was returned. The defined function takes one argument, an expression, and returns true if the argument is defined and false if that argument is undefined. For example

```
unless(defined($Yummy = pop(@Bonbons)))
    { print "There are no more bonbons left." }
```

After executing this, the variable $Yummy contains the value popped off the @Bonbons list. However, if the list is empty, the defined function will return false, Perl will print the message, and $Yummy will hold the undefined value.

Location, Location, Location

As you remember from Chapter 5, strings are groups of characters. Sometimes you will want to look at a *substring*, a string that is part of a larger string. The substr function lets you view just a part of a string in many different ways. The function returns a string that is a substring of a larger string. Its format is

```
substr(FULLSTRING, POSITION, LENGTH)
```

The first character is at position 0, the second character at position 1, and so on. If you want to count from the right side of the string instead of the left side, you can use a negative position.

For example

```
$Small = substr("This is a long string", 5, 4);
print $Small;
```

displays

```
is a
```

because those are the four letters (remember that a space is a letter) that start from position 5 from the left side of the string. However,

```
$Small = substr("This is a long string", -5, 4);
print $Small;
```

displays

```
trin
```

because these are the four letters that start from the fifth position from the right side of the string.

You do not have to include the length argument. If you leave it off, Perl returns everything from the position to the end of the string. For example

```
print substr("This is a long string", 5);
```

displays

```
is a long string
```

You can also use the substr function on the left side of an assignment to add a substring into a string. In this case, the first argument is the name of the string variable you want to change, and the length is the number of characters you want to delete from the full string at the position that the substring is being added. You can probably understand this function better by staring at a few examples than by reading my words, so here goes. . . .

To add a substring in without removing anything that is already there, set the length to 0:

```
$TestStr = "Long string";
substr($TestStr, 4, 0) = "er";
print $TestStr;
```

Perl displays

```
Longer string
```

To delete some characters as you add others, set the length to the number of characters you want to delete:

```
$TestStr = "Long string";
substr($TestStr, -3, 3) = "ange trip";
print $TestStr;
```

displays

```
Long strange trip
```

Instead of looking in a string by location, you want to look in a string to see if a particular substring is in there. The index function is great for this. The format of the function is

```
index(FULLSTRING, SUBSTRING, POSITION)
```

This tells Perl to look for the substring in the full string, starting at the given position. If you do not fill in the position, Perl starts at the left side, position 0.

Perl returns the first position where the beginning of the substring is found. If the string isn't found, Perl returns -1, meaning the position before the first position. For example

```
print index("Will call", "ll");
```

displays

```
2
```

But note that

```
print index("Will call", "L");
```

displays

```
-1
```

The rindex function is the complement of the index function: It returns the position of the last match for the string:

```
print rindex("Will call", "ll");
```

displays

```
7
```

Fancy Formatting for Text and Numbers

The `print` statement is very flexible, but it isn't good at restricting what it prints. For example, you might want to print a column of numbers, some which are two-digit numbers and some of which are three-digit numbers. Here is an example:

```
for($i = 98; $i <= 101; $i += 1) { print "$i\n" }
```

This statement displays

```
98
99
100
101
```

However, you might want the right side of the numbers to all line up nicely:

```
98
99
100
101
```

There is no easy way to do this with `print`. However, `print` has a cousin called `printf` that lets you specify a format for each argument you print. The function looks like

```
printf(FORMAT, LIST)
```

where the format is a string that tells Perl the format of the output, and the list is a list of items that will be formatted using that string. There is an almost-identical function, `sprintf`, that is used for assigning strings. `sprintf` returns what `printf` would have printed so that you can then assign that to a string variable.

`printf` is very powerful and gives you lots of flexibility in how you format your strings and numbers. Unfortunately, the format strings are not all that easy to understand. Well, to be honest, they're downright terrible, and many Perl programmers have to look in the book every time they use format strings. However, you should learn how to use the format strings because the results are so handy.

Each format string starts with a percent sign (%). The format string consists of four parts, the first three of which are optional:

  ✔ A flag to indicate what will come before the output

  ✔ The minimum field width

  ✔ The precision

  ✔ The field type

It actually makes sense to look at these in reverse order because the last parts are more important. Don't worry if you get a tad lost in these descriptions: I provide really thorough examples at the end of this section.

The **field type** tells Perl the type of format to use. The options are listed in Table 9-1.

Table 9-1	Field Type Options
Type	**Description**
s	String
d	Integer
f	Real number
g	Compact real number
u	Unsigned integer
x	Hexadecimal (lowercase)
X	Hexadecimal (uppercase)
o	Octal
e	Scientific notation (lowercase)
E	Scientific notation (uppercase)
c	Single character (by value)
ld	Long integer
lu	Long unsigned integer
lx	Long hexadecimal
lo	Long octal

The **precision**, which is optional, is expressed as a period (.) followed by a number. For real numbers and scientific notation, this is the number of digits shown after the decimal point in the resulting string. For strings, this is the maximum number of characters extracted from the beginning of the string.

The **minimum field width** tells Perl that it should pad a number or string to a certain width. This is quite useful in getting columns to line up. In the previous example of two- and three-digit numbers, you would set the minimum field width to 3 to get the padding on the left of the two-digit numbers. Note that if the number will not fit in the minimum field width given, Perl will use more characters as needed to print the number correctly.

The **flag** can be one of five values. The flags are mostly relevant to numbers, not to strings and characters. Table 9-2 shows the meaning of flags.

Table 9-2	Flags and Their Meanings
Flag	*Meaning*
+	There should always be either a + or - in the output.
-	Left-adjusts the output; this also works with strings.
	A space indicates that a space should be put before positive numbers so that they line up with negative numbers.
0	Perl uses zeros to pad the number instead of spaces, if needed.
#	Alternate form. For hexadecimal, this causes 0x or 0X to be put before the number; for octal, this causes a 0 to be put before the number.

Got all that? Yeah, right. Don't worry if you didn't. It will become clearer when you see some examples. For instance, the following shows how to format a real number so that only two decimal places show:

```
$TestNum = 283.357;
printf("%.2f", $TestNum);
```

This displays

```
283.36
```

Note that Perl correctly rounded the number before truncating the extra digits. Here is a similar example, using scientific notation:

```
$TestNum = 283.357;
printf("%.2E", $TestNum);
```

This displays

```
2.83E+02
```

The format string can have text other than the format string in it. As long as your other text doesn't have any percent signs (%), Perl interprets the other text as text to be displayed:

```
$TestNum = 283.357;
printf("The answer is %.2f, give or take.", $TestNum);
```

This displays

```
The answer is 283.36, give or take.
```

If you want to display a percent sign, you must use two percent signs together:

```
printf("Two thirds is about %.3f%%.", ((2/3)*100));
```

This shows as

```
Two thirds is about 66.667%.
```

So far, all the examples have had just one number formatted. The format string can specify many values with different formats:

```
$Str = "Two thirds is about ";
$Num = (2/3)*100;
printf('%s%.3f%s', $Str, $Num, '%.');
```

This is another way of displaying the same string as before:

```
Two thirds is about 66.667%.
```

The sprintf function works just like printf, except that it returns strings instead of printing them. For instance, you might use it as

```
$Answer = sprintf("The answer is %.2f.", $TestNum);
```

Listing 9-1 is a pretty exhaustive program that shows you all the different interesting permutations of the formats. The output is shown in Listing 9-2. The program shows a way to use printf to get two columns of text to line up when the length of the material in the first column changes. By using printf with a format of %-29s, the program forces the second column to start in position 30, regardless of what was in the first column. The program also uses a subroutine, which you will learn about in the next chapter.

Please note, however, that some versions of Perl on different computers may put out slightly different answers than what you see in Listing 9-2.

```
$Str = 'Dummies';
$Num = 3.141593;
$Int = 4142;
@StrFmts = ('s', '4s', '.4s', '4.4s', '10.4s',
    '10.9s', '-10.9s' );
print "The original string is \"$Str\"\n";
&OutList(@StrFmts, $Str);
@NumFmts = (
    'd', '4d', '.4d', '4.4d', '10.4d', '10.10d',
    '-4.4d', '+4.4d', ' 4.4d', '04.4d',
    'f', '4f', '.4f', '4.4f', '10.4f', '10.10f',
    '-10.4f', '+10.4f', ' 10.4f', '010.4f',
    'e', '4e', '.4e', '4.4e', '10.4e', '10.10e',
    '-10.4e', '+10.4e', ' 10.4e', '010.4e',
    'g', '4g', '.4g', '4.4g', '10.4g', '10.10g',
    '-10.4g', '+10.4g', ' 10.4g', '010.4g',
);
print "\nThe original number is $Num\n";
&OutList(@NumFmts, $Num);
@HOFmts = ('x', 'X', '3x', '.3x', '3.3x', '10.3x',
    '10.10x', '#x', 'o', '#o' );
print "\nAnd a few hexa and octal examples on $Int.\n";
&OutList(@HOFmts, $Int);

sub OutList {
    local($TestStr) = pop(@_);
    local(@TestFmts) = @_;
    local(@OutFmts, $Fmt);
    foreach $Fmt (@TestFmts) {
        unshift(@OutFmts, sprintf("%s%$Fmt%s", ("%$Fmt=|",
            $TestStr, "|")));
    }
    until(@OutFmts == 0) {
        printf('%-29s%-29s%s',
            pop(@OutFmts), pop(@OutFmts), "\n");
    }
}
```

```
The original string is "Dummies"
%s=|Dummies|                    %4s=|Dummies|
%.4s=|Dumm|                     %4.4s=|Dumm|
%10.4s=|      Dumm|             %10.9s=|   Dummies|
%-10.9s=|Dummies   |

The original number is 3.141593
%d=|3|                          %4d=|   3|
%.4d=|0003|                     %4.4d=|0003|
%10.4d=|      0003|             %10.10d=|0000000003|
%-4.4d=|0003|                   %+4.4d=|+0003|
% 4.4d=| 0003|                  %04.4d=|0003|
%f=|3.141593|                   %4f=|3.141593|
%.4f=|3.1416|                   %4.4f=|3.1416|
%10.4f=|    3.1416|             %10.10f=|3.1415930000|
%-10.4f=|3.1416    |            %+10.4f=|   +3.1416|
% 10.4f=|    3.1416|            %010.4f=|00003.1416|
%e=|3.141593e+00|              %4e=|3.141593e+00|
%.4e=|3.1416e+00|              %4.4e=|3.1416e+00|
%10.4e=|3.1416e+00|           %10.10e=|3.1415930000e+00|
%-10.4e=|3.1416e+00|          %+10.4e=|+3.1416e+00|
% 10.4e=| 3.1416e+00|         %010.4e=|3.1416e+00|
%g=|3.14159|                  %4g=|3.14159|
%.4g=|3.142|                  %4.4g=|3.142|
%10.4g=|     3.142|           %10.10g=|   3.141593|
%-10.4g=|3.142     |          %+10.4g=|    +3.142|
% 10.4g=|     3.142|          %010.4g=|000003.142|

And a few hexa and octal examples on 4142.
%x=|102e|                      %X=|102E|
%3x=|102e|                     %.3x=|102e|
%3.3x=|102e|                   %10.3x=|      102e|
%10.10x=|000000102e|           %#x=|0x102e|
%o=|10056|                     %#o=|010056|
```

What Time Is It?

All computers are good at keeping time, and Perl gives you easy access to the time through four functions. You can use these in your programs for doing things like displaying the current time and date, determining how long something takes to run, how old a file is, and so on.

The `time` function, which has no arguments, is the number of nonleap seconds since January 1, 1970. (In MacPerl, it is the number of seconds since January 1, 1904.) You use this function with the `localtime` and `gmtime` functions to find out the month, day, and so on.

By itself, the `time` function isn't all that useful:

```
print time;
```

This prints

```
842654401
```

(Well, that's what it printed when I wrote this chapter.)

The `localtime` function takes a time as its argument and returns a list of nine elements:

- ✔ Second
- ✔ Minute
- ✔ Hour
- ✔ Day of month
- ✔ Month (January = 0, February = 1, . . .)
- ✔ Years since 1900
- ✔ Weekday (Sunday = 0, Monday = 1, . . .)
- ✔ Day of the year (January 1 = 0, January 2 = 1, . . .)
- ✔ Whether the local time zone is using daylight savings time (true or false)

Here is a typical way to use the `localtime` function to receive information on the current time:

```
($Second, $Minute, $Hour, $DayOfMonth, $Month, $Year,
    $WeekDay, $DayOfYear, $IsDST) = localtime(time);
$RealMonth = $Month + 1;
print "$RealMonth/$DayOfMonth/$Year";
```

This displays

```
9/13/96
```

Note in this program that you have to add 1 to the month before you use it in a date string. If you forget to add 1 to the month (as many people do), your month will be off by 1.

Also note that the year is the number of years since 1900, not the two-digit year number. Thus, in a few years, the program above will display something like 9/13/101, which looks completely silly.

The gmtime function returns the time as Greenwich Mean Time, which is not all that interesting for most people.

If you want to display the date and time in a standard format (each number using two digits), you have to use the printf function that you just learned about. Here is a good example:

```
printf('%02d:%02d:%02d %02d/%02d/%02d', $Hour, $Minute,
    $Second, $RealMonth, $DayOfMonth, $Year);
```

This displays

```
15:40:01 09/13/96
```

If you want to use list slices instead of explicit variable names, you might use something like this:

```
@DayNames = ('Sun', 'Mon', 'Tues', 'Wed', 'Thur',
    'Fri', 'Sat');
@TimeArr = localtime(time);
print $DayNames[$TimeArr[6]];
```

Here, $TimeArr[6] is the element that is the weekday of the time right now and is used to pick the element out of @DayNames for today's day name.

Another time-related function is sleep. The argument is the number of seconds you want Perl to take a nap. For instance, if you want your program to do nothing for two seconds, you would use

```
sleep(2);
```

Making Life a Bit More Random

A few programming tasks require random numbers. For instance, if you use Perl to write games, you might want to have the equivalent of dice rolling. You may also need to generate some random numbers if you want to pick a random record from a database.

The rand function returns a somewhat random real number between 0 and the argument. If you don't have an argument, rand returns a somewhat random real number between 0 and 1. For example, to get a random integer between 1 and 10, you would use

```
$PickANumber = int(rand(10)) + 1;
```

Because rand here chooses a number between 0 and 10, the int function is going to produce integers between 0 and 9. To make the range between 1 and 10, you add 1 to the result.

Perl's rand function does not produce truly random numbers. In fact, if you do not tell Perl what seed to use, Perl produces the same series of numbers each time you run it. This, of course, isn't very good if you want numbers that look really random, so you should always set the seed for the random values with Perl's srand function. The srand function takes a single argument that is used as the seed. If you do not specify an argument for srand, it uses the current value from time.

```
srand();
$PickANumber = int(rand(10)) + 1;
```

The rand function is not meant to be used in strong cryptography or other applications that require truly random numbers. Unless you use a good method for picking a pseudo-random seed for srand, a hacker who knows that you are using Perl can probably figure out the random number seed with very little effort.

Twiddling Bits

The logic that you learned in Chapter 8 applies to entire numbers: Either a number was false (that is, has a value of 0), or true (that is, has any value other than 0). Those readers who know much about bits and bytes know that logic goes to a much deeper level than that.

Novices are free to skip this section. The number of people who actually use bit-level logic is quite small. Of course, feel free to read through the material here, but don't worry if this bit-level stuff is beyond your skills (or interest!).

Each bit in a byte has a value of either 1 or 0. For bits, a 1 means true and a 0 means false. You can think of a byte, which has eight bits, as something that holds eight ordered true-false values. You can operate on these bits in numbers using logical operators similar to those you saw in Chapter 8.

The three basic bit-level logical operators for combining two numbers are | (or), & (and), and ^ (exclusive or). You always want to use these operators on integers. Perl won't even let you use them on real numbers: It will truncate a real number before using the operators. Normally, bit-wise logic is used on hexadecimal and octal numbers. However, Perl normally tries to display numbers as real numbers, so you need to use printf to display your results in hexadecimal.

Here is an example:

```
$H1 = 0xfed0; $H2 = 0xedc4;
$Result = $H1 & $H2;
printf("The 'and' of %x and %x is %x", $H1, $H2, $Result);
```

The printf statement displays

```
The 'and' of fed0 and edc4 is ecc0
```

The printf is necessary to get Perl to print the hexadecimal values. If you had instead used

```
print "The 'and' of $H1 and $H2 is $Result";
```

Perl would display

```
The 'and' of 65232 and 60868 is 60608
```

Perl also has a unary bit-wise negation operator, ~. This turns all 1 bits into 0 and 0 bits into 1:

```
$H3 = 0xfed0;
$H4 = ~$H3;
printf("The negation of %x (%d) is %x (%d)",
    $H3, $H3, $H4, $H4);
```

Perl prints

```
The negation of fed0 (65232) is ffff012f (-65233)
```

Note that the negation operator here (as well as the ^ exclusive-or operator) work on values that are 32 bits long. Most systems that run Perl use 32-bit integers, but not all do. This means that bit-moving logic that runs fine on one operating system may not on another.

You can shift numbers a bit at a time with the << and >> operators. These operators move the number to the left of the operator by the number of bits to the right of the operator. As you might guess, << shifts bits left and >> shifts bits right.

```
$H3 = 0x0f30;
$H4 = $H3 << 2;
printf("The left shift of %x (%d) by 2 bits is %x (%d)",
    $H3, $H3, $H4, $H4);
```

Perl displays

```
The left shift of f30 (3888) by 2 bits is 3cc0 (15552)
```

Converting Lists to Strings

Okay, enough fiddling with tiny little bits. It's time to move on to much bigger things, namely lists. So far, you have seen how easy it is to print the other two data types, numbers and text. However, as you saw in Chapter 7, printing lists is not nearly as useful.

```
@Nums = (2.7, 80, 46.2);
@Strs = ("Who's", "on", "first?");
print @Nums, "\n";
print @Strs, "\n";
```

The fairly unpleasing result is

```
2.78046.2
Who'sonfirst?
```

Because this is such a common desire, Perl has a nifty way to convert a list into a string with whatever characters you want between each list item. The join function takes two arguments: the thing you want as the separator and the list. The separator can be as many characters as you want.

```
@Nums = (2.7, 80, 46.2);
@Strs = ("Who's", "on", "first?");
print join('-', @Nums), "\n";
print join(' ', @Strs), "\n";
```

The result is

```
2.7-80-46.2
Who's on first?
```

Much better, eh? The join function is also handy for printing things on separate lines:

```
@Nums = (2.7, 80, 46.2);
print join("\n", @Nums), "\n";
```

Remember that join returns a string, so it is also useful outside of the print function. For instance, to make a string that is a tab-delimited record, you could use

```
@Nums = (2.7, 80, 46.2);
$TheRecord = join("\t", @Nums);
```

Rearranging Lists

You saw in Chapter 7 how to put lists together, how to look at just parts of lists, how to pull items out of lists, and how to stuff (er, splice) items into lists. However, you didn't see how to rearrange the order of the elements in lists.

If I said to you, "Name two ways you might want to change the order of some of your lists," you might reply "reverse the order" and "sort the items." Perl, being the handy language that it is, has simple functions to do both of these tasks.

The reverse function reverses the items in its argument. Don't you just love it when Perl uses such nice function names?

```
@Strs = ("Who's", "on", "first?");
print join(' ', reverse(@Strs));
```

This displays

```
first? on Who's
```

As you may have guessed, you use the `sort` function to sort lists. The `sort` function returns a list that is the original list in sorted order. Perl lets you define how `sort` will sort.

If you want to sort your list in alphabetical order, use the `sort` function with a single argument, namely the list:

```
@Strs = ('cognition', 'attune', 'bell');
print join(' ', sort @Strs);
```

This displays

```
attune bell cognition
```

A second, and a bit more complicated, form of the `sort` function lets you define the method Perl will use to sort. In this form, there are two arguments: a block or subroutine that tells Perl how you want to sort, and the list. You'll learn about subroutines in Chapter 10, so for now let's just look at using a block. To tell Perl how to sort, your block compares two values, `$a` and `$b`, and returns a -1, 0 or 1 depending on how `$a` compares to `$b`. The `cmp` and `<=>` operators you learned about in Chapter 8 come in really handy here.

For example, assume that you want to sort a list of strings by their length (ignoring their alphabetical order). You would use

```
@Strs = ('cognition', 'attune', 'bell');
print join(' ', sort { length($a) <=> length($b) } @Strs);
```

This displays

```
bell attune cognition
```

If you want to know how to use `sort` with subroutines, this example would look like

```
sub lensort { length($a) <=> length($b) }
@Strs = ('cognition', 'attune', 'bell');
print join(' ', sort lensort @Strs);
```

So Where Are You Now?

You now have enough understanding of Perl to start writing your own useful programs. All those text, numeric, and list operators and functions, all that lovely logic; that's pretty much what you need to go ahead. The chapters in the next part show you more about how programs go together, how to read from and write to files. These chapters contain lots of examples of what many people want: Perl programs that are useful on the Internet.

Part III
The Nuts and Bolts on the Perl

The 5th Wave   By Rich Tennant

MODERN MARRIAGE

CRICHTENNANT

WE'RE AGREED ON THE SILVER PATTERN, WALLPAPER AND CARPET SCHEME, BUT WE'RE STILL HASHING OUT THE CODE.

In this part . . .

Okay, you're almost there. The chapters in this part describe some of the "intermediate" things you need to know to put together useful, interesting programs. You'll also find out a lot about how to use Perl and the Internet together.

Chapter 10

Putting Together a Perl Program

. . . .

In This Chapter
▶ Leaving your programs gracefully
▶ Creating subroutines
▶ Using parts from other programs

. . . .

*P*erl is a great language for creating simple programs. As you've seen, you can write a single-line program in Perl. A surprising number of significant Perl programs running on the Internet are fewer than five lines long. Unlike other languages, you don't have to have long sets of lines at the beginning of your program to "set up the language" for your program.

Of course, Perl also has plenty of features that make your programs more efficient and run better if you want. These involve a bit more work than the simplest programs, but not much. This chapter covers the structural ways you can improve your program. The statements covered in this chapter don't do anything like math or string handling; instead, they all relate to how you structure your program.

Exiting

Perl programs end when Perl runs out of statements to execute. If you know other programming languages, you may have noticed that the Perl programs you've seen in this book do not end with any statements that look like they say "Hey, this is the end of the program." Perl doesn't require anything like this: When it gets to the last line of the program, it is smart enough to know that you really intended that line to be the end of the program.

Of course, you can tell Perl that you want to end a program if you want to. If you have read previous chapters, you have seen the die function used in many examples. This function causes Perl to print a message and then stop the program immediately.

Actually, die is like print: It displays its argument (which can be a list) so that you're not restricted to displaying a single string. If the last value in the list does not end with a newline character, Perl also prints the name of the program and the line number, followed by a newline character. If you are in an input loop, Perl also prints the number of times you've gone through the loop.

The exit function is the more traditional way to end a program. Instead of displaying a list, exit takes a numeric argument and returns that argument to the program from which you ran your Perl program. So far, you have only seen how to run a Perl program from your operating system, so Perl returns the value in exit to the operating system.

For most people, this won't mean anything, because their operating systems ignore the return code, or at least don't do anything interesting with it. However, if your operating system does do something interesting with it, such as display the return code of programs when they exit, you might find the exit function useful. If you don't supply an argument to exit, Perl uses 0.

die and exit are often used on the right side of the or operator in logical expressions, as shown in Chapter 8. If there is something in your program that absolutely has to be true, you can exit the program immediately if it is false. Many programmers use these functions with if and unless for the same reasons. For instance, the following two examples do the same thing.

```
unless($Now > ($StartTime + 3)) { die "It's too soon.\n" }
($Now > ($StartTime + 3)) or die "It's too soon.\n";
```

You should have a \n at the end of the string you use in die; otherwise, Perl adds its own text at the end of what it prints telling you the program name and the line number. If you had instead not used the "\n" at the end of the string

```
($Now > ($StartTime + 3)) or die "It's too soon.";
```

Perl would display some thing like

```
It's too soon. at LabMonitor.pl line 12.
```

As you can see from the many examples throughout this book, I prefer die to exit. It's almost always nice to tell the users something as the program ends so that they do not stare at the screen wondering what happened. You can create plenty of useful lines with die, such as

```
Program ended because the file 'input.txt' was not found.
All done. Thank you!
Finished at 08:27:52 in .03 seconds.
Unable to find the specified file; exiting.
```

Remember that you should use error messages in your program that you would want to see yourself if you were running a program you weren't familiar with. And don't forget that you should always make the messages that the user sees when the program ends friendly, and even humorous if you dare. We've all seen incomprehensible error messages, and the best way to help remind people to write better error messages is to do so yourself.

Avoiding Repetition with Subroutines

The section of Chapter 9 that describes `printf` contains an example of a program that uses the same set of statements in a few different places. However, instead of repeating the lines in each place they are needed, that program uses a *subroutine* to define the set of lines and then uses *calls* to that subroutine. The main purpose of subroutines is to consolidate repeated sets of statements into a single block. This has many advantages:

✔ If you later want to change the block of lines, you can do it in just one place instead of having to search the program for all the places where that set of lines appears.

✔ Your program will be shorter and will thus run faster.

✔ In long programs, subroutines can act like named "subprograms" to help you organize the program.

Warning without exiting

Perl has another function, `warn`, that acts like `die` except that it does not cause the program to quit. Instead, it just prints out a warning. For most people, this means that `warn` just does the same thing as `print`.

The difference between `warn` and `print` is that `warn`, displays its message on the output stream called STDERR. Most readers of this book will have no idea what that means until Chapter 11, where output streams are discussed. Because most operating systems make whatever appears on STDERR also appear on the standard output stream, `warn` and `print` are indistinguishable for most people. The reason I mention `warn` here is that, like `warn`, `die` actually puts its argument on STDERR. In other words, don't worry about it for now.

In my mind, the first reason (having everything in a single place so updates are easier) is by far the most important. I can't tell you how many times I've gotten lazy when writing a program and didn't use subroutines, only to be bitten later when I wanted to change the repeated lines.

For example, imagine a program that has a dozen or so lists, and at different points in the program you want to print just the last item in each list and put a copy of that item into the @Big list. Without subroutines, it might look like the following:

```
. . .
printf("Price: \$%.2f\n", $ListPrice[$#ListPrice]);
push(@Big, $ListPrice[$#ListPrice]);
. . .
printf("Price: \$%.2f\n", $CustPrice[$#CustPrice]);
push(@Big, $CustPrice[$#CustPrice]);
. . .
printf("Price: \$%.2f\n", $NewPrice[$#NewPrice]);
push(@Big, $NewPrice[$#NewPrice]);
. . .
```

Now imagine that you want to change the way that @Big is formed and push the last two items onto the end of @Big instead of just the last item. You would have to search for each push, make sure it's one that is pushing onto @Big, and change the item that is there now to a slice:

```
push(@Big, @ListPrice[$#ListPrice-1..$#ListPrice]);
```

As you can imagine, this task would be really tedious. You would also be prone to error, particularly after you make your 15th replacement by hand.

Subroutines fix this problem completely. The program here would be changed by adding a subroutine and changing the pairs of printf and push statements to a single subroutine call. It would look like this:

```
# Print the price and push it on @Big
sub PrintPushBig {
    @TheList = @_;
    printf("Price: \$%.2f\n", $TheList[$#TheList]);
    push(@Big, $TheList[$#TheList]);
}
. . .
&PrintPushBig(@ListPrice);
. . .
&PrintPushBig(@CustPrice);
```

```
. . .
&PrintPushBig(@NewPrice);
. . .
```

Notice the difference here. Instead of repeating the lines, they're contained in the subroutine. To make the previously described change to the subroutine, you would simply change the `push` statement to

```
push(@Big, @TheList[$#TheList-1..$TheList]);
```

After you change those statements, the change will be reflected each time the subroutine is called.

The parts of a subroutine

Creating a subroutine is easy. The `sub` statement has this format:

```
sub NAME { BLOCK }
```

The rules for making subroutine names are the same as for making variable names: no spaces, the only punctuation you can use is the underscore (_), and the case of the letters is significant.

To call a subroutine, you use the ampersand (&) character followed by the subroutine name. If the subroutine takes arguments, you include those in parentheses just like you do for Perl's built-in functions. In Perl 5, you don't have to use the & character if there is an argument in parentheses. But it certainly doesn't hurt to use ampersands, plus they let everyone reading the program know that this is a subroutine, not one of Perl's built-in functions.

Inside the block, you can do whatever you please, just as you can in any other Perl block. However, there are a few things that happen in most subroutines. Because most subroutines have arguments, you need a way to use those arguments in your block. Perl makes the argument called available in the special list @_. In the preceding example, the argument was a list, so @_ is the entire list.

It is also common to have subroutines that have one or two arguments that are scalars. In this case, you can use `shift` to get the arguments out of the @_ list in the order they went in. Here is an example:

```
sub JustAdd {
    $First = shift(@_);
    $Second = shift(@_);
    return($First + $Second);
}
```

Perl creates the variable $First to hold the first argument and $Second to hold the second argument. You can then treat these variables as you would any others.

Also, most subroutines return a value, just like most Perl functions. The return function, described a bit later in this chapter, is the most common way to return a value. Some subroutines also change the values of variables in the main program, but most don't. Instead, most subroutines make no changes to variables and let the program make the changes itself by looking at what is returned.

Incidentally, you could replace the first two lines of the preceding subroutine with

```
($First, $Second) = @_;
```

Of course, you don't really have to create new variables in your subroutines. If you want, you can just use slices of @_, although that can get cumbersome if you have many arguments or your subroutine is long. For instance, the JustAdd subroutine could have been written as

```
sub ShorterJustAdd { return(@_[0] + @_[1]) }
```

Although this is nice and compact, the longer form is easier to read.

Keeping your subroutines clean

You're not going to like hearing this, but the subroutines already shown have a major flaw in them. In order to make these first examples easier to read, I didn't do one thing that is very important. They work fine, but they are dangerous due to this omission.

In both PrintPushBig and JustAdd, the first steps are to assign values from @_ to variables. That makes sense, but what if those variables were being used in the program? For instance, in JustAdd, you might have already had a variable called $First that you were using for something like keeping track of who's on first. (I hear an Abbott and Costello routine coming on . . .) In this case, when you called JustAdd, Perl would wipe out the previous value of $First, which is probably not what you wanted to do.

Perl makes it easy to avoid these situations. The my and local functions cause Perl to create a *local* copy of the variable for the block that the function is in. For most cases, the two functions do the same thing, but my is faster. However, my does not exist in Perl 4; Perl 4 users must use local instead.

You use my and local when you first declare a variable. You can declare a variable at any time in a block, but most programmers prefer to do it at the very beginning of a block so they know where to look for their variable declarations. This preference is probably a holdover from other programming languages, because most other languages *require* that you declare all your variables before you use them. Perl is nice enough not to require predeclaration: You just create a new variable when you feel like it. However, if you are going to use my or local to safely declare a variable, you have to do it before using that variable.

my and local can be used as statements by themselves or on the left-hand side of an assignment. If you just want to declare that a variable will be local, you can say

```
my($AirCondNum);
```

If you want to also set its value when you first declare it, you can say

```
my($AirCondNum) = 3;
```

As I said earlier, the subroutines already shown don't declare their variables as local even though they should have. You could change JustAdd to

```
sub JustAdd {
    my($First) = shift(@_);
    my($Second) = shift(@_);
    return($First + $Second);
}
```

This causes Perl to create new copies of the variables $First and $Second that are only used inside the subroutine. If there is also a $First and $Second somewhere else in the program, they are unaffected by a call to the subroutine.

Another way to think about this is that my and local cause Perl to remember other variables that have the same name and store them off to the side. When the subroutine finishes, Perl throws away the new instances of the variables and restores the old ones that it saved to the side. This is why theses functions are said to create "local" variables: They only exist while the subroutine is being run.

You can declare variables with my and local in any block, not just the block of a subroutine, although they're mostly found only in subroutines. Perl acts the same way in any kind of block: It preserves any variable with the same name, creates a local version, and then destroys the local version at the end of the block.

To make life easier, you can declare as many variables as you want in my or local. For example, if you know you are going to use $i, $j, and $k as loop variables in a block, you can define them all at once with

```
my($i, $j, $k);
```

It is a good habit to use my religiously when you write subroutines. Even though you might be sure that you haven't used any variable with the same name in the program when you create the subroutine, you never know if you will use that name *later,* having forgotten that you had used it before. Furthermore, you will see later in this chapter how you can include code from other Perl programs in your program. This is a handy way of creating subroutines that you will use in other programs. In that case, you certainly want to use my for every variable in those subroutines.

Note, however, that sometimes you *want* a subroutine to modify something outside of it. Take a look at the (corrected) PrintPushBig subroutine from earlier in this chapter:

```
sub PrintPushBig {
    my($TheList) = @_;
    printf("Price: \$%.2f\n", $TheList[$#TheList]);
    push(@Big, $TheList[$#TheList]);
}
```

The purpose of this subroutine was to both print something and to change the value of a list that is in the main program, namely @Big. Thus, this subroutine has side effects outside the subroutine, namely to add an element to @Big.

If you write subroutines that change variables in your program, it is a good idea to put a very clear comment at the top of the subroutine so that you don't later forget this and can't figure out why the variable in the program keeps changing.

Some programmers are absolutists about subroutines not changing anything in the program. They would say, possibly rightly so, that this leads to mysterious results later when you have forgotten what gets changed. If you subscribe to this theory, and I must admit that I go in and out on this debate, you can return one or more values and force the calling program to do its own variable changing. Return values are described a little later in this chapter.

As I said earlier, Perl 4 users have to use local instead of my because my was introduced in Perl 5. Perl 5 users can choose between the two. For most programs, there is no noticeable difference between the two. However, more advanced programmers may want to be aware of the slight difference.

Using my hides a variable from all other blocks, both those that call the one with my, as well as subroutines called from the subroutine with my. Using local, on the other hand, only hides the variable from the enclosing block and makes the variable visible to subroutines that are called from the block with local in it. Here's a short example to show the difference:

```
# Simple subroutine to print the value of $J at the moment
sub PrintJ { print "The value of \$J is $J\n" }
# Simple subroutine to print the value of $K at the moment
sub PrintK { print "The value of \$K is $K\n" }
# Here's the test
my($J) = 5;
local($K) = 10;
&PrintJ;
&PrintK;
```

Here is the result:

```
The value of $J is
The value of $K is 10
```

You receive this result because $J is undefined in the PrintJ subroutine and $K is passed through to it.

Handing back a value from your subroutine

Every Perl function returns a value to the program that called it. Sometimes you care about what is returned, but sometimes you don't because you called the function only for a side effect of the function. For instance, the chomp function described in Chapter 5 returns a value (the character or characters it chomped), but most of the time you don't pay attention to that and just use the function to hack off characters at the end of strings.

Your subroutines also return values, which you can pay attention to or ignore. The best way to return a value is with the return statement. This statement causes the subroutine to end and returns the list that you give as its argument. Thus, in the JustAdd subroutine, return is used to return the value of the two arguments added together:

```
sub JustAdd {
    my($First) = shift(@_);
    my($Second) = shift(@_);
    return($First + $Second);
}
```

You can also use `return` with no argument, in which case Perl returns the value 0.

You don't have to use `return` in your subroutines, although it makes them easier to read. If you don't have a `return` statement when Perl hits the end of the subroutine's block, the subroutine ends and Perl returns the value of the last statement. Thus, you could write the `JustAdd` subroutine as

```
sub JustAdd {
    my($First) = shift(@_);
    my($Second) = shift(@_);
    $First + $Second;
}
```

As you can see, using `return` makes things a little clearer because the last line of this subroutine doesn't look like it's *doing* anything, even though it is returning the value of the expression. I like seeing functions that look like verbs, such as `return`, instead of plain values dangling there.

The `return` function is also handy if you want to stop a subroutine before you get to the end. You can use `return` somewhat like the `last` statement in loops, and your subroutine can have many `return` functions in it. Here is an example:

```
# Subroutine that returns the string "long" if the
#    argument is longer than 10 characters
sub IsLong {
    my($TheStr) = pop(@_);
    if(length($TheStr) > 10) { return('long') }
    else { return('short') }
}
```

You can return either a scalar or a list. For example, you might have a subroutine that returns a number raised to the second, third, and fourth power:

```
# Returns the argument raised to 2, 3, and 4
sub Raised {
    my($Sq, $Cub, $Quad);
    my($Val) = pop(@_);
    $Sq = $Val ** 2; $Cub = $Val ** 3; $Quad = $Val ** 4;
    return($Sq, $Cub, $Quad);
}
```

You might call this subroutine

```
@Powers = &Raised(12.3);
```

or

```
($TheSq, $TheCube, $TheFourth) = &Raised(12.3);
```

Returning a list is a handy way to return more than one value. As I mentioned earlier, some programmers absolutely insist that subroutines should not change any variables in a program. Instead, they should return values that the program can use to change its own variables.

Who am I?

Here's a fun little oddity for you. If you're in a subroutine and want to know the name of the program that called you, you can use the `caller` function to find out. Now, this function may not be all that useful, because this information will rarely be important, but it's a cute little function. In a list context, its format is

```
($PackageName, $FileName, $LineNum) = caller;
```

Packages are described later in this chapter.

In a scalar context, `caller` simply returns true if you are in a subroutine, inside of an `eval` function (described in Chapter 18) or a `require` function, described later in this chapter.

Using Imported Perl Code in Your Programs

Once you start writing many Perl programs, you're going to want to start reusing old programs that you wrote before in your new programs. For instance, imagine you wrote a really handy subroutine that reads a file and creates a list of all the capitalized words in the file. You did this in a program that you wrote six months ago. Now you find yourself wanting that same subroutine in a program you're writing today.

You could just copy the subroutine from the old program to the new one using your text editor. However, if you want to use 10 or 20 old subroutines, your new program will be very long before you have even started writing the new code. Instead, you can put the subroutines in one or more separate files and simply call those files into your new program.

If you end up using Perl a lot (and I certainly hope you do), you'll find that each time you create a new, useful subroutine, you'll put it in a file. You can put many subroutines in a single file, or each in their own files. Then, you'll be able to use this library of subroutines whenever you need it.

You may not even need to write many of your own subroutines, however. The CD-ROM that comes with this book has gazillions of well-written programs that you can use. They almost all use Perl's object-oriented features that are described in Chapter 19, so you may not be able to use them quite yet. But you can include programs in your own programs by using the same function you use for including your own subroutine library.

And that function is the `require` function. It takes one argument, the name of the file that you want to include in your program. For instance, if you have a subroutine you want in the numsubs.pl file, you could include all those subroutines in your current program with this simple statement:

```
require('numsubs.pl');
```

It is common to see the `require` function without parentheses:

```
require 'numsubs.pl';
```

A requirement for included files

Unfortunately, putting your subroutines in files isn't quite as easy as I have just described it, but almost. The small hitch is that the `require` function requires that whatever it reads in a file return a true value. As it turns out, just having a subroutine in a file doesn't cause Perl to return a true value. So, you must have at least one statement in the file outside a subroutine, and that statement must return true. The common way to do this is to have just this statement

```
1;
```

somewhere in the file, usually at the end. This is a statement, and the statement returns the value 1, which is a value for true. Thus, you usually see such a line, or a line with just a string, at the end of every file that is intended to be included with `require`.

Requiring a particular Perl version

The `require` function has another purpose in Perl 5: to specify what version of Perl you must be running in order to run this program. If you use a number as the argument to `require` (instead of the file name you saw above), Perl stops the program if the version of Perl isn't that number or higher. For example

```
require 5.003;
```

indicates that Perl must be version 5.003 or higher. If it isn't, Perl will stop and you'll get an error message that tells you what version was required and which was running. For example, the current version of Perl-Win32 is only 5.001, so this `require` function would cause the program to stop.

Where Perl finds included files

The `require` statement expects a file name so that it knows what file to open. However, as you know, a file can reside in lots and lots of places on your computer. You can specify exactly where a file should be, or you can put the file in one of the directories in Perl's search path.

The more exact way to do things is to give a full specification for where the file is located. This is a bit tedious, however. For instance, the following three `require` statements might appear in Perl programs under Windows, MacOS, or Unix:

```
require('C:\LANGS\PERL5\LIBS\NUMSUBS.PL');
require('Felicity:Perl 5:My Libraires:numsubs.pl');
require('/usr/home/phoffman/libraries/numsubs.pl');
```

When you use a full path name to your library, you have the further disadvantage of not being able to move your libraries without rewriting all your Perl programs to point to the new library location. A much better method is to put your libraries in one of those places that Perl knows to look for libraries and then let Perl search through those places.

The `@INC` special variable holds the list of places Perl looks for libraries. This list is a set of directory names where Perl will look for the file you name. For example, `@INC` in Perl for Windows might contain

```
('C:\perl5\lib\i386-win32', C:\perl5\lib')
```

In MacPerl, the default value is a single value of the lib folder where MacPerl was installed, such as

```
('Felicity:Perl 5:lib')
```

On Unix, the list usually has a few different places, such as

```
( '/usr/local/lib/perl5/i386-bsdos/5.003',
   '/usr/local/lib/perl5',
   '/usr/local/lib/perl5/site_perl/i386-bsdos',
   '/usr/local/lib/perl5/site_perl')
```

If you put your libraries in one of the directories listed in @INC, you need to use only the file's name in the require function:

```
require('numsubs.pl');
```

Every implementation of Perl I've ever seen has a sensible definition for where to look, but even if it doesn't, you can change this variable yourself. For instance, if you are a Windows user and you want to store all your libraries in the C:\PROGR\PERL5\MYSUBS directory , you could add this directory to the @INC list before you use any require statements:

```
push(@INC, "C:\PROGR\PERL5\MYSUBS");
require("numbsubs.pl");
```

You would use a similar push statement for other operating systems, of course.

Packages

You learned about my and local for subroutines earlier in this chapter. Perl has a different method of keeping variable definitions local to a set of subroutines: *packages*. A package is a set of things for which you want a set of local variables. An included file is an excellent example of something that would want to have its own set of variables.

The package declaration tells Perl to start a new package. Until you use package the first time, Perl has everything in the default package, called main. To name a package, simply use the declaration followed by the package name:

```
package NetworkStuff;
```

If you have included a few files that have different packages, you must refer to subroutines in those packages with their package names. The subroutines you saw earlier in this chapter were all in the same package (main) as where you were calling them, so you didn't have to specify a package name. This is because you can have two subroutines in different packages with the same names, and you must be able to differentiate them.

When you want to call a subroutine that is in a different package, you must list that package name, followed by a double colon (::). In Perl 4, you use a single quotation mark (') instead of the double colon. For instance, if you have a package called "NetworkStuff" and a package called "MySubs," you might invoke your subroutines with

```
&MySubs::Router;          # Perl 5
&NetworkStuff::Router;    # Perl 5
&MySubs'Router;           # Perl 4
&NetworkStuff'Router;     # Perl 4
```

Although you will rarely use this you can also refer to variables in other packages using the same double colon. For example, to refer to the variable $i in the package called "MySubs," you would use $MySubs::i.

Including code other than subroutines

So far, I've talked about using require with files that contained only subroutines. Actually, a file you include using require can contain any kind of Perl code. For example, you could include statements that set variables or print text. However, this if often a bad idea because you may not always remember what an included file does when you use require.

In fact, I'd say that it is always a good idea to only use subroutines in the files that you use with require. These subroutines should also be *very* careful about changing any variable and should declare every variable they use (other than Perl's special variables) with my and local.

Running programs in eval

There's yet another way to run programs in Perl: using the eval function. As the name implies, eval causes Perl to evaluate its argument. After it evaluates it, it runs it. You use eval to include parts of a program if you don't know what they will be until the program runs.

For example, if you want to let the user see the value of any desired variable while the Perl program is running. You might have something like

```
print "Name of the variable do you want to see: ";
$Resp = <STDIN>;
print eval($Resp);
```

eval is usually only used by advanced programmers, so you don't need to worry about it much. However, you may find as you are creating a program that you can't do what you want without knowing something at the time the program is running, and eval may be the only way to do so.

Chapter 11

Perl and CGI: Web Server Programs Made Simple

● ●

In This Chapter

▶ Getting realistic about CGI and the Web

▶ Creating simple HTML

▶ Reading requests from URLs

▶ Using Web user information

▶ Processing Web forms

● ●

*O*ne of the events that has done more for promoting Perl than anything else is the rise of the World Wide Web, better known as just "the Web." Unless you have spent the past few years in a cave, you probably have heard lots (maybe too much) about the Web and the wonders that it will bring to all of us.

What is legitimately confusing to many people is why the popularity of the Web should have such a positive effect on the popularity of a programming language like Perl. In fact, the relationship is tenuous at best, but the Web has certainly done a great deal to bring more people into the Perl fold.

By the way, if you're really not at all interested in the Web, feel free to skip this chapter. There are no new functions or statements or operators presented here. This chapter covers how to use Perl in conjunction with Web servers to make Web pages more useful. It is just one application of Perl, albeit a popular one these days. But if you're sure you're not going to have to make Web sites work, feel free to go on to the next chapter.

If you do want to find out more, this chapter will show you how easy it is to use Perl to help control your Web server. However, it is important to understand that there are dozens of different kinds of Web servers, and they all have different requirements for how to interact with Perl. Thus, this chapter does *not* cover how to set up your server to interact with Perl, just what to do after you have followed the directions that come with the server software to hook the server together with a programming language like Perl. The methods covered here are for typical Unix Web servers, because that's what many Windows and Macintosh servers try to emulate.

This chapter also assumes that you understand HTML because you really should understand it before you do much with a Web server. There are zillions of books on HTML, such as the popular *HTML For Dummies,* by Ed Tittel and Steve James (IDG Books Worldwide, Inc.). In fact, there are even a couple of short introductory chapters about it in my *Netscape and the World Wide Web For Dummies* book. The most interesting part of HTML, as it relates to Perl, is HTML forms, which most books about HTML cover in depth. What they don't cover in depth is how to process a form after a user has filled it in; that's one of the things covered in this chapter.

Making the Web More Interesting

If you create Web sites, you can just put up static, unchanging information such as pages of text and graphics. It is more common, however, to put up information that can change depending on the desires of the person visiting the Web site. There are many ways to determine how the user's interaction will change what he or she sees on the site, but all of them involve programming on some level.

Each time a user chooses a Web page to go to, that choice gets transmitted to the Web server. The Web server then determines what to do with the choice. If it is a simple choice, like "show me this page of information," the Web server simply retrieves that information from disk and transmits it back to the user. If, however, the request is something like "here's a filled-in form, do something with it" or "please search for this text" or "let me look at this restricted area," you need to use a program of some sort to figure out what the user is requesting so you can give the user what he or she wants.

As you may imagine by now, Perl is great for more complicated requests. Perl can take a text request, even a very complex one, and easily break it into its constituent parts. Perl is also good at pulling together different pieces of information and presenting them in a single coherent form, which is precisely what you often want to do on Web pages.

CGI: It's Less Than You Think

From the earliest days of the Web, Web servers needed a way to interact with programming languages. The early Web server writers decided to use a single, standard method instead of inventing a different one for each server and each language. This made it easy for people to have their programs run from the Web server. That single, standard method is called *CGI,* which stands for "Common Gateway Interface."

Learning CGI is simple. In fact, many people say it's trivial. I'll tell you almost everything you need to know about it in one sentence. CGI passes a user's request to a program using some special variables and/or standard file input; the program passes information to the user using standard file output. I describe "standard file input" and "standard file output" in the next chapter. They are fairly easy to deal with, and you don't really need to know what they are in order to use CGI. (Incidentally, CGI programs are often called *scripts*.)

Yup, that's it. All you need to know now is the format of the input and the kind of information in the special variables. The output you create is the same output that would normally be sent by your Web server, such as HTML or just plain text. Again, because I do not want to define how you should format your output, I use HTML for the examples in this chapter because that's what you see most of on the Web.

What you need to know

In order to write Web server programs with Perl, then, you need to know two things:

- ✔ How to tell what the user asked for
- ✔ How to tell the user what you want to say

The first part, the input, is more difficult than the second, the output. In fact, I'll spoil the suspense of the latter part by telling you what you have probably already guessed: You do your output using the `print` statement. The input's a bit more difficult but still easy to handle for anyone who has gotten this far in the book.

Who are you talking to?

One thing that is important to understand is that your Perl program works with the Web server software, not around it. Web users coming to your Web site do not run your programs directly. Instead, they access the Web server, and the Web server software launches your programs. Thus, you have to write your programs to work with the Web server.

The reason this chapter isn't the end-all-be-all reference on how to write CGI programs in Perl is that different Web servers have different requirements and perform different actions when you run a CGI program. For example, some Web servers require that all your CGI programs be in one place and that they must follow certain naming rules; other servers let you put them where you want and give them whatever names you want.

Thus, it is very important that you read the instructions with your Web server before trying to write CGI programs in Perl. This isn't to say that it's going to be hard: Most Web servers try to make using CGI programs fairly easy. However, many people do not receive any results at all on their first few attempts because they didn't follow the rules of whatever Web server they are using.

Environment Variables

As I have mentioned already in this chapter, there are two ways to get information from the Web server: through special variables called *environment variables,* and through the standard file input (which is described in Chapter 12). For many requests, you use environment variables; however, for most HTML forms, you use standard file input. You need to learn both methods, but environment variables are easier to grasp, so I'll cover them first.

Beyond CGI

In the old days, CGI was the only game in town for interfacing Web servers and programming languages. Now, almost every server still supports CGI, but the most popular servers also support their own programming interfaces, usually to their own programming languages. For instance, the Web servers from Netscape run a language called JavaScript, which interfaces to the server through a different interface than CGI.

The only reason you should know about this is that CGI is pretty limited, even if the programming languages to which it attaches aren't. The custom *application programming interfaces*, or *APIs*, used by newer Web servers give you many more capabilities than plain old CGI. If you get serious about creating programs that work with your Web server and

your server has its own API, you should probably strongly consider learning it. (Of course, the API might not be nearly as easy to use as Perl, but few languages are!)

If your Web server runs on Windows 95 or Windows NT, it may use an extended version of CGI that most Windows Web servers use. The interface is called Windows CGI. Although it is much more complicated than standard CGI, it has many features not available in standard CGI.

If you are running on Unix and are using the Apache Web server, you can embed Perl directly into the server. This makes launching Perl scripts from your Web server much, much faster. See your Apache instructions about how to embed Perl.

The term "environment" comes from Unix, although it also applies to Windows as well. Environment variables are variables that are set in the operating system. They are similar to text variables in Perl. Perl can read operating system environment variables and use them just like other Perl variables. (Macintosh users: The Mac doesn't really have environment variables, but MacPerl pretends to have them for use in CGI programs.)

Unix has dozens of environment variables, but this chapter covers only those that are specific to running CGI programs. They are set by the Web server software as a way to communicate information to programming languages such as Perl. The CGI standard defines many of these variables, but only a few of them are useful to most people.

Getting at the variables

The method you use to get the values of the environment variables won't be described until Chapter 16, but it's fairly easy to use without understanding it completely. Like Perl variables, environment variables have names; the environment variables in CGI have their names in all capital letters. To get the value of an environment variable with the name VARNAME, you would use

```
$ENV{"VARNAME"}
```

Note that there is a $ before the ENV, but *not* before the "VARNAME".

For example, there is a variable called REMOTE_HOST that has the domain name of the computer making the request. You can set a variable $TheUserHost in your Perl program with

```
$TheUserHost = $ENV{"REMOTE_HOST"};
```

Just to give you a feel for the variables' names and the typical values you might see, here's a list of them for a typical Web request:

```
    GATEWAY_INTERFACE — CGI/1.1
                HOME — /
        HTTP_ACCEPT — image/gif, image/jpeg, */*
          HTTP_HOST — www.mycompany.com
    HTTP_USER_AGENT — Mozilla/3.01b1 (Macintosh; I; PPC)
    PATH_TRANSLATED — /usr/local/wn/scripts
       QUERY_STRING — eastern
        REMOTE_ADDR — 169.207.113.247
        REMOTE_HOST — jl12.cs.cmu.edu
     REQUEST_METHOD — GET
```

(continued)

(continued)

```
        SCRIPT_NAME — /telltime.cgi
        SERVER_NAME — www.mycompany.com
        SERVER_PORT — 80
    SERVER_PROTOCOL — HTTP/1.0
    SERVER_SOFTWARE — WN/1.14.2
       WN_DIR_PATH — /usr/local/wn/scripts
           WN_ROOT — /usr/local/wn/scripts
```

You need to use only a few environment variables to get information from the user; you rarely need to use the others. Thus, I'll describe the important ones first, and leave the rest for near the end of the chapter, after I've described what you want to do with the useful ones.

The query

When a user clicks on a link to your program, it causes the Web server to launch the program. Your program may need to know certain things about what the request was, so the Web server sets a few variables with this information.

The QUERY_STRING variable has all the text after the ? in the user's request. For example, your home page might have the following as part of it:

```
<p>
```

To see what time it is in the central time zone, choose

```
<a href="/amy/telltime.cgi?central">this link</a>.
```

To see what time it is in the eastern time zone, choose

```
<a href="/amy/telltime.cgi?eastern">this link</a>.
```

When the user chooses this link, the value of QUERY_STRING will be either central or eastern. Thus, your Perl program might have something in it like this:

```
$TheTime = time();
$DesiredTimeZone = $ENV{"QUERY_STRING"};
if($DesiredTimeZone eq 'central')
    { $TheTime += 3600 }   # Add one hour
elsif($DesiredTimeZone eq 'eastern')
    { $TheTime += 7200 }   # Add two hours
```

Remember that the query string is assigned by you in your HTML pages. To allow the user to make choices on an HTML page, you need to use HTML forms, which are described later in this chapter.

Pretty much, QUERY_STRING is the only variable you really need for most things other than for handling forms. There are a raft of other environment variables that are of only marginal value for what you really want to do, which is to figure out what the user wants so that you can give it to him or her. The rest of the environment variables (other than two described immediately in the following section) are described at the end of this chapter.

Where the request came from

You may find two more environment variables of interest because you can use them to log accesses to your Web site. These variables, REMOTE_HOST and REMOTE_ADDR, tell you which computer made the request to your Web server. Note that these identify the *computer,* not the *user.* REMOTE_HOST is the domain name of the computer making the request (if the Web server was able to determine this), while REMOTE_ADDR is the IP address of that computer.

Some people use these values to determine what information is given in the message returned. For instance, you might want to give more information to someone on a computer you recognize. However, this is an incredibly unsafe practice. It is possible for someone to pretend to be a particular computer by subverting the addresses on the Internet. It is probably best just to ignore the values in REMOTE_HOST and REMOTE_ADDR.

REMOTE_HOST may be a null string if your Web server could not translate the IP address that it got with the request into a domain name. Most people would prefer to see host names in their logs rather than IP addresses, so they may check whether or not REMOTE_HOST has a value, and if not, use REMOTE_ADDR instead. You can do this with something like the following:

```
# Get the host name or IP address for the log
unless($ENV{REMOTE_HOST} eq '')
    { $TheWhere = $ENV{REMOTE_HOST} }
else { $TheWhere = $ENV{REMOTE_ADDR} }
```

Getting Requests from HTML Forms

Using a query string (stuff after the ? in a URL) is a simple, direct way to get one piece of information from the user. However, you often want much more than just one piece of information. For example, you might want to know the user's name, answers to a few yes-no questions, and so on. For this, you want the user to fill out a form.

The particulars of HTML forms are beyond the scope of this book because they really have nothing to do with Perl. If you aren't familiar with how to put together an HTML form, you should find a good tutorial on them. The following assumes that you understand enough HTML to put together your own form but need to know what to do with the results.

There are two parts of an HTML form that are relevant to CGI programs: the HTTP method used in the form, and the names of the elements in the form. Beyond that, the rest of the form consists mostly of formatting that makes it easier for the user to enter information.

The method for submitting forms can be either GET or POST. The GET method puts the responses to the form in the query string, while the POST method puts the responses into the body of the HTTP reply that you can read from the standard file input that you will learn about in Chapter 12. Most people use POST instead of GET because some Web clients have a hard time handling long GET strings and some forms allow you to enter arbitrarily long responses. However, either can be used, depending on your fancy.

For instance, the following is a very short, very simple form.

```
<hr><form method=POST
    action="http://www.bigstate.edu/accts/namecolor.pl">
First name: <input name=FirstName size=30><br>
Last name:  <input name=LastName size=30><br>
Favorite color: <select name=FavColor>
<option>crimson<option>apricot<option>saffron
<option>emerald<option>sapphire<option>magenta
<option>pearl<option>coal<option>chestnut
</select>
<br><input type="submit" value="Send">
</form><hr>
```

Figure 11-1 shows this little form.

This form returns values for the three named elements: FirstName, LastName, and FavColor. CGI returns values in a very compact and hard-to-decipher fashion: as a single string with each element listed as elementname=elementvalue, with spaces in the values turned into + characters and & characters between each element. For example, if a person named Sharon Fulton who really likes purple fills in the form, the returned string returned will look like this:

```
FirstName=Sharon&LastName=Fulton&FavColor=magenta
```

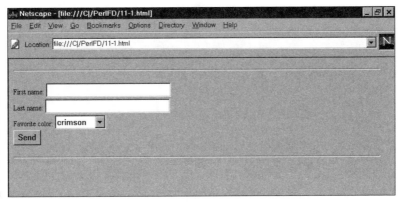

In fact, it gets a bit more complicated than that. Many "special" characters get encoded as a percent sign (%) followed by the hexadecimal value of the character. For instance, if Sharon had entered Sharon & Pete instead of Sharon, the returned string would have been

```
FirstName=Sharon+%26+Pete&LastName=Fulton&FavColor=magenta
```

Two ways to get the form data

As I have already mentioned, you can use either GET or POST as the HTTP method for submitting the form to the Perl program. The way you get the form data depends on which method you use.

✔ For GET, the response comes back in the QUERY_STRING environment variable, which you can read with $ENV{"QUERY_STRING"}.

✔ For POST, the response comes in the content of the reply, which you read from the standard file input.

The environment variable REQUEST_METHOD tells you which method was used. People use the POST method more commonly than the GET method. To read the right amount of information, you need to know how long the content is, and then read that many characters using Perl's read function. The environment variable CONTENT_LENGTH tells you how long the response is. Thus, you can put the data into the variable $TheResp with this statement:

```
read(STDIN, $TheResp, $ENV{"CONTENT_LENGTH"});
```

The read function is described in Chapter 13, so you have to take it on faith for now that this does what it is supposed to.

If you want your Perl program to be robust, you would check for both methods:

```
if($ENV{"REQUEST_METHOD"} eq 'GET')
    { $TheResp = $ENV{"QUERY_STRING"} }
else
    { read(STDIN, $TheResp, $ENV{"CONTENT_LENGTH"}) }
```

What to do with the mess

Okay, so now you know how to get the user's responses. However, that smooshed-together response looks like this:

```
FirstName=Sharon&LastName=Fulton&FavColor=magenta
```

Perl is great at handling data just like this. You can write a program that will split this string into pairs of items such as FirstName and Sharon, LastName and Fulton, and so on.

However, because of all the rules given earlier for the special cases, you should let someone else write the program for you. As you can imagine, because this kind of program is needed by everyone who uses Perl to read HTML forms, someone has already written this program. In fact, many people have already written this program; you can find a variety of programs on the CD-ROM for working with HTML forms. The easiest of these programs is called CGI_Lite. It's a Perl 5 program, and it uses some of the object-oriented features covered in Chapter 19. However, you can use this program without understanding its object-oriented features.

To use CGI_Lite, you have to make it available to Perl. The best way to do this is to copy the CGI_Lite file, called CGI_Lite.pm, into one of the directories in Perl's search path. Chapter 10 shows you how to locate these directories (they are listed in the special @INC list). After you have copied CGI_Lite.pm into one of the directories on Perl's search path, start your Perl program with something like the following:

```
use CGI_Lite;
$InCGI = new CGI_Lite();
@FormData = $InCGI->parse_form_data();
```

The use statement tells Perl to read the CGI_Lite module into this one. use is a bit like the require statement described in Chapter 10, but it has some extra object-oriented features. For now, assume that it is a way to get a Perl object-oriented module into your program.

The next line causes Perl to create an object described in CGI_Lite, and the third line tells Perl to use the parse_form_data method in the object. The point of all this is to create an array, @FormData, whose items are the names and elements returned. In fact, for Sharon and her preference toward purple, @FormData would contain

```
('FirstName', 'Sharon', 'LastName', 'Fulton',
    'FavColor', 'magenta')
```

Of course, you now want to do something with the values in the array, namely put them in Perl variables that you can use in your program. You can do this quickly for element names you know by looking through the array for the name you know and then picking the next item in the array for your Perl variable:

```
# Fill in $FormFirst with the name given
for($i = 0; $i <= $#FormData; $i += 1) {
    if($FormData[$i] eq 'FirstName') {
        $FormFirst = $FormData[$i + 1];
        last;
    }
}
```

This is actually not the best way to handle the data. In fact, it is an ugly kludge. You will see in Chapter 16 how to use *associative arrays* to deal with lists that are in the form "name, value, name, value . . ." much better than this. However, associative arrays take much more introduction than I have room for here.

Sending Out the Result

So far, you've only learned how to read the data from the users, but you haven't told them anything yet. Of course, the interesting part is giving the users information. After you know a few quick rules for how to put out information, you can create your own programs to tell the users whatever you want.

Every message sent from a Web server to a Web client consists of two parts: header information and the main message. The header information might be very short, but it must be there. If it isn't included, most Web browsers assume that the main message is a plain text file.

A few servers pass their own header information, but your Perl program isn't supposed to pass any. Most servers pass some of the information, but not the most important piece: the MIME content type. MIME stands for Multipurpose Internet Mail Extension, and it's used in the Web as well as in Internet mail. MIME types are more properly called *Internet media types,* but the name MIME has stuck and is almost universally used instead.

For our purposes, MIME tells the Web client what kind of information is in the response. The Web client then uses this information to decide how to show the information. For instance, a Web client will do something different when you say "this is an HTML document" or "this is a GIF image" or "this is compressed program file."

The header that you send to the client before you start sending your own information starts with the string Content-type: followed by a space and then the MIME type. There are dozens of different MIME types, most of which you can probably ignore. Table 11-1 contains the MIME types that you are most likely to want to send.

Table 11-1	MIME Types for Common File Formats
MIME Type	*Description*
text/html	A regular HTML document
text/plain	A plain text file that will appear exactly as you send it
application/binary	A binary file that will be saved to disk
image/gif	A picture in GIF format
image/jpeg	A picture in JPEG format
audio/aiff	A sound in AIFF format

For example, if you are going to send back an HTML document to the user, your Perl program would print the following before it does anything else:

```
Content-type: text/html
```

The header information is separated from the body of the message by a blank line. Thus, you have to use \n\n at the end of your Content-type line.

A few servers send out the Content-type line to the client for you, meaning that you should not put it out yourself. Again, see your server's documentation for information on what you should be sending out in your CGI programs.

That's it! That's all you need to know about how to send information back to the user. For example, here's a really short Perl CGI program that ignores any client input and returns a short message formatted as HTML:

```
print "Content-type: text/html\n\n";
print "<b>Thank you</b> for running my Perl program.";
```

This short program doesn't have any of the HTML header information and other things that it should, but it does work. Here's a longer and more interesting example, called thetime.cgi:

```
# CGI program to tell the user what time it is.
#    The user either got here with a URL of
#    "central" or "eastern" or nothing.
$TheZone = "Pacific";
```

```
if ($DesiredTimeZone eq 'central') {
    @TimeArr = localtime(time + 3600);
    $TheZone = "Central";
}
elsif($DesiredTimeZone eq 'eastern') {
    @TimeArr = localtime(time + 7200);
    $TheZone = "Eastern";
}
$Hour = $TimeArr[2];
$Minute = $TimeArr[1];
$TimeString = "$Hour:$Minute";
print <<"EndOfStuff"
ContentType: text/html

<html><head><title>At the tone...</title></head><body>
In the <b>$TheZone</b> time zone, it is now $TimeString.
</body></html>
EndOfStuff
```

The HTML document that refers to this program might look like this:

```
Which time zone do you want to see the time for?
<br>
<a href="/cgi-bin/thetime.cgi?pacific">Pacific</a>?
<br>
<a href="/cgi-bin/thetime.cgi?central">Central</a>
<br>
<a href="/cgi-bin/thetime.cgi?eastern">Eastern</a>
```

Creating HTML on the Fly

Many people use CGI programs to take requests from the users and combine them into a single response. This is useful when the information you are sending is short and the user will want to see many different items.

For instance, assume that you sell musical instruments. You could have a master page with links to descriptions of each instrument, but that means that users who are interested in comparing three instruments have to go back and forth from the main page to each of the other pages. Instead, you would like them to be able to see all of the instruments they are comparing at the same time.

To let them compare many items at once, you might have an HTML form like this:

```
<form method=POST action="/cgi-bin/dispguit.cgi">
Please pick the instuments from the following list. You
may choose as many as you want.
<br><input type=checkbox name=GoyaStandard>
Goya standard guitar
<br><input type=checkbox name=GoyaConcert>
Goya concert guitar
<br><input type=checkbox name=VegaArtistGrand>
Vega Artist Gran guitar
<br><input type=checkbox name=HarmonySteel>
Harmony steel guitar
<br><input type="submit" value="Show me">
</form>
```

The dispguit.cgi program might look like Listing 11-1. The GetData subroutine would be something that gets information from a database or from a file. It would return a string containing the desired information.

Listing 11-1:
Program for displaying information about guitars based on user requests.

```
#  First get the form data. CGI_Lite will only return
#    the values of checkboxes that are selected by
#    the user, so you don't have to check for "on"
#    and "off"
use CGI_Lite;
$InCGI = new CGI_Lite();
@FormData = $InCGI->parse_form_data();

print <<EndOfTop;
Content-type: text/html

<html><head><title>Guitar Information</title></head><body>
Thank you for considering our guitars. Here is the
information you requested.
EndOfTop

while(@FormData) {
    $ThisGuitar = shift(@FormData);  # The item name
    $ThisOn = shift(@FormData);  # Toss this out
    $DisplayThis = &GetData($ThisGuitar);
    print "<hr>$DisplayThis";
}

print "</body></html>\n";
```

Redirection

It is very common to find links on one Web server that point to a different Web server. It is also common for Web administrators to want to track who comes to their servers and who follows their links to other servers. For example, if you list a dozen different sites on your server, you might want to be able to tell the administrator of those sites, "I sent 100 people to your site last week."

The common way to send someone to another site is to simply have a link to that site. However, when a user accesses one of those links, you do not know it. A less-common method to link to other sites is through *redirection,* which requires that you have a CGI program that sends a special HTTP message to the user's browser that then links them to the other site. By using redirection, you can also log how many times you sent people to each site.

Listing 11-2 shows a long program called ad-url.cgi which is used to track redirections. I wrote the program for a newspaper I write for, *MicroTimes.* The editor of *MicroTimes,* when creating our Web site, wanted to be able to list all the advertisers who had their own Web sites and have us link to them.

Listing 11-2:
Program for
redirecting
Web
clients.

```perl
$WebPerson = 'webmaster@yourcompany.com';

# Look at the string they handed to us in the URL
$TheSearch = $ENV{QUERY_STRING};

# Look in the search string
unless($TheSearch eq '') {
    $RefURL = '';  # The URL we will send them to
    # Open the database
    open(IN, 'AdURLs') or die "Could not open the URL " .
        "database. Please send mail to $WebPerson so " .
        "we can fix this.\n";
    # Read the database line-by-line
    while (<IN>) {
        $TheString = $_; chomp($TheString);
        # Split the line into two parts, based on
        #    whitespace between them
        ($TheName, $TheURL) = split(/\s+/,$TheString, 2);
        # Check if the part we just got is the same as
        #    the part in the search string
        if ($TheName eq $TheSearch) {
            # If so, set some variables and leave
            $RefName = $TheName;
            $RefURL = $TheURL;
```

(continued)

(continued)

```
            last;
        }
    }
    close(IN);
    unless ($RefURL eq '') {    # We found a match
        &PrintFound;
    }
    else {    # We didn't find a match
        &PrintNotFound;
        # Change the $RefName for the log
        $RefName = "ErrorNotInDatabase:$TheSearch";
    }
}
else {  #The search string was empty
    print "HTTP/1.0 400 Bad Request\n";
    print "Content-Type: text/html\n\n";
    print "<head><title>Incorrect Request</title>" .
        "</head><body>\n";
    print "There was no query.\n";
    print "</body>\n";
    $RefName = 'ErrorNoRequest';  # This is for the log
}

#  We displayed what we wanted to, now make a log entry

# Get the time right now into a bunch of variables
($Second, $Minute, $Hour, $DayOfMonth, $Month, $Year,
    $WeekDay, $DayOfYear, $IsDST) = localtime(time);
$RealMonth = $Month + 1;  # Since $Month starts at 0
# Format the variables to be two digits long
$DateAndTime = sprintf("%02d/%02d/%02d\t%02d:%02d:%02d",
    $RealMonth, $DayOfMonth, $Year, $Hour, $Minute,
    $Second);

# Get the host name or IP address for the log
unless($ENV{REMOTE_HOST} eq '')
    { $TheWhere = $ENV{REMOTE_HOST} }
else { $TheWhere = $ENV{REMOTE_ADDR} }

# Open the log and write the line
open(ADLOG, '>>AdLog') or die "Could not append to the " .
    "URL log. Please send mail to $WebPerson so we can " .
```

```
    "fix this.\n";
print ADLOG "$DateAndTime\t$TheWhere\t$RefName\n";
close(ADLOG);

sub PrintFound {
        print <<"EndFound";
HTTP/1.0 302 Found
Location: $RefURL
Content-Type: text/html

<head><title>Redirection Information</title></head><body>
If you are reading this, your Web browser does not support
redirection. That's OK: simply select <a href=\"$RefURL\">
this</a> and you will be taken to the advertiser you
selected.
</body>
EndFound
}

sub PrintNotFound {
        print <<"EndNotFound";
HTTP/1.0 404 Not Found
Content-Type: text/html

<head><title>Incorrect Request</title></head><body>
There is no entry in the URL database for '$TheSearch'.
This may indicate an error in our database of URLs.
If you are sure you got this message by simply choosing
one of the links on our page, please send email to
<a href=\"mailto:$WebPerson\">$WebPerson</a>.
</body>
EndNotFound
}
```

In order to use this redirection program, your Perl CGI program must be the only one sending any HTTP headers. Thus, this program does not work on all Web servers, because many servers send out their own HTTP headers as well. However, you will find that most servers allow you to prevent them from sending out headers for some CGI programs using special settings. See your Web server documentation to determine how you can tell it to not send any HTTP headers out for this program.

The *MicroTimes* Web site contains pages with links to a database that we have. The HTML for these pages looks something like this:

```
<h3>Computer Systems</h3>
<a href="ad-url?ACME">ACME Micro-System, Inc.</a><p>
<a href="ad-url?AdvancedComputer">Advanced Computers
and Technology</a><p>
<a href="ad-url?Airt"> AIRT Computers</a><p>
```

and so on. The database is a simple text file with lines like this:

```
ACME    http://www.acmemicro.com/
AdvancedComputer  http://www.plgrn.com/adv-comp.html
Airt     http://www.airtcomp.com/
```

The first section of the program sets up a variable, $WebPerson, that is used in many places in the program. It then fills $TheSearch with the request that the user made.

The program then checks $TheSearch to see if it is blank, which it shouldn't be. If it isn't blank, the program opens the AdURLs file and reads through it a line at a time (see Chapter 12). Each line is split into two variables, $TheName and $TheURL, and the program compares $TheName to $TheSearch. If they match, the program sets some variables and jumps out of the loop.

After the loop, the program sees whether or not any entry in the database matched the search. If it did, the PrintFound subroutine prints the appropriate HTTP redirection headers; if not, the PrintNotFound subroutine prints an error message. The HTTP headers put out by the PrintFound subroutine cause almost any modern Web client to automatically go to the specified URL, but in case they don't, the text in the message will let the user go there manually.

The sections in the middle of the program create the log entries using the functions described in Chapter 9. The log is opened, appended to, and closed using statements you'll learn about in Chapter 12.

Security and CGI Programs

You're probably anxious to go out and start writing your own CGI programs now, and that's great. You can do lots with Perl and CGI that will make your Web site more attractive and useful. However, you can also do plenty of stuff that is detrimental to the security of your site.

When you write your CGI programs, you should be very careful about reading and writing files on your system. People who would be happy to break into your system and cause havoc are always on the lookout for programs that might be poorly written so that they can take advantage of these programs.

You should be particularly aware of CGI programs that take input from a user and then use that input as a command for the computer. There are many pitfalls in doing this kind of thing, some of which are described in Chapter 18. Before you write any Perl CGI program, you should read the Web Security FAQ document that can be found on the Web at /http://www-genome.wi.mit.edu/WWW/faqs/www-security-faq.html/. This document lists many of the common security mistakes people make when creating CGI programs.

Less Interesting Environment Variables

There are a bunch of other environment variables available to your CGI programs, but few of them are useful. This section runs through the remaining variables not described earlier in this chapter.

Additional client information

The CONTENT_TYPE variable holds the MIME type of the form handed to the CGI program. This is often left blank, but it can be set in the HTML <form> tag with the enctype attribute, if you really want.

Most Web clients also send a few additional HTTP headers when they make requests. These headers appear in environment variables that have HTTP_ before the header name and hyphens changed to underscores. For example, the User-Agent header put out by most clients can be accessed from the HTTP_USER_AGENT environment variable. Note that not all Web servers set all the environment variables that the Web client gave them.

Server information

Table 11-2 contains the environment variables that tell you about the Web server from which the CGI program was launched.

Table 11-2	Server Information Variables
Variable	*Description*
SERVER_SOFTWARE	The name and version of the Web server software
SERVER_NAME	The domain name that the server is running from
SERVER_PORT	The TCP port on which the request was made
SERVER_PROTOCOL	The version of HTTP that the server is running
GATEWAY_INTERFACE	The version of CGI that the server is using

Some Web servers also create server-specific environment variables. Unfortunately, these don't have standard names, so you can't find them easily. For example, my favorite Web server software on Unix, WN, creates environment variables called WN_DIR_PATH and WN_ROOT; other servers create similar variables.

User authentication

If your Web server supports user authentication, REMOTE_USER has the name that the user was authenticated with. AUTH_TYPE is the protocol used to authenticate the user. If your Web server supports the Internet IDENT protocol, and the user's computer does as well, the REMOTE_IDENT variable will hold the user name of the person.

Do not rely on the IDENT protocol for any security. It is easy, nay, trivial to fool an IDENT server, and you might think that a user is someone who he or she is not.

Program information

SCRIPT_NAME is the path to the CGI program being run, in case you need to know what directory you are in.

Some Web servers process incoming URLs in such a way that the CGI program that gets executed is not the one at the end of what looks like the directory path in the URL. In this case, the PATH_INFO variable is set to the extra path information, and PATH_TRANSLATED is set to the actual path that the server used. These features are rarely used anymore.

Chapter 12
The Files Go In, The Files Go Out

. . . .

In This Chapter

▶ Learning about files

▶ Opening and closing files

▶ Reading and writing text files

▶ Finding information about your files

▶ Using STDIN and STDOUT

. . . .

*T*he sample programs you used in Chapters 3 and 4 read information from text files. I promised that I'd explain to you how Perl handles files, and here it is Chapter 12 and I haven't done so yet. It's not that file handling is all that hard, but it isn't trivial either. Further, file handling is related to lots of other parts of Perl, so I had to show those parts first. This is one of the hard parts of laying out a book about a programming language: You want to put everything first.

Be that as it may, you're now ready to learn about how to read and write files in Perl programs. When you're done with this chapter, you'll be able to write programs that read text files for information and write text files that contain results from your programs. For instance, you might want to write a program that reads a text file and writes out the same file in a different format. With Perl, such a program might be only a few lines long.

What Is a File, Anyway?

When you use a computer, it is sometimes easy to take simple things for granted. It is easy to forget that some of the things you use every day have a deeper meaning than you would expect. When you think of files, you probably think of "those things on my disk." They have names, they have stuff in them, and that's about it.

Very simply, one could say that a file is an ordered set of bytes stored on disk with a file name. The bytes in a file are ordered so you know where the beginning and end of the file are, they're stored on disk, and you can access a file by its file name.

For most users, this definition is good enough. However, Perl's roots in Unix make describing a file much more difficult than that. Unix's files do not have to reside on disk. They can be any stream of ordered bytes that a program can access. Things like the output of a program or a stream of data coming in from the network can be viewed as a file in Perl.

For now, don't worry about this. You'll see at the end of this chapter some pretty snazzy things you can do with special files that don't reside on disk, but for the rest of this chapter, just think of files as disk files.

That definition of a file talks only about the file in a very general way, without dealing with what's inside the file. The bytes in a file can have any value. The contents of a file are only relevant to things that read that file. That is, you don't care about the contents of a file that you don't read.

You can divide files into two broad categories based on their contents: *text* files and *binary* files. There are no hard-and-fast rules for this separation, but a reasonable definition is that a text file only has bytes whose values are displayable characters plus a few special characters, and a binary file is any file that isn't a text file. Not too scientific, but good enough for us.

Text files contain values that you can see on the screen, such as letters, digits, and punctuation, as well as the special characters for space, carriage return, line feed, and the tab character. Text files are often human readable, but many text files are meant to be read by programs. Binary files are not human readable because they contain nonprinting characters; they are almost always only meant to be read by programs.

You should know the difference between the two kinds of files because Perl has some handy features that only apply to text files. Because so many of the files that Perl programmers want to read are text files, Perl makes text file handling as easy as possible. This isn't to say that handling binary files is inherently hard, just that if you know a file is a text file, your programs for reading from and writing to those files will be shorter and easier to follow.

The First Step: Opening Files

When you either want to read from or write to a file, you must first open it. Every operating system has a different way of opening files, but Perl takes care of all the differences behind the scenes. Regardless of your operating system, you use Perl's open statement the same way. The format of open is

```
open(HANDLE, FILENAME);
```

The *handle,* sort of like a nickname, is a name that you will use in the program to talk about the file. It is a new kind of thing that you haven't seen before. File handles are shown in Perl programs without any special character in front of them. File handle names have the same rules as variable names. It has become a Perl convention to always use all uppercase letters in file handle names.

For example, here is a typical open statement:

```
open(INFILE, 'sample.txt');
```

It is also common to use a variable to hold the file name and use that variable as the second argument to open:

```
$TheFile = 'sample.txt';
open(INFILE, $TheFile);
```

In both these cases, the file handle is INFILE. This is an arbitrary choice; you can name your file handles however you want, following the rules for variable names you saw in Chapter 3.

File modes

When you open a file, Perl needs to know what you want to do with the file. You can open a file for reading, for writing, or for appending. If you want to program with files, you must understand the difference between these three tasks.

- ✔ Opening a file for reading means that you want to look through the file and not change its contents in any way. You can read a file in any order, but people usually read a file from beginning to end. Of course, you can only read from a file that already exists.

- ✔ Open a file for writing means that you want to write new information into a file. You can write to a new file, which is how you would create a file, or you can write to an existing file, in which case you will immediately wipe out everything that is already in the file. Opening a file for writing is like starting fresh, regardless of whether or not there is anything in that file.

✔ Opening a file for appending means that you are going to write into the file, but only at the end. This is different than opening a file for writing in that appending doesn't wipe out the current contents; it only inserts at the end. You can open a nonexistent file for appending, which is the same as opening it for writing because you are adding to the "end" of this new file in both cases.

Note that you cannot both read and write to a file at the same time. At first, you may be frustrated by this fact, but there is a very good reason why you can't do both. If you write into some part of the file and then attempt to read near the place you wrote, Perl is not sure whether it should read strictly what is on disk or whether it should read what is on disk plus what you wrote. Perl would be absolutely sure only if you wrote out what you wanted to disk.

You have to tell Perl in the open statement which of the three modes you want to open the file in. It would have been nice if you could do it with something like

```
open(INFILE, 'read', 'sample.txt');
```

but you can't. Instead, Perl looks at the first character or two of the file name you give it and determines the mode from that. This is a bit dweeby and very Unix-ish, but it's the only way you can do it.

✔ To read a file, you precede the name with < or with no special character

✔ To write a file, you precede the name with >

✔ To append to a file, you precede the name with >>

Here are some examples:

```
open(INFILE, '<sample.txt');  # For reading
open(INFILE, 'sample.txt');   # Also for reading
open(INFILE, '>sample.txt');  # For writing
open(INFILE, '>>sample.txt'); # For appending
$TheFile = '>sample.txt';     # Prepare for writing
open(INFILE, $TheFile);       # This will open for writing
```

How to tell if it really opened

As described in Chapter 8, the open statement returns a value of true if the open was successful. For reading, open returns true if the file exists and is readable. For writing or appending, open returns true if the file can be written to. If the file exists, it must not be set "read only" in the operating system. A file doesn't have to exist to be written to, but you cannot always create a file that you can write to, such as if you do not have permission to write to the directory in which the file is located.

If an open statement does not work, it will return a false value. This is the catalyst for the "open or die" statements contained in the sample programs in Chapters 3 and 4. These kind of statements mean "quit the program immediately if the open failed."

Using Files

After you've opened a file, all the other Perl statements that you use on that file have the file handle as an argument. Specifically, you use the file handle and not the file name because not every Perl file has a name. Also, file handles are usually much shorter than file names:

```
open(THEDATA, "C:\EMPLOYEE\DATA\NAMES.DB");
```

Typical things you do on open files is read from them, write to them, investigate where you are in reading and writing, and so on. Perl has many statements for files. Most of them are pretty direct and are covered in the rest of this chapter and in Chapter 13.

Note that you can have many files open in a single program. In fact, it is quite common to have two or more files open if your program does some sort of conversion on a file into a new one. In this case, your program would have open statements near the beginning like this:

```
open(ORIG, 'original.txt') or die "Can't open input.\n";
open(NEW, '>new.txt') or die "Can't open output.\n";
```

The rest of the statements in the program would then use the ORIG file handle when reading from the file being converted and the NEW file handle when writing into the new file.

When You're Done: Closing Files

When you're done processing a file, you can close it with Perl's close statement. If you forget to close a file, it is no big deal: Perl closes all open files when a program ends. The close statement takes one argument, the file handle of the file you want to close:

```
close(ORIG);
```

Note that you want to close a file that you opened for writing or appending as soon as you are done with it because Perl won't necessarily write out the last part of the file to disk until the file is closed. Also, if some other program opens the file for reading before you have closed the file, that program may think the file is shorter than you expect it to be because Perl hasn't written out the last part. Thus, you should always use an explicit close for any file that you are writing or appending just in case your computer crashes before the program finishes.

If you want to open a file right after closing it, you don't need to close it at all. Perl notices that the file is open when it goes to open it a second time and automatically closes it before doing the new open.

File Names for Different Operating Systems

Most of the file names I've used in this book are pretty generic and work on all of the operating systems covered (Windows 95, Windows NT, MacOS, and Unix). However, each operating system has different rules for naming files. Perl allows you to use any valid name in the operating system you are using. For instance, here is an open statement that would work on a Mac but not on a PC:

```
open(POOL, "Betting pool results");
```

Chapter 11 explains how Perl searches in different directories for files that you include with the require statement. The open statement does not search for files, however. You must give an explicit path to the file in the file name; otherwise, Perl looks only in the current directory for that file. For example, if you want to read a file and have the statement

```
open(IN, 'jan97.dat');
```

that file must be in the directory from which you started Perl or Perl won't find the file.

To explicitly state the default directory that you want to be in, use Perl's chdir function. This takes one argument, a string with the name of the directory you want. For example, on Unix you might use

```
chdir('/usr/bin/accounting/data');
```

This function returns false if Perl couldn't change to that directory, so you should write things like this:

```
chdir('/usr/bin/accounting/data') or die "Could not " .
    "change to the accounting data directory.\n";
```

If you use the `open` statement to open a file for writing or appending and do not specify the directory into which you want to write, you should be very sure you know which directory you are in before opening the file. If you are in a directory different than you expect, you could wipe out or alter a file that you did not intend to. At a minimum, you might have a hard time finding the file that you create if you're not sure what directory you're in.

Directory names on different computers

The way that you specify directories in the different operating systems differs. Under Windows 95 and Windows NT, you use a file letter, followed by a colon, and then the directories names separated with the backslash character (\):

```
open(IN, "D:\ORDERS\DATA\JAN97.DAT");
```

On the Mac, you use the disk name and folder names separated with colons:

```
open(IN, "Main:Order entry:Data files:January 1997 data");
```

On Unix, you use the standard path name to a file, separated with slash characters (/):

```
open(IN, "/usr/home/orders/data/jan97.dat");
```

You could use *relative references* rather than absolute file names. A relative reference refers to a directory relative to the current directory. For instance, under Windows and Unix, the directory named .. indicates the directory above the current directory. On the Mac, you specify the folder above the current folder with two colons (::). Thus, you could specify that you want to open for writing the process.log file in the directory above the current directory with the following:

```
open(PLOG, '>..\process.log');  # for Windows
open(PLOG, '>::process.log');   # for the Mac
open(PLOG, '>../process.log');  # for Unix
```

Opening files is more fun on the Mac

Okay, time for the Mac lovers to gloat a bit. So far, all you have seen is how to specify a file by its name. MacPerl also lets you specify a file's name by using the standard file interfaces that you use with the Open and Save commands in every Mac program. (Perl-Win32 should have features for this but doesn't yet.)

To create a file name string using the Mac interface, you must include the library called StandardFile.pl. Thus, you must have this line near the beginning of your program:

```
require 'StandardFile.pl';
```

This library contains subroutines called GetFile and PutFile. You use GetFile just like the Open command in programs: to select a file. You use PutFile, on the other hand, just like the Save command in programs: to choose a folder and enter a name for the file you want to save.

The arguments for these two subroutines are a bit confusing, but you are safe to use them with no arguments. The obscurity of the arguments comes from the way that the Macintosh handles file calls internally. For example, to get the full file name for a file that already exists, you would use something like

```
$InFile = StandardFile::GetFile();
open(INPUT, $InFile);
```

Similarly, to get from the user the name of a file that they want to create, you could use

```
$NewText = StandardFile::PutFile();
open(TEXTOUT, ">$NewText");
```

Reading from a Text File, the Easy Way

The examples in Chapters 3 and 4 use an operator that you are probably not familiar with. The *file input operator* consists of angle brackets around the name of a file handle. For instance, counter1.pl contains this statement:

```
while(<INFILE>) {
. . .
}
```

Here, the file handle INFILE is surrounded by the file input operator.

The file input operator returns a line from the named text file. By "a line," I mean all the text up to and including the next line separator. The first time you use the file input operator on a file handle, Perl returns the first line of text. The next time you use the file input operator on the same file handle, you get the next line, and so on until there is no more text to be read from the file.

Imagine that your text file contains these contents:

```
What I Did Over Summer Vacation

I wanted to go to the park and play ball a lot, but my
mother made me read a bunch of boring books instead.
The first one I read was about a dumb programming language
. . .
```

If this file has the handle IN, the first thing returned by <IN> is the string What I Did Over Summer Vacation\n (that's a single linefeed character at the end of the string, not the \ and n characters). The next thing returned by <IN> is the single character \n, the next returned is I wanted to go to the park and play ball a lot, but my\n and so on. The important thing to remember here is that every string returned by the file input operator ends in a line terminator.

There are two ways to get the result of the file input operator. One is to assign a string to the input:

```
$ThisLine = <INPUT>;
```

The other is to use Perl's $_ special variable, which gets assigned by the file input operator.

You see the file input operator in Perl programs most often as part of while loops. For instance, here is a tiny Perl program that prints a file:

```
open(A, "somefile.txt");
while(<A>) { print $_ }
```

Many people also assign $_ to a variable as soon as they are in the loop:

```
while(<INPUT>) {
    $ThisLine = $_;
    chomp($ThisLine);
    . . .
}
```

If you intend to use the line you got from the file input operator in more than one statement, you should immediately assign $_ to a variable and use that variable instead of $_ because another statement may wipe out $_ and put in its own results.

The while(<HANDLE>) syntax is very handy because it does a few things at once. The file input operator will always return a true value as long as there is text left in the file. Thus, the while gets a true value when there is text in the file and a false value as soon as there is no more text in the file to be read.

For some programs, you want to use both a variable assignment and a loop with the file input operator. For example, if you are not sure that the file you are opening is the right file, you might check the first line before processing the file. You would use something like this:

```
open(THEFILE, $FileName);
$FirstLine = <THEFILE>;
unless($FirstLine eq "What I Did Over Summer Vacation\n")
    { die "This is not the right file.\n"}
while(<THEFILE>) {
    $Line = $_;
    . . .
}
```

So far, you have seen the file input operator used only in the scalar context. In scalar context, Perl reads one line and puts it into the variable. In list context, however, Perl reads the *entire* file into a list in one step. Thus, you do not use the file input operator in list context in a loop because everything happens in one call.

Of course, if your text file is big, using the file input operator might consume a lot of memory in your computer. If the file is small, there's no danger in using the file input operator. The simple file printing program, using the list context, would look like

```
open(A, "somefile.txt");
@B = <A>;  # reads the whole file
print @B;
```

You could also use a while loop to read each element of the list:

```
open(A, "somefile.txt");
@B = <A>;  # reads the whole file
while($Line = shift(@B)) { print $Line }
```

These two programs do the same thing. Note, however, you cannot do the following because shift doesn't put the value it got into $_:

```
while(shift(@B)) { print $_ }   # This is WRONG
```

The file input operator is intended for use with text files only, not binary files. It should work just fine with binary files, but it is slower than using the binary file statements described in Chapter 13.

Writing Text to a File, the Easy Way

Okay, so now that you know how to read text from a file, you want to learn how to write it to a file. The funny thing is that you already know how to, almost. The print and printf statements have a second format that let you put strings into a file instead of on the screen:

```
print HANDLE LIST;
printf HANDLE FORMAT LIST;
```

Please note that you do *not* have to put a comma after the file handle.

For example, this short program creates a file with ten lines in it.

```
open(OUT, '>lineout.txt') or die "Couldn't open the " .
    "lineout.txt file for writing.\n";
for($i = 1; $i <= 10; $i += 1)
    { print OUT "This is line $i\n" }
```

This program doesn't display anything: instead, it creates a file called lineout.txt whose contents are

```
This is line 1
This is line 2
```

and so on.

The printf statement is similar:

```
open(OUT, '>lineout.txt') or die "Couldn't open the " .
    "lineout.txt file for writing.\n";
for($i = 1; $i <= 10; $i += 1)
    { printf OUT "This is line %.2d\n", $i }
```

This creates a file with these lines:

```
This is line 01
This is line 02
```

and so on.

That's it! No new statements, nothing new to learn. And as an extra special bonus, you'll discover in Chapter 13 that you use print and printf to write to binary files as well. Not bad, eh?

When used without file handles the print and printf statements print to the screen. (Actually, they print to the *standard output,* which is described at the end of this chapter.) When you want to print to a file, you normally use that file's handle in the print and printf statements. However, Perl lets you change where it will print when you don't use the file handle.

The select statement tells Perl to cause print and printf to start printing to the specified file handle:

```
open(OUT, '>lineout.txt') or die "Couldn't open the " .
    "lineout.txt file for writing.\n";
select(OUT);
for($i = 1; $i <= 10; $i += 1)
    { printf "This is line %.2d\n", $i }
```

The printf will write to the lineout.txt file because of the select statement.

select returns the file handle that it is replacing. This makes it easy to use it temporarily and then switch back:

```
select(FH1);
print "This will go to the file with FH1.\n";
$TempHandle = select(FH2);
print "This will go to the file with FH2.\n";
select($TempHandle);
print "This will go to the file with FH1.\n";
```

I do not recommend using select. If you use it and later in the program forget that you did, you might get very confused when a print statement doesn't show anything on the screen. The only advantage that select gives you is that print and printf statements are a bit shorter, but that isn't worth the confusion that it causes.

Testing Things about Files

Reading and writing text files is all well and good, but you might also want to find out about a file before you open it. Perl has a large set of file test functions that lets you determine things like whether or not a file exists, how long it has been since it was created or last updated, its size, and so on. All of these file tests are in this form:

```
-X FILENAME
```

where X is the letter of the test, and the file name is, as you might guess, the name of the file. Note that the file tests take file names, not file handles. There's a good reason for this: You may want to test a file before opening it. Also, you might want to test a whole slew of files because it takes less time to run simple file tests than to open and close several files.

For example, the -w test is used to find out whether or not you can write to a file. You might use it as

```
if(-w 'somefile.txt') { open(CLIST, '>somefile.txt') }
```

The tests are pretty easy to use. Note, however, that some of the tests are specific to Unix and other multi-user operating systems and make no sense on a single-user operating system. If you are running on a system like Windows 95 or MacOS, you should not use the multi-user file tests because the results are undefined.

The most common file tests are common to all operating systems. See Table 12-1 for those that return true or false.

Table 12-1	Common File Tests
Test	*What It Tells You*
-e	File exists
-r	File can be read
-w	File can be written to
-z	File is exactly 0 bytes long
-d	Named item is a directory, not a file
-T	File is a text file (The first hunk of a file is examined, and it's a text file if fewer than 30 percent or so of the characters are nonprintable.)
-B	File is a binary file (this is the exact opposite of the -T test)

Some of the file tests only make sense on Unix. (Well, some of these make sense on Windows NT as well, but they aren't implemented in Perl-Win32 yet.) These tests, which are also true-false, are contained in Table 12-2.

Table 12-2	Unix-specific File Tests
Test	What It Tells You
-x	File can be executed
-o	File is owned by effective user of the running program
-R	File is readable by real user of the running program
-W	File is writable by real user of the running program
-X	File is executable by real user of the running program
-O	File is owned by real user of the running program
-u	File has its setuid bit set
-g	File has its setgid bit set
-k	File has its sticky bit set

A few of the file tests return numbers. The -s test tells you how large a file is. -M, -A, and -C tell how long it has been (in days) since the file was created, accessed, or updated. The values returned by these three tests are measured from when the program started (see Table 12-3).

Table 12-3	File Tests That Return Numbers
Test	What It Tells You
-s	Size of the file in bytes
-C	Creation age of file
-A	Access age of file
-M	Modification age of file

These tests are useful for programs that are supposed to execute on files that are older than a certain age. For instance, if you write a backup program that checks if a file has been modified in the last 12 hours, you could use something like this:

```
if((-C $TheFile) < 0.5) { &BackupThis($TheFile) }
```

Advanced users can use some of these file tests on items that are not standard file names. Table 12-4 contains these true-false tests that are rarely used, even by high-powered dweebs.

Table 12-4	Advanced File Tests
Test	*What It Tells You*
-f	Named item is a plain file (not a special file or a directory)
-l	Named item is a symbolic link
-p	Named item is a pipe
-S	Named item is a socket
-b	Named item is a block special file
-c	Named item is a character special file
-t	Named item is a file handle that is opened to a terminal

The stat function returns values for many of the things that file tests test for; it is covered in Chapter 13.

Not Really Files: Standard In, Standard Out, and Standard Error

Perl's roots in Unix show up at times I wish they wouldn't. Some features are so ingrained in Unix users' heads that they never imagine that non-Unix folk would not understand them. A case in point is Unix's *standard file* metaphor. Most Unix dweebs can use these reflexively, just like breathing, but forget that lots of other people can't figure them out at all, much less use them effortlessly.

The concept of "standard file I/O" runs throughout Perl's file handling. I've navigated around it so far in this chapter because it usually completely stumps those who cannot grasp it, and this misunderstanding gets in the way of the real business of programming in Perl. However, understanding standard file input and output is useful for getting ahead in Perl, and thus I present them here. If after reading this section you have no idea what I'm talking about, don't worry; you can still use Perl's file handling for most normal tasks, as you have seen.

To most of us, a file is a set of bytes on disk. Unix, and Perl by extension, has a much wider definition of files, which is that a file is an ordered stream of bytes that can be identified by the operating system. If that stream of bytes is a set of bytes on a disk, then the definition matches what we all already understand. However, the stream can also be from anywhere to anywhere.

The big three

There are three such file streams that have special properties in Perl. The three are called standard file I/O because they are standard to all Unix implementations. They are *standard file in, standard file out,* and *standard error,* but are usually referred to by their nerdy abbreviations STDIN, STDOUT, and STDERR. You can also drop the "file" part and call them *standard in*, *standard out*, and *standard error*.

STDIN is the byte stream that is associated with the keyboard. This is, when you type something while a Perl program is running, what you type becomes the contents of STDIN. STDOUT, on the other hand, is a stream that is sent to your computer screen. When you write to STDOUT, it's like saying "instead of writing to a file, write to the screen."

STDERR is a bit more problematic. It is a defined file stream, but different operating systems handle it differently. For instance, most versions of Unix display characters sent to STDERR on the screen, just like STDOUT. However, you can also tell Unix to send these error messages to a file instead of to the screen. This is handy if you want to keep a log of error messages but not of the regular text displayed on the screen.

Perl lets you use `STDIN`, `STDOUT`, and `STDERR` as predefined file handles. This means that you don't have to use `open` to name them. For example, you can say

```
$GetALine = <STDIN>;
```

This causes Perl to wait for you to type something on the keyboard, followed by an end-of-line character; it then assigns what you typed to the `$GetALine` string.

If you want to print to `STDERR` instead of `STDOUT`, you could use something like this:

```
print STDERR "Bad user input.\n";
```

Perl allows you to use the empty file input operator, <>, instead of <STDIN>, if you do not give arguments on the program's command line. In this case, <> means "all of the files listed on the command line." This is pretty darn confusing, and you should probably avoid <> because of it. It isn't all that hard to use <STDIN>, after all.

Not files at all: Running programs

If you think of a file as a stream of bytes, there are other things on your computer that can take in a stream of bytes or put out a stream of bytes that you might want to process. Unix lets you use *pipes* to give a stream to, or take a stream from, a program through the standard file input and output. You can use pipes in Perl's open statement.

Windows 95 and Windows NT users can also use stream input through some MS-DOS programs in the MS-DOS box that Perl runs in, but doing so may crash your system. Mac users can't use the features described here unless they have a programming environment with the ToolServer program. Thus, this section (which is the end of the chapter) is really only of interest to Unix users.

Using pipes is pretty technical, but if you understood the stuff in the previous section about STDIN and STDOUT, you may want to give it a try. A program that uses STDIN (the standard name for input from the keyboard) to take in data can also take in data through a pipe. A program that puts out its data on STDOUT can put out its data through a pipe. The pipe acts as a conduit for data going from one source to another.

For instance, Unix's uptime program displays how long the system has been up and the load averages. It displays these by sending them to STDOUT, so you can capture this information with a Perl open statement that has a pipe from uptime to a file handle:

```
open(UPIN, 'uptime |');
```

This tells Perl "run the uptime command and take its STDOUT output and feed it into the UPIN file handle." uptime only puts out one line, and you can read it with something like this:

```
$UptimeInput = <UPIN>;
```

For Unix programs that put out many lines, you would probably use a `while` loop just as you have for reading from actual files. For instance, here's a way to find out which directories exist under the /tmp directory on your system:

```
open(LSIN, 'ls -l /tmp | ');
while(<LSIN>) {
    $TheLine = $_;
    chomp($TheLine);
    if(substr($TheLine, 0, 1) eq 'd') {
        $LastSpace = rindex($TheLine, ' ');
        $DirName = (substr($TheLine, $LastSpace +1));
        print "$DirName is a directory\n";
    }
}
```

You can also use pipes to write to other programs, although this is less common. A few Unix programs do much more than Perl by taking input from STDIN. For example, the `mail` program allows you to send mail with the message coming from STDIN. Thus, you might have a program like this:

```
$MTo = 'someone@someplace.com';
$MSubject = 'Data from the accounting program';
open(DOMAIL, "| mail -s $MailSubject $MTo");
print DOMAIL <<"EndOfMessage";
Your department has a balance of $DeptBal.
If you have questions about this, please send mail
to accounting@someplace.com.
EndOfMessage
```

The rule for using pipes in `open` statements is that piping *from* a `print` statement has the pipe on the left of the Unix command, and piping *to* a file handle has the pipe on right of the Unix command.

Chapter 13

More on Files and Directories

••

In This Chapter

▶ Reading and writing binary files and databases

▶ Changing file settings

▶ Handling directories

••

The preceding chapter explains how to open files and how to read and write text files (as well as other important things about files). This chapter tells you a zillion other things about files, such as what to do if you want to read and write a nontext file, how to change information about files, and how to deal with directories.

Reading and Writing Files, the Slightly Harder Way

You learned in Chapter 12 that to read a text file line by line, you use the file input operator:

```
$TheLine = <ACCTFILE>;
```

However, the file you want to read from may not be a text file: It might be a binary file. In this case, you use a set of functions that lets you read from any part of any file. Incidentally, you can use these functions on text files if you want.

To read from a binary file, open it using the open statement just like you open a text file. Then you use the read function to read from the file. The format of the read statement is

```
read(HANDLE, VARIABLE, LENGTH, POSITION);
```

The variable is the place where you want to read into, the length is the number of bytes to read, and the position is the byte in the file to start reading from. Perl uses 0 as the position for the first byte in the file (just like it uses 0 for the first item in lists).

For example, to read the first seven bytes from the file that has the handle ACCTDATA, you would use

```
read(ACCTDATA, $Start, 7, 0);
```

The read statement returns the number of bytes actually read. That number is handy if you don't know how long the file is so that you can know whether or not you read "off the end" of the file. For example, you might want to detect this with something like

```
$NumGot = read(ACCTDATA, $Start, 7, 0);
if($NumGot < 7)
    { print "You read off the end of the file.\n" }
```

Perl keeps track of where you have read in a file. For instance, after the read in the example above, Perl would set the file position keeper for the ACCTDATA file handle to 6, the position that was the last read. You can use the eof function to test whether the next read would start at the end of the file. It returns true if the keeper is at the end of the file. (By the way, "eof" is common dweebspeak for "end of file.")

```
unless(eof(ACCTDATA)) {
    $NumGot = read(ACCTDATA, $Start, 7, 0);
    if($NumGot < 7)
        { print "You read off the end of the file.\n" }
}
else { print "Already at end of the file.\n" }
```

Note that eof won't tell you if you are near the end, only at the end. That's why you need to check how many characters you receive with each read to be sure you don't receive fewer than you expected.

The seek statement lets you place the file position keeper to anywhere you want. Its format is

```
seek(HANDLE, RELATIVEPOSITION, FROMWHERE);
```

The third argument lets you say where the position in the second argument is relative to: 0 means from the beginning of the file, 1 means from the current file position, and 2 means from the end of the file. Thus, to move the position forwards 12 positions, you would use

```
seek(ACCTDATA, 12, 1);
```

To move it to the second byte in the file, you would use

```
seek(ACCTDATA, 1, 0);
```

The file position keeper is handy so that you don't always have to remember where you read to if you're reading through a file from start to finish. You can leave the last argument off of the read function, and Perl will instead use the file position keeper. For instance, to read a file ten bytes at a time until the end of the file, you could use the following:

```
seek(ACCTDATA, 0, 0);  # If it wasn't at the beginning
while(read(ACCTDATA, $Start, 10)) {
    # $Start is now the next ten bytes of the file
    #    If this is the last chunk of the file, it might
    #    be less than ten bytes long, however.
}
```

If you want to know where the file position keeper is now, use the tell function:

```
$FilePos = tell(ACCTDATA);
```

Writing to a binary file

So, you use read to read from a binary file: What do you use to write to it? If you said write, you'd be wrong. Perl's write function has nothing to do with writing to a binary file. Instead, you use print with a file handle, as described in Chapter 12.

To write nontext data with print, you can use many of the things explained in Chapter 5, such as the chr function and the special characters. For instance, to write the five characters whose values are 23, 97, 192, 12, and 0, you could do something like this:

```
@PrintThese = (23, 97, 192, 12, 0);
foreach $Item (@PrintThese) { print ACCTDATA chr($Item) }
```

Forcing binary reads

Some operating systems treat binary files differently than text files. If you are running Perl on such an operating system and are using read, you must first use the `binmode` function so that Perl can tell the operating system to do binary reads. Yes, this is incredibly lame, but an unfortunate necessity in some cases. The function is called as

```
binmode(ACCTDATA);
```

It is always safe to use `binmode` in your programs that use `read` even on operating systems where binary mode is the default. If you later copy the Perl program to a different, less intelligent operating system, you don't have to remember to search through your programs for `read` functions.

Getting one character the very slow way

There is an additional method for reading characters from a file, but you should probably not use it because it is very slow. `getc` returns the next character from the named file; if you are at the end of the file, it returns a the null character:

```
$TheChar = getc(ACCTDATA);
if($TheChar eq '') { print "At the end of the file.\n" }
```

Changing Things about the Files

Perl gives you pretty complete access to doing anything with your files within your programs. For instance, you can rename a file and even delete it from a Perl program.

Renaming files

The `rename` function takes two arguments: the old name and the new name. It returns true if successful. Here is an example:

```
unless(rename('somedata.txt', 'somedata.old'))
    { print "The rename failed.\n" }
```

On Windows, the extension of a file is significant. For instance, double-clicking on a file that has the .txt extension causes Windows to do something completely different than double-clicking on a file that has the .exe extension. The `rename` function is handy for changing file extensions. For example, assume you want to change the extension of a file from whatever it is now to .old. If the file name is kept in `$FileName`, you could use the following:

```
$PeriodPos = index($FileName, '.');
if($PeriodPos == -1) { $BareName = $FileName }
else
    { $BareName = substr($FileName, 0, $PeriodPos) }
$NewName = "$BareName.old";
rename($FileName, $NewName);
```

Changing file times

You can also change the times that your computer thinks that a file has been accessed or modified. The utime function takes as its argument a list that has an unusual format:

```
(ACCESSTIME, MODIFICATIONTIME, FILE1, FILE2, ...)
```

For instance, if you want to change the access and modification time of a file to right now, you can use

```
$Now = time();
utime($Now, $Now, 'somedata.txt');
```

Deleting files altogether

To delete a file, you use the unlink function. This odd name comes from the technical way that Unix deletes files from a directory (by unlinking them from the directory structure). The unlink function takes a list of the names of the files you want to delete and returns the number of files deleted.

```
unless(unlink('a.dat', 'b.dat') == 2)
    { print "One of the files didn't get deleted.\n" }
```

Hacking off the ends of files

In a slash-and-burn mood? The truncate command tells Perl to whack off the end of a file. It takes two arguments: the name or file handle of the file and the length you want the file to be. For example, to make the nowshort.txt file exactly 100 characters, merrily discarding whatever was already in the file beyond that point, you would use

```
truncate('nowshort.txt', 100);1
```

Unix users beware: `unlink` does not delete a file if it has multiple links to it. It simply removes the link for that file in that directory. A file isn't really deleted from the system until you remove all links to the file.

Great Big Globs of Files

Perl 5 has an humorously named feature called *file globbing* that lets you easily create a list of files based on matching characters in the file names. In the `glob` function, you can use the asterisk (*) as a wildcard character just like you do in Windows or Unix file commands.

For you Macintosh users who haven't had the pleasure of working with Windows or Unix, or those others who might have forgotten, the asterisk wildcard character is used to match one or more other characters in file names. When you search for files in a directory, you can match one or more files using the asterisk in your test file name to indicate that you want to find any file that has one or more other characters in that place.

For example, imagine that you have a directory with five files whose names are

```
chartab1.pl
counter1.pl
edata.txt
empdata1.pl
hexchart.pl
```

Searching for the file *c** would match *chartab1.pl* and *counter.pl* because both file names start with the letter *c* and have one or more characters after the *c* in the file name. Similarly, searching for **pl* would match *chartab1.pl, counter.pl, empdata1.pl,* and *hexchart.pl* because all of these files have one or more characters followed by the letters *pl*.

The `glob` function returns a list of files in the current directory that matches the text argument. For example, to get a list of all the files that start with the letter *m,* you might use

```
@XFiles = glob('m*');
```

You can use the results of the `glob` function to process groups of files that you know have similar names. For instance, imagine that you want to delete all the files in a directory that have *.tmp* at the ends of their names. You would use

```
unlink(glob('*.tmp'));
```

Or suppose that you want to create one big file that contains the contents of every file that starts with the letters *flow*. You would do something like this:

```
open(BIG, ">bigflow");
@AllFlow = glob('flow*');
foreach $FileName (@AllFlow) {
    open(IN, $FileName);
    print "Inserting the file $FileName\n";
    print BIG <IN>;
    close(IN);
}
close(BIG);
```

File Features for Unix

Perl was created for Unix system administrators, and there are many parts that are really only useful to those folks. However, some of Perl's file features are also useful to mere mortal Unix users, those who have figured out how to navigate the Unix file system and use Unix's file commands.

Unix-like chown *and* chmod

You Unix folks probably are familiar with the chmod and chown commands in Unix: They change the access privileges and the owner of files. Perl has its own chmod and chown functions that act like the Unix commands.

The chmod function takes a list as its argument. The first item of the list is the numerical permission you want on the files, and the rest of the list is the files you want changed. If you're not familiar with the numerical permissions under Unix, you should certainly stay away from this function, because changing the permissions can make a file unavailable.

Most Unix systems display the numeric file permissions in octal, and you can use these permissions directly in chmod. For example, to make a file readable and writable by the owner and group, but with no permissions to others, you would use

```
chmod(0660, 'somefile', 'someotherfile');
```

The octal value 0660 is certainly cryptic, just the way Unix systems folks like it. Unfortunately, Perl's chmod doesn't let you use the more readable alphabetic file permissions like "rw-rw——".

The chown function also takes a list as its argument. The first item in the list is the numeric user ID, the second item is the numeric group ID, and the rest are the files you want to change:

```
chown(100, 12, 'somefile', 'someotherfile');
```

Links in Unix

Unix's file system lets you create file names that are nothing more than links to other files on the computer. If you're a Unix user and familiar with symbolic links, you can use Perl to create both hard links and symbolic links. The link and symlink functions take two arguments: the existing file and the link you want to create.

link is like the Unix command ln with no arguments, and symlink is like the Unix command ln -s. For instance, to create a new file in the current directory, TheLog, that is a symbolic link to the /var/log/maillog file, you would use

```
symlink('/var/log/maillog', './TheLog');
```

The readlink function, whose argument is a file name, returns the value of a symbolic link, which is the name of file that the symbolic link is to. For example, to see the name of the file to which the symbolic link TheLog is linked, you would use

```
print readlink('./TheLog');
```

Nitty-Gritty File Details

The file tests shown in Chapter 12 let you look at lots of information about a file using true-false settings. You may, however, want to get all this information at once in a list. Of course, Perl obliges you.

The stat function, which takes either a file handle or a file's name as its argument, returns a wealth of information about the file. Most of the values have no meaning except on Unix, as you can see in Table 13-1.

Table 13-1	Information Returned by the `stat` Function
Element	*Information Returned*
0	Device number (Unix only)
1	Inode number (Unix only)
2	Inode protection mode (Unix only)
3	Number of links to the file (Unix only)
4	User ID of owner
5	Group ID of owner
6	Device type (Unix only)
7	File size (in bytes)
8	Time of last access (seconds from OS base time)
9	Time of last modification (seconds from OS base time)
10	Time of last file status change (seconds from OS base time)
11	Optimal block size (Unix only)
12	Number of blocks allocated for the file (Unix only)

None of this is terribly useful except to Unix hackers, I'm afraid, particularly because you can get the good information from the file tests. One last hint: On Unix, if you're looking at a file that is a symbolic link, the `lstat` function returns the information on the file that is linked to, not the link itself. That's useful if you want the real fine information, not just the information about the link.

Directories: Dealing with Gangs of Files

Dealing with files one at a time is interesting, but many times you may want to process a whole directory. For example, you may want to find out about each file in a directory before you decide what to do next. Perl has a set of functions that handles directories similar to the way you handle files. Instead of looking at the characters in a file, however, they look at the files in a directory.

The directory functions use *directory handles,* which are very similar to file handles except that you use them for directories. Directory handle names have the same rules as file handle names and are used in functions in pretty much the same way.

Directory functions

To tell Perl to start processing a directory, you use the opendir statement. Yes, it's almost like the open command for files. It takes two arguments: the name of the directory handle you want to use and the name of the directory. There is an equivalent closedir function as well:

```
opendir(DOCS, 'C:\TREES\DOCS');
```

You can also open directories relative to the current directory. In this case, you use just the directory name, not the full path to the directory

```
opendir(TEMP, 'temp');
```

To open the current directory, you use the special directory name "." on Unix and Windows (Mac users use ":"). To open the directory above the current one, you use the special directory name ".." (Mac users use "::").

The readdir function, when used in a scalar context, returns the next file name or subdirectory name in the directory:

```
$ThisName = readdir(DOCS);
```

In list context, readdir returns all of the file names and subdirectory names at once in a list:

```
@AllNames = readdir(DOCS);
```

telldir returns the value of the directory position keeper, and seekdir changes the position of the directory position keeper. Of course, these functions are similar to read, tell, and seek for files, except that readdir can only return one file name whereas read can read one or more characters. You can also use rewinddir to set the directory position keeper to the beginning of the directory list.

The main problem with these functions is that there is no way to tell when you get to the end of the directory except to check if readdir returns a null string. Unfortunately, there is no directory equivalent of the eof function. Thus, it is usually easier to use readdir in a list context, which causes it to return all of the file names at once into your list.

Walking through directories

readdir returns the names of the files or subdirectories in no apparent order. Well, there is some order, but it's the internal order given by the operating system, which is usually not alphabetical or size order.

It is important to note that readdir returns both file names and subdirectory names. In fact, on Unix and Windows systems, it also returns the special directory entries "." and ".." (Mac users don't have to worry about this). Thus, when you look through the results of readdir, you must not assume that you have received a file name.

For example, assume that you want to find out the total size of all the files in the current directory. You would use something like this:

```
opendir(HERE, '.');  # Mac users would use ':' instead
@AllFiles = readdir(HERE);
$TotSize = 0;
foreach $Name (@AllFiles) {
    if(-d $Name) { next }  # It's a directory: skip it
    $TotSize += (-s $Name);  # Add its size to the total
}
```

On the other hand, you may want to know what the subdirectories of a directory are:

```
opendir(HERE, '.');  # Mac users would use ':' instead
@AllFiles = readdir(HERE);
foreach $Name (@AllFiles) {
    if(-d $Name) { print "$Name\n" }
}
```

Creating and destroying directories

There are two additional directory functions, mkdir and rmdir. They don't use directory handles, however; instead, they use directory names. Both functions return true if they are successful, false if they aren't.

To make a new directory, you use the mkdir function. It takes two arguments: the name of the directory you want to create and a mode. The mode is only relevant on Unix systems and is ignored on Windows and the Mac. On Unix, it is the read and write permissions for the directory:

```
mkdir('subdir', 0770);
```

To delete a directory, you use rmdir, which takes one argument: the name of the directory to delete

```
rmdir('subdir');
```

Chapter 14

String Magic: Pattern Matching and Regular Expressions

● ●

In This Chapter

▶ Understanding regular expressions

▶ Searching for strings in strings

▶ Changing text selectively

▶ Translating strings into others

● ●

*C*hapters 5 and 9 show you lots of functions and operators that work on text. In a few places in those chapters, I refer forward to this chapter without much explanation, other than to say that this chapter is more advanced.

Perl has one consistent way of matching text, called *regular expressions,* which you use in many ways. For example, you can search through a string for tab characters and turn them into line breaks. Or you can quickly determine if a string has one of the letters J, K, or L anywhere in the string. You can change every instance of two spaces into one or make sure that every period has a space after it.

All of these tasks first search for text in the string and then do something. Different programming languages and operating systems have different methods for letting you say, "I want to name some text that isn't exact." Perl chose Unix's regular expressions for this. Therefore, Unix users may already understand how to specify searches, or at least they may have been exposed to it. Because regular expressions come from the murky world of Unix, many people find them difficult to understand.

In this chapter, I describe the simple (yet powerful) regular expressions first and leave some of the more advanced regular expression features for the end of this chapter. You certainly don't need to know about the ones at the end of the chapter for most of your day-to-day use of Perl.

What's So Regular about Regular Expressions?

You shouldn't feel that all regular expressions are difficult to understand. In fact, you've already seen a number of them without knowing what they were. The split function that has appeared in various programs takes a regular expression as its first argument. Remember that the split function searches through a string for a particular substring and then splits the string into smaller strings at the positions where the substring is found. So far, you've had to go on faith that you express these arguments with a slash (/), followed by the exact text, followed by another slash:

```
@TheFields = split(/\t/, $TheRecord);
```

This code will return a list of strings in $TheRecord, where each string is the text between the tab characters (remember that \t indicates a tab character). Thus, if $TheRecord contains "Speakers", followed by a tab character, followed by "2", followed by another tab character, followed by "High", the split function above would return

```
('Speakers', '2', 'High')
```

Thus, the simplest kind of regular expression is just the exact characters you want to specify, such as a single tab character in the preceding example. You can put more than one character between the slashes. For example, assume that you have a database in a text file in which you use three hash characters (###) between fields instead of the tab character. Thus, if $TheRecord contains "Speakers###2###High", you would use

```
@TheFields = split(/###/, $TheRecord);
```

Simple true-false searches

The split function is good for some things, but it isn't great for showing all the features of regular expressions. Thus, now is a good time to take a slight break from regular expressions and take a look at the m// operator, which returns true or false depending on whether it finds what it is searching for. It's very handy when you're learning regular expressions because you can write tiny programs to test strings.

The m operator is followed by the regular expression that you want to test. Because most people use the slash (/) character at the beginning and end of their regular expressions, many people call the m operator the m// operator instead (and it makes it easier to pick out on the page!). The m//

operator tests this against something that is given to its left, preceded by the =~ operator. For example, to test whether the string "abc#def" contains the string "#", you could use

```
if("abc#def" =~ m/#/)
    { print "True\n" } else { print "False\n" }
```

Of course, running this string prints True on your screen.

You can, of course, also use variables on the left side of the =~ operator:

```
if($Test =~ m/#/)
    { print "True\n" } else { print "False\n" }
```

(For the rest of this chapter, I'm going to drop the second line of this little program to keep things clearer.)

You may also want to generate a true value if the pattern is *not* found. For this task, use the !~ operator instead of the =~ operator:

```
if($Test !~ m/#/)  # If there is no hash character...
```

You can use variables in your search. For example, if $Find contains the string you want to search for and $Test is the string you want to search in, you would use

```
if($Test =~ m/$Find/)
```

However, you must watch out for patterns that evaluate to the null string. If the pattern you give is the null string, Perl uses the value in $_ as the search pattern, and you may have no idea what's in $_ at the time. Thus, if you use a variable as the search pattern, be sure you know what's in it.

Getting even shorter

Perl needs to know where your regular expressions begin and end. More programmers use the slash character (/) than any other character to signal the beginning and ending of expressions. However, you can delimit your regular expression with any character, such as a vertical bar (|):

```
if($Test =~ m|#|) . . .
```

However, because almost every Perl program I've seen uses the slash character, that's what I'll use in order to keep things less confusing.

Even though you can use characters other than the slash character, you may want to use the slash character because doing so allows you to use the short form of the m// operator. If you use the slash character, you don't have to include the m.

```
if($Test =~ /#/) . . .
```

In fact, most Perl programmers use the short form of the m// operator.

And, to get things even more compact, if you are searching in Perl's special variable $_, you don't need the =~ at all. Remember from Chapter 12 that the file input operator <> puts the next line of the file into $_. Thus, you may see something like this:

```
while(<INFILE>) {
    if(/Proprietary/) {   # The line has the keyword
    . . .
```

However, I'll mostly use the =~ // form in this chapter because it is safer — some things change the value of $_ unexpectedly.

Those pesky backslashes

As you are about to see, regular expressions have many special features that use characters you may want to search for. For example, you are about to see that the vertical bar (|) has a special meaning in a regular expression. However, if you want to search for a vertical bar and not assign it a special meaning, you have to precede the vertical bar with a backslash.

Thus, to search for a vertical bar, you would use

```
if($Test =~ /\|/) . . .
```

Yes, this looks kind of goofy, but it's the only way to tell Perl not to treat this vertical bar as anything special.

The quick ones among you may be asking "Okay, how do I search for a backslash?" Good question, same answer: You have to precede it with a backslash:

```
if($Test =~ /\\/) . . .
```

These special characters are called *metacharacters*. The following characters need this special treatment (when you don't want them to have a special meaning, that is):

```
^ $ + * ? . | ( ) { } \ [ ]
```

The slash (/) is also in that list if you use it as the delimiters for your regular expression.

Here's a maniacal one: See if a string has the pattern "slash, backslash, vertical bar, slash, vertical bar, backslash, caret" in it:

```
if($Test =~ /\/\\\|\/\|\\\^/) . . .
```

For extra credit in your geography class, name the mountain range that this string of code resembles.

If you're not sure whether a string has metacharacters in it, you can use the quotemeta function in Perl 5. This function takes a string and returns a string with backslashes in front of all metacharacters.

Inexact Matches in Regular Expressions

The previous examples use exact matches for the regular expressions: You give the exact characters you want to match. However, you often don't know the exact characters for which you are looking. For example, you may be searching for "the letter x or the letter X," or "one or more hash characters," or even "a hash character followed by any other character followed by a hash character." Regular expressions make these kind of inexact matches fairly easy.

To indicate that you want to match either one character or another, you use the vertical bar (|) between each character you may want to match. This is called *alternating* because you give Perl a list of alternates to look for. For example, to search for either "x" or "X", you may use

```
if($Test =~ /(x|X)/) . . .
```

This code will match exactly one "x" or "X".

Like in numeric equations, you can use parentheses around a group of related items in your regular expression. You can have more than one kind of thing in a regular expression, such as a fixed expression and alternating list. For example, to search for "candle", "candy", and "cancer", you could use

```
if($Test =~ /can(dle|dy|cer)/) . . .
```

Matching any character

If you don't know which character you want to match, you use a period as a wildcard character. For example, if you want to match "the letter N followed by any character followed by the letter T," you would use

```
if($Test =~ /N.T/) . . .
```

This code returns true for "NET" and "N3T" and "N+T", but returns false for "NEST" (because NEST has *two* characters between the "N" and the "T"). Note that the example would return false for "net" (because upper- and lowercase characters are considered different in regular expressions).

Note that the period wildcard matches any character, printable or not, other than \n. Thus, it won't match across a line break but will match anywhere else.

Characters with class

Regular expressions can also match on *character classes,* which are lists of single characters to be matched. To specify a character class, you use square brackets and list the characters. For example, you have already seen how to use alternation to match "x" or "X":

```
if($Test =~ /(x|X)/) . . .
```

To do the same thing with a character class, you would use

```
if($Test =~ /[xX]/) . . .
```

You can use the caret character (^) in front of a list to indicate that you want to match any character *not* in that range. For example, to indicate any character that is not one of the first five capital letters, you would use

```
if($Test =~ /[^ABCDE]/) . . .
```

Character classes are more compact and easier to understand when you want to search for many single characters, such as "any digit." With alternation, you would use this:

```
if($Test =~ /(0|1|2|3|4|5|6|7|8|9)/) . . .
```

With a character class, you would use this:

```
if($Test =~ /[0123456789]/) . . .
```

Character classes can be specified as ranges using a hyphen (-). Thus, the "any digit" example can be simplified even more:

```
if($Test =~ /[0-9]/) . . .
```

If you want to test for "any upper- or lowercase letter," you can use the following:

```
if($Test =~ /[A-Za-z]/) . . .
```

Note that this range is different than the range operator (. .) described in Chapter 5.

Because these ranges are so commonly used in Perl, you can use a couple of shortcuts so that you don't have to specify the actual range (see Table 14-1). These shortcuts are like the backslash codes used for special characters (like \t for tab character), except that they indicate a range to be matched.

Table 14-1	Shortcuts for Character Ranges	
Code	**Replaces**	**Description**
\d	[0-9]	Any digit
\w	[a-zA-Z_0-9]	Any alphanumeric character
\s	[\t\n\r\f]	A whitespace character
\D	[^0-9]	Any nondigit
\W	[^a-zA-Z_0-9]	Any nonalphanumeric character
\S	[^\t\n\r\f]	A nonwhitespace character

Thus, you could reduce your "any digit" search to the following:

```
if($Test =~ /\d/) . . .
```

You can test for "A capital letter followed by two digits" by using this:

```
if($Test =~ /[A-Z]\d\d/) . . .
```

To find "a word that has three letters," meaning "three alphanumeric characters that are preceded by and followed by a whitespace character," you would use

```
if($Test =~ /\s\w\w\w\s/) . . .
```

Some Special Locations

Frequently, you may want to match in a string only if what you're looking for is at the very beginning or end of a string. In this case, you should use the carat (^) to indicate the beginning of the string and the dollar sign ($) to indicate the end of the string. For example, to check if the string starts with "Beg", you would use

```
if($Test =~ /^Beg/) . . .
```

This code would not find the string "I Beg Your Pardon".

To see if the string ends in "don", you would use

```
if($Test =~ /don$/) . . .
```

The $ character has two wrinkles. If the last character in the string is the newline character, $ forces the search to happen only at the end of the line. Thus, if $Test is either "I Beg Your Pardon" or "I Beg Your Pardon\n", searching for don$ will return true. (The second wrinkle is more advanced and discussed later in the chapter.)

Perl also lets you specify that it should start searching at a word boundary with the \b code. This is the point between a \w and a \W, or between a \W and a \w. The \b code is useful for finding some text at the beginning of a word. For example, to find if a word in the string starts with the letter "Y" you would use

```
if($Test =~ /\bY/) . . .
```

Likewise, to find the letter "J" at the end of a word you would use

```
if($Test =~ /J\b/) . . .
```

The \B code indicates the opposite of the \b code: a location that is not on a word boundary (that is, in the middle of a word).

Quantifiers Give You Multiplicity

Sometimes, you may want to match on an unknown number of repetitions of a string. For example, if you want to find "one or more hash characters," you could use something like

```
if("abc#def" =~ /#|##|###|####/) . . .
```

But this isn't really general enough. Instead, you can use some other special characters outside the slashes to indicate how many copies of what's inside the slashes to match on. These counting characters are called *quantifiers* because they let you tell Perl the number of times that the string they follow can exist to be matched. See Table 14-2 for a list of the quantifiers.

Table 14-2	Pattern-Matching Quantifiers
Symbol	*Meaning*
+	Match 1 or more times
*	Match 0 or more times
?	Match 0 or 1 time
{n}	Match exactly *n* times
{n,}	Match at least *n* times
{n,m}	Match at least *n* but not more than *m* times (these values must be less than 65,536)

Thus, to search for "one or more hash characters," you would use

```
if($Test =~ /#+/) . . .
```

To search for "exactly three digits," you would use

```
if($Test =~ /\d{3}/) . . .
```

You can combine quantifiers with character classes to do some pretty neat things. For example, to search for a word that ends in a digit, you could use

```
if($Test =~ /\w+\d/) . . .
```

This means "one or more alphanumeric characters followed by one digit."

Most regular expressions that use quantifiers use the + quantifier. However, you can find good use for the * quantifier as well. Remember how (earlier in the chapter) you saw this test:

```
if($Test =~ /N.T/) . . .
```

This code would match "NET" but would not match "NEST" (because NEST contains too many characters). This code also would not match "NT" because NT has too few characters. If you want to match "N followed by one or more arbitrary characters, followed by T," you would use

```
if($Test =~ /N.+T/) . . .
```

If you want to match "N followed by zero or more arbitrary characters, followed by T," you would instead use

```
if($Test =~ /N.*T/) . . .
```

The latter example of code would match "NT", "NET", "NEST", and so on.

What Perl Returns from a Match

So far, you have seen only how to get Perl to tell you whether a match happened. However, with things like inexact matches, it would be nice to find out *what* got matched. For example, if

```
if($Test =~ /N.*T/) . . .
```

returned true, it would be nice to know what string actually matched.

Using the match results in your program

To get the result of a test, you have to use grouping parentheses in the regular expression and then check Perl's special variables $1, $2, $3, and so on:

```
$Test = 'NESTING';
if($Test =~ /(N.*T)/)
    { print "True\n" } else { print "False\n" }
print "$1\n";
```

When you run this program, Perl displays

```
True
NEST
```

$1 matches the result of the first set of parentheses, $2 matches the result of the second set, and so on.

```
$Test = 'NESTING';
if($Test =~ /(N.)S(.I)/)
    { print "True\n" } else { print "False\n" }
print "$1\n$2\n";
```

When you run this program, Perl displays

```
True
NE
TI
```

If for some odd reason you want to suppress $1, $2, and so on from getting assigned, add a ?: after the left parenthesis. This only works in Perl 5:

```
$Test = 'NESTING';
if($Test =~ /(?:N.)S(.I)/)
    { print "True\n" } else { print "False\n" }
print "$1\n";
```

When you run this program, Perl displays

```
True
TI
```

You'll see later in this chapter how this construct affects the split function in a useful but very confusing way.

Greedy matching

So far, so good. However, some of you are probably asking, "How much does Perl return when there are more than one match?" For example, what would you expect Perl to print when you run the following?

```
$Test = 'NITWITS';
if($Test =~ /(N.*T)/)
    { print "True\n" } else { print "False\n" }
print "$1\n";
```

The result is

```
True
NITWIT
```

By default, Perl always uses what is humorously called *greedy matching*. It's greedy because it matches as much as possible on the first try. Perl sees quantifiers as a great excuse to get greedy.

You can suppress Perl's greedy ways by following a quantifier with a question mark (?). When you do this, Perl matches the shortest possible string instead of the longest string. For example, note the small change to the previous program:

```
$Test = 'NITWITS';
if($Test =~ /(N.*?T)/)
    { print "True\n" } else { print "False\n" }
print "$1\n";
```

Here is the new output:

```
True
NIT
```

Advanced Use of the m// Operator

Believe it or not, you can do even more with the m// operator. Almost all of what you've learned so far in this chapter has do to with regular expressions, not with m//. You'll see in the rest of the chapter that many functions and operators work with regular expressions.

Scalar and list context

So far, you've only seen the m// operator in scalar context, where it returns true or false depending on whether the string is matched. In list context, however, the m// operator returns a list of the things matched in the parentheses. This is essentially like creating a list of $1, $2, and so on that you saw earlier in this chapter:

```
$Test = 'NESTING';
@Birds = ($Test =~ /(N.)S(.I)/);
print join("\n", @Birds);
```

When you run this program, Perl displays

```
NE
TI
```

If there are no parentheses, however, Perl returns the list (1), meaning a list with a single true value in it.

Introduction to modifiers

The m// operator has *modifiers* that change the way m// works to search. The modifiers come after the closing slash character, such as the i modifier in the following:

```
if($Test =~ /(N.*T)/i) . . .
```

Table 14-3 shows the modifiers.

Table 14-3	Modifiers for m//
Modifier	*Description*
g	Returns each occurrence (global search)
i	Ignores case
m	Allows multiple lines in the string
o	Compiles the pattern once (rarely used)
s	Treats as a single line
x	Allows whitespace for comments

The m, s, and x modifiers are new in Perl 5.

The i option is the easiest to explain: It simply forces Perl to ignore case when searching. For example, if $Test is "nest",

```
if($Test =~ /(N.*T)/i) . . .
```

would be true.

The o modifier prevents Perl from using variable substitution in the pattern when the variable changes. This makes your program slightly faster but prevents you from using variable substitution in the pattern. Generally, the speed increase caused by using the o modifier is teensy, relative to the speed of the whole program.

The new x modifier lets you add spaces and line breaks in your regular expressions as a way of making them more readable. You usually need to add spaces and line breaks only to complex regular expressions. For example, instead of

```
if($Test =~ /(N.)S(.I)/) . . .
```

you could use

```
if($Test =~ /
    (N.)  (?# Start with N and any letter)
    S  (?# ...followed by the letter S)
    (.I)  (?# ...followed by another letter, then I)
    /x) . . .
```

On the other hand, I don't think that these kind of comments make most regular expressions more readable than a regular Perl comment on the line before them.

Global searches in the m// operator

The g modifier causes Perl to do a "global" search on the string. This may at first sound odd, because Perl is supposedly *already* searching the whole string. The *global* here refers to the way that Perl returns different results based on the g modifier.

In a list context, Perl returns a list of the strings matched using parentheses, as you have already seen. However, if the regular expression contains no parentheses, Perl creates a list of each matched item:

```
$Test = 'NESTING';
@Birds = ($Test =~ /N./g);
print join("\n", @Birds);
```

When you run this program, Perl displays

```
NE
NG
```

This is a handy way to find all the matching strings if you don't know how many there will be.

In scalar context, however, Perl returns true and false for each match in the string. Perl remembers where in the string it found the last match and starts from there for the next search. This is a good way to determine how many matches exist without looking at the matches:

```
$Test = 'NESTING';
$i = 0;
while($Test =~ /N./g) { $i += 1 }
print "There were $i matches.\n";
```

You can use the pos function to determine where Perl is going to start the next global search in scalar context. The argument to pos is the string:

```
$Test = 'NESTING';
$i = 0;
while($Test =~ /N./g) {
    $i += 1;
    print "Now at " . pos($Test) . ".\n";
}
print "There were $i matches.\n";
```

When you run this program, Perl displays

```
Now at 2.
Now at 7.
There were 2 matches.
```

If you want to change where Perl will start looking on the next round of searching this string, you can set the position to any number you want in the string. For example, to start searching two characters further ahead than you were going to, you may say

```
pos($Test) += 2;
```

Multiple lines in a string

You saw earlier in the chapter how the ^ and $ characters match the beginning and end of a string. However, you may want ^ to match the beginning of lines and $ to match the end of lines in a string that has more than one line in it.

In Perl 4, to get ^ and $ to match the beginning and end of each line in a string, you set the $* special variable to 1 before the test. By default, $* is set to 0, so ^ and $ match the beginning and end of the string, not lines in the string.

In Perl 5, you use the m modifier on your regular expression to get ^ and $ to match the beginning and end of each line in a string:

```
if($Test =~ /^\t/m) . . .
```

This statement finds a tab character at the beginning of any line in the string. The s modifier does the opposite of the m modifier — it makes things work like in Perl 4. It isn't really needed, because it is Perl's default.

The special characters \A and \Z can be used in a regular expression to indicate the beginning and end of a string regardless of whether the m modifier is used. That is, these always mean "the string" and not "the line."

The Unix Geek's Favorite: grep

If you want to do a search for the same regular expression in every element in a list, the grep function is for you. It takes two arguments: a regular expression or a block, and a list. It then evaluates the regular expression or block on each element of the list and looks for true and false results. In list context, grep returns the elements from the list for which the regular expression or block returns true; in scalar context, it returns the number of elements that return true.

For example, assume that you want to look through the list @LastNames for all names that start with the letter "S". To get the names, you would use

```
@JustSNames = grep(/^S/, @LastNames);
```

To simply find out how many names started with "S", you would use

```
$TotSNames = grep(/^S/, @LastNames);
```

The grep function also lets you use a block instead of a regular expression. In this case, the special variable $_ is set to the value of the list element being tested. This is very similar to the map function described in Chapter 8.

As you become more comfortable with regular expressions (well, *if* you become more comfortable with regular expressions), you will find many uses for grep. If you have read all the lines of a file into a list with a statement such as the following:

```
@TheFile = <INFILE>;
```

You can then create other lists that contain certain kinds of lines. For example, you could create a list of all the lines that have whitespace at the end of the line:

```
@RealLines = grep(/\s$/, @TheFile);
```

The name of the `grep` function comes from a very handy Unix utility of the same name. The Unix command's name was derived from an almost-acronym for "global regular expression and print." Perl's `grep` function doesn't print. But because it checks the regular expression globally on each item in the list, it's pretty similar.

Simple Substitutions

So far in this chapter, you have learned only how to search in strings for text using regular expressions. Well, you've learned *lots* of ways of doing that, but so far all you could do with this skill is to then find out whether a particular string matches a regular expression.

You may desire to change a string. Chapters 5 and 9 contain many different ways to change strings, but there are even more ways using regular expressions. The `s///` operator acts much like the `m//` operator except that you specify what you want to replace the found string with. You put the replacement between the second and third slashes.

The `s///` operator returns the number of times it substituted. It takes the same modifiers as the `m//` operator.

Suppose that you want to change all the lowercase "e" characters to uppercase "E":

```
$Count = ($Test =~ s/e/E/g);
```

A slightly more complex example would be to change all the vowels to the letter "V":

```
$Count = ($Test =~ s/[aeiouAEIOU]/V/g);
```

Like the `m//` operator, if you don't use the `=~` operator before the `s///` operator, Perl assumes that it is working on the special variable `$_`. Thus, you may use something like the following:

```
while(<INFILE>) {
    s/\t/|/g;  # Change the tabs to vertical bars
    . . .
}
```

However, it is usually safer to assign `$_` to a variable and work with that variable instead.

You can certainly use variables in either part of the s/// operator. For example, you can search for a group of digits at the beginning of a string and change it to the value of $NewLabel:

```
s/^\d+/$NewLabel/;
```

Using the match results in your substitution

You saw earlier how to use $1 and $2 in your Perl programs to find out what was matched by the m// operator. In the s/// operator, using these variables is quite handy because you may want to replace what you found with something related to it.

For example, if you want to find all the lines that start with a number and change them into "Line" followed by that number, you could use

```
$Test =~ s/^(\d+)/Line $1/;
```

Here is a more complex example that changes the strings that are formatted as "Lastname, Firstname" to "Firstname Lastname":

```
$Test =~ s/([^,]+), (.+)/$2 $1/;
```

The test finds first all the characters up to the comma and puts those into $1. The regular expression [^,]+ means "find all characters other than a comma." The expression matches the comma and the space, and then it matches the rest of characters and puts those into $2. The substituted text is $2, followed by a space, followed by $1.

You can also use \1, \2, and so on in the second part of s/// operators, but you should probably use $1, $2, and so on instead, because doing so is much clearer. Perl allows you to use the backslashes as a way to make people who are familiar with some Unix programs feel better, but it makes your Perl programs harder to read.

Expressions in the second argument

You have seen how you can use variables in the second part of the s/// operator. The s/// operator has one modifier that the m// operator doesn't: the e modifier. This modifier causes Perl to evaluate the second part as an expression rather than a string.

Using an expression as what will be replaced is often useful if you want to base the replacement on $1, $2, and so on but need to change the results. For example, assume that you want to find the first number on the line and change it to one greater than that number. You could use

```
$Test =~ s/(\d+)/$1 + 1/e;
```

In this case, if Test is "Line 23: go", it would be changed to "Line 24: go".

Another Look at Splitting

Okay, time to revisit one of Perl's best functions — split. The first argument in split is a regular expression, not just a string. So far, you've seen split used only with very simple regular expressions, but now you will see some other nice uses.

For example, assume that you have someone creating a database using a text editor. You told them to use only a tab character between fields, but you suspect that they may have slipped in one or more spaces before or after the tab character in some records. Instead of this simple split

```
@TheFields = split(/\t/, $TheRecord);
```

you may use

```
@TheFields = split(/ *\t */, $TheRecord);
```

This regular expression says "look for zero or more spaces, followed by exactly one tab, followed by zero or more spaces."

Note that you could also have preprocessed the record with s/// to get rid of the bad typing before splitting:

```
$TheRecord =~ s/ *\t */\t/g;
```

```
@TheFields = split(/\t/, $TheRecord);
```

Quoting words, the shorter way

If you use `split` to split on whitespace (`\s`), Perl 5 has a quoting operator that makes this easier to read. Instead of the following

```
@TheFields = split(/\s+/, $TheRecord);
```

you can use the `qw` function:

```
@TheFields = qw($TheRecord);
```

Here, `qw` is short for "quote words," which is exactly what this function does.

Returning delimiters in `split`

As you have seen, the `split` function does not return the delimiters in the items in the list. However, that's not always true: If you use parentheses in your regular expression, `split` returns whatever is in the parentheses as items in the list:

```
$TheRecord = "Serling|Rod|Twilight Zone|";
@TheFields = split(/\|/, $TheRecord);
```

When you run this program, Perl returns

```
('Serling', 'Rod', 'Twilight Zone')
```

However, when you run this program

```
$TheRecord = "Serling|Rod|Twilight Zone|";
@TheFields = split(/(\|)/, $TheRecord);
```

Perl returns

```
('Serling', '|', 'Rod', '|', 'Twilight Zone','|')
```

You can suppress this action by using the (?: extension to regular expressions:

```
$TheRecord = "Serling|Rod|Twilight Zone|";
@TheFields = split(/(?:\|)/, $TheRecord);
```

Perl returns

```
('Serling', 'Rod', 'Twilight Zone')
```

Letter-for-Letter Translations

The s/// operator is great for simple one-to-one changes. Sometimes, you may want to do a many-to-many change, such as translating uppercase letters to lowercase letters. For this, you can use the tr/// operator.

The tr/// operator lets you specify individual letters, or ranges of letters with a hyphen (-). For example, you can use the following to change the case of the uppercase letters in $Test:

```
$Test =~ tr/A-Z/a-z/;
```

The tr/// operator returns the number of changes that it makes. It also has some modifiers that are quite different than those for m// and s///. See Table 14-4 and note that the tr/// operator does *not* use regular expressions, only actual characters and character ranges.

Table 14-4	Modifiers for tr///
Modifier	*Description*
c	Complement of the first argument is used
d	Deletes matching characters that are not replaced
s	Removes duplicate replace characters

The c modifier is useful to keep the list of characters between the first and second slash short. For example, if you want to change all characters other than digits into linefeeds, you could use

```
$Test =~ tr/0-9/\n/c;   # Note that "c" to invert range
```

The d modifier allows you to delete instead of replace certain characters. For example, if you want to delete all the nondigits, you would use

```
$Test =~ tr/0-9//cd;   # Change non-digits into nothing
```

The s modifier is useful for collapsing duplicate characters. It causes Perl to treat all the found characters as one before doing the translation. For example, you may want to change all instances of two or more adjacent commas into just one comma:

```
$Test =~ tr/,/,/s;
```

For historical reasons, the y/// operator exists, but it does exactly the same thing as the tr/// operator.

Part IV
Advanced Perl Is Still Somewhat Easy

In this part . . .

Even though this book is for novices and intermediate users, it's good to go into a bit about the advanced features of Perl. The chapters in Part IV cover subjects that are useful for more advanced programmers, but still accessible to most beginners. You don't *need* the material in this part, but you may find it very useful.

Chapter 15

Perl as a Gateway to the Internet

● ●

In This Chapter

▶ Creating your own Internet clients

▶ Doing the Web the Perl way

▶ Checking POP mailboxes

● ●

*I*nternet users have gotten used to having fancy graphical interfaces to the Web through programs like Netscape's Navigator and Microsoft's Internet Explorer. These programs make it easy to get things from the Web by pointing and clicking. Many Internet users also use graphical interfaces to read and send mail, using programs like Qualcomm's Eudora, the mail program in Netscape's Navigator, or one of the mail programs from Microsoft.

These programs are easy to use, but they do not provide the flexibility that everyone wants. To be specific, they are difficult or impossible to program. For example, suppose that you have a list of 100 domain names that host Web sites and that you want to download the home pages of each site for later viewing. Programs like Navigator and Internet Explorer do not have point-and-click interfaces for this kind of thing. Of course, this sounds like a job for Perl. There are already lots of good Internet tools written in Perl, so you don't have to reinvent the wheel. In fact, the tools are fairly easy to use, and you can do things like getting FTP files in just a few lines of programming code. Note that the result is *not* a graphical program, but a very character-oriented one. However, that might be just what you want.

This chapter covers how to use a few of the Internet tools from the CPAN library. These tools are all on the CD-ROM, so they're easy to load and run. Each of the tools is a Perl 5 module, so you must install the module in a place where Perl can find it, namely in one of the directories in @INC.

All the programs described in this chapter are written for Unix. Some of them may also work on Windows and the Macintosh, but they usually require some modifications in order to work. There are a few folks out there in the Perl community who work for free to make these modifications, but they don't always keep the programs up to date. Also, some of the programs described here require a recent subversion of Perl 5, such as version 5.003;

at the time I'm writing this, however, the stable versions of Perl for Windows and the Macintosh are both Perl 5.001. The best way to be sure that the Internet Perl program you want to use works is to check the Web sites for Perl-Win32 and MacPerl, both of which are listed in Chapter 23.

Getting at the Web with libwww-perl

The world seemed to sit up and take notice of the Internet once the Web became popular two or three years ago; the Internet hasn't been the same since. To many people, the Internet is the Web, and thus the way to get to the Internet is through their Web browsers. Maybe by the time you read this more people will think that e-mail is more interesting than the Web, but (sadly) I doubt it.

Be that as it may, you may have many reasons for wanting to create a Perl program that knows how to go out and snag pages from the Web. For example, you might want to create a robot to get all the Web pages from one site or from many sites. Or you might want to send a particular Web request every hour to see if there is any change in the information from the previous hour. Or you may want to check a list of Web links to make sure they are all still valid. All these tasks take some programming and can't easily be done with a standard Web client like Netscape.

The best Perl library for accessing the Web is called libwww-perl. This somewhat awkward name comes from the fact that the Perl library is based on the earlier libwww library written in C. We don't want those C programmers mistaking our library for theirs, do we? libwww-perl consists of many parts, and it must be installed from the installation program that comes in the library. In fact, the libwww-perl library does much more than just access the Web: It contains modules for accessing FTP, Usenet news, Gopher, files on your computer, and even sending mail. In technical terms, this means that libwww-perl can handle all the following types of URLs:

- http:
- ftp:
- news:
- gopher:
- file:
- mailto:

Installing libwww-perl

You can find the libwww-perl library in its compressed form on the CD-ROM. You have to be the system administrator to install it on your Unix system because some of the parts of the library go into directories that are usually restricted to only sysadmins. However, the installation takes about a minute, so even a harried sysadmin shouldn't object too much to a request to install it.

Getting documents from the Web and FTP

libwww-perl is a set of Perl 5 modules, so you normally use Perl's object-oriented syntax (described in Chapter 19) when interacting with it. However, the folks who wrote libwww-perl, Gisle Aas and Martijn Koster, included a simple interface so that even nonobject folks could easily use the basic parts.

At the beginning of your program, you tell Perl that you want to use the Simple package in LWP:

```
use LWP::Simple;
```

Table 15-1 contains the four functions in the LWP::Simple package that get the contents of a document based on its URL.

Table 15-1	LWP::Simple **Functions**
Function	*Description*
get($URL)	Gets the document at the URL and returns it
getstore($URL, $Filename)	Same as get but writes the document on disk into the named file
getprint($URL)	Same as get but prints the return to standard file out
mirror($URL, $Filename)	Same as getstore but only gets the document if it is newer or a different size than the file on disk

Thus, get returns the document into a string, getstore puts it in a file, getprint puts it out on standard file output, and mirror only gets the file if it needs to. For example, if you just want to print the contents of a Web page, you might use this very short program:

```
use LWP::Simple;
getprint('http://www.dummies.com');
```

If you want to download a file from an FTP site, you might use this one:

```
use LWP::Simple;
getstore('ftp://ftp.internic.net/rfc/rfc822.txt',
'rfc822');
```

This program gets the file from the FTP site and stores it on your hard disk with the name rfc822.

If you give an invalid URL to `get` or `getstore`, such as the name of a Web site that does not exist or a file name that is spelled wrong, `LWP::Simple` returns an empty string. `getprint`, on the other hand, fills the string with an error message that looks something like this:

```
<HTML>
<HEAD>
<TITLE>
An Error Occurred
</TITLE>
</HEAD>
<BODY>
<H1>An Error Occurred</h1>
404 - Access denied, or file does not exist
</BODY>
</HTML>
```

Making it a program

Of course, you didn't decide to learn Perl just to get Web pages one at a time. You might want to get a whole group of them with a single program. Another example of a program that is commonly desired is one that checks whether or not all the links from one Web page actually work. Listing 15-1 shows the linkchck.pl program that reads a Web page, picks out all the links from the page, and then goes out and tests whether or not those links are valid.

Listing 15-1:
Program for checking the links from a Web page.

```
$TheURL = $ARGV[0];  # Get the URL from the command line

use LWP::Simple;
$TheMain = get($TheURL);  # Get the main page

if($TheMain eq '')
    { die "The starting URL was not valid.\n" }

$TheMain =~ tr/A-Z/a-z/;   # Lowercase everything
$TheMain =~ s/\"/'/g;      # Double quotes to single
$TheMain =~ s/\n/ /g;      # Get rid of the linefeeds
$TheMain =~ s/\s+/ /g;     # Compress spaces/tabs

# First find any "base href='URL'" for relative URLs.
$BasePos = index($TheMain, '<base href');
if($BasePos > -1) {
    $OpenQuote = index($TheMain, "'", $BasePos);
```

```
        $BaseStart = $OpenQuote + 1;
        $CloseQuote = index($TheMain, "'", $BaseStart);
        $BaseLen = $CloseQuote - $OpenQuote - 1;
        $URLBase = substr($TheMain, $BaseStart, $BaseLen);
}
else { $URLBase = '' }

# Keep a list of the URLs we find
@URLList = ();
while(1) {  # Loop forever, rely on "last"
        $TheA = index($TheMain, '<a href');  # The next link
        if($TheA == -1) { last };
        # Find the URL in the quotes
        $OpenQuote = index($TheMain, "'", $TheA);
        $URLStart = $OpenQuote + 1;
        $CloseQuote = index($TheMain, "'", $URLStart);
        $URLLen = $CloseQuote - $OpenQuote - 1;
        $TheURL = substr($TheMain, $URLStart, $URLLen);
        # Put the URL into @URLList
        push(@URLList, $TheURL);
        # Chop off beginning of $TheMain to our position
        $TheMain = substr($TheMain, $CloseQuote);
}

@CheckURLs = ();
foreach $TheURL (@URLList) {
        # Determine which URLs are relative. Absolute URLs
        #    start with 'http:' or 'ftp:' or 'mailto:';
        #    others are relative to the base. Relative URLs have
        #    $URLBase added to the beginning.
        unless($TheURL =~ /^(http:|ftp:|mailto:)/)
            { $TheURL = $URLBase . $TheURL }
        # Don't check URLs starting with 'mailto:'
        unless($TheURL =~ /^mailto:/)
            { push(@CheckURLs, $TheURL) }
}

# Now check each URL in the list for error messages
foreach $TheURL (@CheckURLs) {
        $TheCheck = get($TheURL);
        if($TheCheck ne "") { print "OK:     $TheURL\n" }
        else { print "Fail: $TheURL\n" }
}
```

The first line tells Perl to get the URL for the page you want to check from the command line. For instance, you might run the program with

```
linkchck.pl http://www.mycompany.com/accts/main.html
```

The next set of lines loads the LWP::Simple package, gets the document, and loads it into the string $TheMain. The program then checks whether that string has anything in it and ends if it doesn't.

The next four lines use many of the techniques you learned in Chapter 14. These lines

- ✔ Convert the document to all lowercase all at once so that you don't have to do it for each string you are looking for.

- ✔ Change all the quotation marks to apostrophes. URLs can be in either single or double-quotation marks, so this conversion makes them easier to find.

- ✔ Change all linefeeds to spaces because some HTML tags might be split over a line break.

- ✔ Change all the multiple spaces and tab characters into a single space. This prevents the program from missing some tags if they have multiple spaces or tabs inside the tags.

The next task for the program is to look for an HTML base tag. If the page you get has a base tag, some of the URLs on the page might be *relative* URLs, meaning that they don't have the full URL, just the last part. At the end of this set of lines, $URLBase is set to either the base URL or the null string if no base URL exists.

The program then goes through the $TheMain string and looks for HTML a tags that are links. The loop is exited when there are no more HTML a tags. This set of statements finds the beginning of the tag and then the quoted URL inside the tag. Each URL is added to the end of the @URLList. $TheMain is then shortened up to the point where the tag was found, and the loop begins again.

The next step is to go through all the URLs found to see whether they are absolute URLs (that is, ones with the full URL syntax) or relative URLs. In the latter case, the program tacks on the base URL to the beginning of the URL. The program also checks if the URL is a mailto: URL, and if so, ignores it because mailto: URLs cannot be checked.

The last section of the program goes out and checks each remaining URL. If the get function is successful, the program prints OK: and the URL; otherwise, the program prints Fail: and the URL. This way, you can quickly see which of the URLs did not come back with documents so you can investigate them on your own.

Using libwww-perl with objects

I would like to emphasize that libwww-perl does *much* more than what you have seen in the `LWP::Simple` package. The `LWP::Simple` package is great because it allows people who don't understand the object-oriented features in Perl 5 to use Perl to get things from Web and FTP servers.

After you have read Chapter 19, which describes object-oriented Perl, I strongly recommend that you go back and take a look in the other parts of the libwww-perl package. The examples in Chapter 19 show a bit about how to use the libwww-perl objects. The libwww-perl package contains many useful features that allow you to do the following:

- ✔ Make Web robots that will download all the documents linked from a particular Web page.
- ✔ React to different HTTP headers that are returned on Web requests.
- ✔ Convert HTML to a somewhat readable form.
- ✔ Traverse directory trees on FTP servers so that you can get all the files in particular directories and their subdirectories.
- ✔ Get and send Usenet news.
- ✔ Send electronic mail.

Getting Your Mail

Lots of the information on the Internet is available only through e-mail and not through the Web or FTP. Many mailing lists contain very valuable sources of information that are not accessible through other means. And, of course, e-mail is a great way to have person-to-person communication over the Internet.

Just as there are many good, graphically based Web clients, there are many good graphically based e-mail clients. Like their Web client brethren, however, few can be programmed to do what you want. For instance, if you are on ten active mailing lists, wouldn't it be nice to have a program filter the messages into different files and look for particular items you are interested in? You may also want to have a program be your interface for e-mail if you use e-mail to receive regular reports from other computers; you can use the program to look for these reports, pull out the information, add it to previous reports, and so on.

The Mail::POP3Client module

Fortunately, if you get your e-mail from a POP server, all this is very easy with the Mail::POP3Client module. This module, which you can find on the CD-ROM that comes with this book, gives you a very simple interface to POP servers. You can use it to check your mail, grab particular messages, and so on. Of course, the module has to be installed before you can use it, and you can (hopefully) get your system administrator to install it.

Unlike the libwww-perl module, there is no nonobject interface to Mail::POP3Client. But you can do so few things with the Mail::POP3Client. You can create useful mail-collecting programs even before you learn about object-oriented programming in Chapter 19.

Like all mail programs, you need to know three things in order to talk to the POP server:

- ✔ The mail account name
- ✔ The mail account password
- ✔ The domain name of the mail server

Thus, your program might begin with a few variables:

```
$Name = 'larry';
$Pass = 'AouerGyvvt';
$Serv = 'mail.yourisp.com';
```

Creating a basic client

To use the Mail::POP3Client, you first include it into your program and create a client object. The client object is the thing that communicates with the POP server. When you create a new client, you supply the user name, password, and server name as arguments. Thus, you might start your program off with the following:

```
use Mail::POP3Client;
$Client = new Mail::POP3Client($Name, $Pass, $Serv);
```

At this point, your Perl program has logged into the POP server. The POP server is waiting for you to send it POP commands. You should understand a few things about POP before writing your programs. After you have logged into a POP server, you can send it commands that give you information about either the entire mailbox or about individual messages. For instance, you can ask for a count of all the messages or for the contents of a particular message. Each message in a POP mailbox has a message number. Message numbers start at 1, not 0 as you have gotten used to in Perl programs.

You use Mail::POP3Client methods to send POP commands to the POP server and to look at the results. Many of the Mail::POP3Client methods take one argument, namely the message number on which you want them to act. Table 15-2 contains a few of the interesting methods.

Table 15-2	Methods for the Mail::POP3Client Module
Method	**What It Does**
Count	Tells how many messages are on the server
Head(num)	Gets the header lines of the message
Body(num)	Gets the body of the message
HeadAndBody(num)	Gets the entire message
Delete(num)	Marks the message for deletion
List	Lists all the messages and their sizes
Close	Closes the connection, deleting any marked messages
State	Tells whether or not the connection is alive

For example, assume that you have a program that mails you a report every day. You want to process your mailbox to find out whether or not the report was sent, and if so, to save the report on disk and delete that message from your mailbox. That way, you can use your graphical client to read the rest of the messages but still process the report automatically. Listing 15-2 shows such a program.

Listing 15-2: Program for checking for a report in a POP mailbox.

```
$Name = 'larry';
$Pass = 'AouerGyvvt';
$Serv = 'mail.yourisp.com';
$Subj = 'Subject: Daily logging report';

use Mail::POP3Client;
$Client = new Mail::POP3Client($Name, $Pass, $Serv);
$TheState = $Client->State;
if($TheState eq 'AUTHORIZATION')
    { die "Bad user name or password.\n" }
elsif($TheState eq 'DEAD')
    { die "Mail server unreachable or unavailable.\n" }

# Find out how many messages there are
$NumMsg = $Client->Count;

#Loop through the messages (starting at 1)
```

(continued)

(continued)

```
for($i = 1; $i<=$NumMsg; $i +=1) {
        $Headers = $Client->Head($i);
        @HeadList = split(/\n/, $Headers);
        foreach $Line (@HeadList) {
                if($Line =~ /^$Subj/) {
                        # Found the message; get the body,
    then delete
                        $Body = $Client->Body($i);
                        $Client->Delete($i);
                        # Process the report and leave
                        &ProcessReport($Body);
                        last;
                }
        }
}

# Close the connection so the delete happens
$Client->Close;

sub ProcessReport {
        my($Report) = pop(@_);
        # Do something here that is processing the report
        return;
}
```

The first few lines set up variables for later in the program. This statement

```
$TheState = $Client->State;
```

uses the `State` method on the client. The three possible results of the `State` method are `TRANSACTION`, meaning things are fine, `AUTHORIZATION`, meaning that the POP server is trying to authorize the client, and `DEAD`, meaning that the POP server wasn't found. If you end up in `AUTHORIZATION` after giving a user name and password, it means that the combination didn't work. The program then gets the number of messages and loops through each one. This statement

```
$Headers = $Client->Head($i);
```

gets the headers for the current message. These are then split into an array and checked for the subject header that identifies the message you want. If it is found, `$Body` gets the body of the message, the message is deleted, the report is processed, and the loop terminates.

Chapter 16

Associative Arrays and Multidimensional Lists

*P*erl has many strengths, and many people would say that one of Perl's biggest strengths is the way that it handles lists. Most other languages do not know anything about lists; you have to use nonstandard methods to make list structures, add items to lists, and so on. Perl's lists are part of the very core of Perl.

The lists you have seen so far are normal lists. You access items in the list using the item's numerical position, such as $Names[4] for the fifth item in the @Names list. You can search through a list for something like "an item whose value is 82," but that item is then defined by its position in the list.

It is time that I told you about a different kind of list that is common in programming. Imagine that you have a paper list that has two columns: employee numbers and names. There is exactly one employee for each employee number, and the numbers are not sequential. For example, the top of the list might look like this:

ID	Name
742	Kathi Stennis
5280	Roberta Wallace
3279	Daniel Exon

You might use this paper list to look up an employee by their ID number or to look up the ID number for the employee's name.

You could make a Perl list that looked like this:

```
(742, 'Kathi Stennis', 5280, 'Roberta Wallace',
    3279, 'Daniel Exon')
```

But this list doesn't really embody the same feeling as the paper list because the even-numbered items are ID numbers, and the odd-numbered elements the names. To search for a particular ID number, you have to look at every other item in the list, not every item.

Associative Arrays

Because these kinds of lists are common in many fields, Perl has a second kind of list, called an *associative array,* that acknowledges that you often don't want to find an item by its position. (Remember that in Perl, *list* and *array* mean the same thing, and that many Perl programmers prefer the nerdier term *array*.) An associative array is a list of *key-value* pairs. That is, instead of looking up an item by its position in the list, you look it up by its key. Each key-value pair is called a *record* instead of an item.

Thus, in the previous example, an associative array would have three records. One record would have the key 742 and the value Kathi Stennis, another record would have the key 5280 and the value Roberta Wallace, and yet another record would have the key 3279 and the value Daniel Exon.

Notice that I didn't say "the first record," "the second record," and "the third record." In an associative array, the order of the records is unimportant and in fact is usually randomized by Perl. To get at the records, you don't use record numbers like you do in normal lists, you use keys. Thus, "the record associated with key 5280" is the one that has "the value Roberta Wallace."

The fact that you always identify records by their key leads to an important attribute of associative arrays: There can be only one record with a particular key. You are guaranteed that when you say "the record with key 5280" there will be either zero or one record with that key. This means that associative arrays are not good for some tasks. For example, if you have a list of telephone numbers and names, you would not want to use an associative array because two people might have the same phone number and one person might have more than one phone number.

Some Perl programmers call associative arrays *hashes* because that is how they are technically stored in your computer's memory. Perl uses a *hash function* to determine how to store the keys and values efficiently; thus the name. However, I strongly prefer the name "associative array" to "hash" because it defines better what they are used for, not how they are implemented. I actually like "associative array" better than "associative list," but I'm not really sure why.

You don't ever need to use an associative array (except in the few cases where they are handed to you by Perl itself). However, they have a couple of major advantages over simple lists for many applications.

For lists of name-value pairs, associative arrays are handy because there are a handful of built-in Perl functions for them. You don't have to create your own functions to do things like find the value based on the name, to delete a name-value pair from the middle of the list, and so on.

More importantly, searching through an associative array is much faster than searching through simple lists if you have lots of data. The "hash" storage has the advantage that finding a particular record in a hash is much faster than looking through every other item in a list. If you think about it, the "average" search through a list of key-value pairs requires Perl to look at half the pairs before finding the one you want. Hashes, on the other hand, take much less processing power to find the same record.

Talking about Associative Arrays

Associative arrays have a different notation than regular lists. You name an associative array with a percent sign (%) instead of the @ you use in regular lists. For example, you might have an associative array called %IDList.

You refer to an element in an associative array by its key. You put the key in curly braces ({ and }) instead of the parentheses you use in regular lists. Thus, the following would assign the value of the record whose key is 5280 to the variable $NextPerson:

```
$NextPerson = $IDList{"5280"};
```

You do not need to use the quotation marks around the key value if it is a single word, but it is always safer to do so.

Creating Associative Arrays

You assign records to an associative array as pairs of items. For example, to create the associative array %IDList, you might use

```
%IDList = (742, 'Kathi Stennis', 5280, 'Roberta Wallace',
    3279, 'Daniel Exon');
```

This may be a bit hard to read, given that you have to view the assignment in pairs. Perl 5 allows you to use the => operator instead of the comma. Many programmers use the => operator between the key and the value (indicating "this key is associated with this value") and commas between records:

```
%IDList = (742 => 'Kathi Stennis',
    5280 => 'Roberta Wallace',
    3279 => 'Daniel Exon');
```

If the key is more than a single word, it should be in quotation marks. For instance, if you have an associative array whose keys are street names and whose values are zip codes, you would use

```
%Streets = ("Pine" => "92484", "North Elm" => "92481",
    "River" => "92484");
```

If you want to start an empty associative array before adding records, you can use the simple

```
%Streets = ();
```

Adding records

To add a record to an associative array, you assign a value to a key. For instance, to add another record to %Streets, you might use

```
$Streets("South Elm") = "92481";
```

When Perl sees an assignment like this, it looks to see if the key South Elm already exists. If so, Perl replaces the corresponding value with 92481; if not, it creates the key and gives it that value. Assigning in associative arrays is just like assigning values in regular lists, except that you use keys instead of offset locations into the list.

Removing records

To remove an existing record, use the `delete` function. It takes as its argument the key you want to remove:

```
delete($Streets{"North Elm"});
```

The `delete` function returns the value of the key it just deleted.

Looking inside Associative Arrays

You saw earlier how to look at the value of a record by giving its key:

```
$ARRAYNAME{"KEY"}
```

Perl has additional functions that let you handle associative arrays in an automatic fashion.

You may want a list of all the keys in an associative array so you can look at each record. The (appropriately named) `keys` function does this. The argument to `keys` is the name of the associative array. For instance, here's a short program that prints the records from an associative array:

```
@AllKeys = keys(%Streets);
foreach $TheKey (@AllKeys)
    { print "$TheKey is the key for $Streets{$TheKey}\n" }
```

The order that the keys are returned is fairly random. Because `keys` returns a simple list, you can sort it before using it:

```
@AllKeys = sort(keys(%Streets));
```

You may have already guessed the next function: `values`. It returns a list of the values in the associative array. Remember that there may be duplicate values (but never duplicate keys):

```
@AllVals = sort(values(%Streets));
print join("\n", @AllVals), "\n";
```

If you have a very large associative array, you may not want to create big lists with `keys` and `values`. Instead, you can use the `each` function to step through the records one at a time. `each` returns a two-element list: the key and the value. When you reach the end of the associative array, `each` returns a false value:

```
while(($TheKey, $TheVal) = each(%BigList))
    { print "$TheKey is the key for$TheVal\n" }
```

The counter used by `each` is reset when you use either a `keys` or `values` function, so you should definitely not use them in your loop. `each` will work correctly if you delete records, but not if you add them.

If you just want to be sure that a particular key is in an associative array, use the `exists` function:

```
unless(exists($Streets{"Main"}))
    { print "Main Street has disappeared.\n" }
```

Do not assume order

Now that you've learned most of what there is to know about associative arrays, you need to be reminded of one of the features mentioned earlier: Perl stores the records in an apparently random order. By "apparently random," I mean an order that makes no sense just by looking at the keys or the values. As soon as you assign a record to the array, Perl determines where in the hash the record should go and puts it there, forgetting the order in which you put the records.

Here is a great example of this:

```
%IDList = (742 => 'Kathi Stennis',
    5280 => 'Roberta Wallace',
    3279 => 'Daniel Exon');
print join("\n", %IDList);
```

When you run this program, Perl displays

```
3279
Daniel Exon
742
Kathi Stennis
5280
Roberta Wallace
```

Thus, you should never use `pop` or `unshift` with associative arrays because you don't know what is at the "end" or "beginning" of the lists. Use the functions described earlier in this chapter instead.

Checking for any records at all

You can find out whether or not there are any records in an associative array by evaluating the name in a scalar context. This will return true only if there are any records:

```
unless(%IDList) { print "The assoc. array is empty.\n" }
```

Associative Arrays and Files

Rarely do you keep all your data in your Perl program. Instead, you keep it in a file on your hard disk and read it into your program. You might also use Perl to change the data in your database and then write the file to disk. You can use files with associative arrays pretty much the same way you use files with simple lists.

For example, you might keep your data as a tab-delimited text file, reading it into your program when it first starts up. You can write your data to the file using something like this:

```
open(STREETOUT, ">streets.txt") or
    die "Couldn't write to streets.txt file.\n";
foreach $Key (sort(keys(%Streets)))
    { print STREETOUT "$Key\t$Streets{$Key}\n" }
close(STREETOUT);
```

You can read this file with a program such as

```
%Streets = ();
open(STREETIN, "streets.txt") or
    die "Couldn't read from streets.txt file.\n";
while(<STREETIN>) {
    $TheRec = $_; chomp($TheRec);
    ($Key, $Val) = split(/\t/, $TheRec, 2);
    $Streets{$Key} = $Val;
}
```

Chapter 17 describes how to use database files with much faster access than the ones described here.

Lists within Lists

As described in previous chapters of this book, Perl's lists are useful for a myriad of applications. You can use them to hold names, addresses, numbers, and so on. But, until Perl 5 arrived, Perl programmers were limited to lists that had scalar items. In my mind, multidimensional lists are one of the greatest features of Perl 5.

It probably occurred to you that you might want to have a "list of lists." For instance, you might want a list of employees. Instead of the items being just the employees' names, you may want each item to be a list of their name, ID number, and telephone number. Or you may want a list of inventory, where each item in the list is a list of the inventory location, item part number, item name, and quantity in stock.

Ask and ye shall receive. Starting in Perl 5, there is an easy way to handle lists whose items are other lists. You can even have associative arrays whose values are lists. Although the technical method Perl uses for these is well beyond the scope of this book, the way you use these is pretty straightforward.

Lists of lists are based on Perl *references* and *pointers*. References and pointers are familiar to most advanced programmers, and most modern programming languages have them. However, they are usually mind-boggling to most novice and intermediate users, and are probably among the hardest things to learn well enough to use on a daily basis.

Because of this, I will show you how to use lists of lists but not what the individual symbols mean. If you want to learn more about these, you can certainly go ahead and read about references in the Perl documentation. However, if you don't seem to be able to grasp them after reading there, don't worry. You can still use lists of lists just fine without understanding why they work.

Two-dimensional lists

Let's use the inventory example to investigate how to put together and use a list that has lists as its items. Our inventory database, @AllInv, is made up of items. Each item has four parts to it:

- Location in the warehouse
- Part number of the item
- Part name of the item
- Quantity in stock

Thus, one item in the database might be

```
('Shelf 17B', '35J912', 'Tool chest, black', 11)
```

Another item might be

```
('Shelf 19A', '20N14', 'Allen wrench set', 47)
```

These kinds of lists are called *two-dimensional* lists because instead of being linear (one-dimensional), they have two dimensions: rows and columns. Each row is a stock item. Each column is a category, such as location or part number.

Suppose that you want to create a list that has these two lists (and many others) in it. Your first guess of how to do this might be

```
#  WRONG, BUT CLOSE
@AllInv = (
    ('Shelf 17B', '35J912', 'Tool chest, black', 11),
    ('Shelf 19A', '20N14', 'Crescent wrench set', 47)
);
#  WRONG, BUT CLOSE
```

In lists of lists, you mark the inside lists with square brackets ([and]), not parentheses. Thus, you really want this:

```
#  THE RIGHT WAY
@AllInv = (
    ['Shelf 17B', '35J912', 'Tool chest, black', 11],
    ['Shelf 19A', '20N14', 'Crescent wrench set', 47]
);
#  THE RIGHT WAY
```

That's it! You now know how to create lists of lists. Just remember that you mark the outermost list with parentheses, just like simple lists, and the inner lists with square brackets.

Accessing one piece at a time

Remember that in a simple list, you access an element with a subscript in square brackets, such as the sixth element of @MyList being $MyList[5]. In two-dimensional lists, you use two subscripts, the row first and then the column. For instance, the fourth column in the second row of @AllInv would be accessed as $AllInv[1][3]. Thus,

```
print $AllInv[1][3];
```

would display

```
47
```

You can set values in lists of lists exactly as you do in simple lists. For example, if you want to decrease the number of crescent wrenches in stock to 35, you would use

```
$AllInv[1][3] = 35;
```

Of course, you can use variables in the subscripts. For instance, to double the number of all the items in your inventory, you would use

```
$NumItems = @AllInv;
for($i = 0; $i < $NumItems; $i += 1)
    { $AllInv[$i][3] *= 2 }
```

You may want to get a whole item as a list instead of each of its pieces. This is easy, but a tad psychedelic-looking due to the way that Perl handles references. Here is the format:

```
@{@ARRAYNAME[ROW]}
```

For example, you might have something in your program like this:

```
@TopRow = @{@AllInv[0]};
```

There is no direct way to refer to an entire column in a similar fashion.

Adding rows and columns to two-dimensional lists

So far, you have seen how to initialize a list of lists and how to change parts one piece at a time. You may want to add items to a list a full row at a time, such as when new items are added to inventory. You can use the venerable push function for this:

```
@NewItem = ('Floor 2J', '82B297', 'Keyhole saw', 18);
push(@AllInv, [ @NewItem ]);
```

If you don't want to use a temporary variable, you could say

```
push(@AllInv, [ 'Floor 2J', '82B297', 'Keyhole saw', 18 ]);
```

Adding a column takes a little more work, but it is still easy. You have to add an item to the end of each list in the main list. For example, if you want to add a column at the end of each list that has the date you last looked at the item, you could do something like the following:

```
# Start by using today's date
($Second, $Minute, $Hour, $DayOfMonth, $Month, $Year,
    $WeekDay, $DayOfYear, $IsDST) = localtime(time);
$RealMonth = $Month + 1;
$Today = sprintf('%02d/%02d/%02d', $RealMonth,
    $DayOfMonth, $Year);
$NumItems = @AllInv;
for($i = 0; $i < $NumItems; $i += 1)
    { $AllInv[$i][4] = $Today }
```

Perl automatically extends each list as you add columns to the end, just as it does for simple lists.

Associative Arrays of Lists

As you saw at the beginning of this chapter, associative arrays are also kinds of Perl lists. It is easy to create associative arrays where the values are lists. In fact, the more you work with Perl, the more uses you will find for associative arrays with lists as values.

A great example of this is the inventory database example I've been using. In @AllInv, you have to search record by record in order to find the information for a part. With an associative array, you can quickly find the record by its key.

You create associative arrays with list values using statements such as this:

```
%AllInvByNum = (
    '35J912' => ['Shelf 17B', 'Tool chest, black', 11],
    '20N14'=> ['Shelf 19A' , 'Crescent wrench set', 47]
);
```

Here, the part number is the key.

You could look at or set an individual item with something like

```
$WrenchCount = $AllInvByNum{'20N14'}[2];
```

You can add records to the associative array with an assignment:

```
$AllInvByNum{'82B297'} = [ 'Floor 2J', 'Keyhole saw', 18 ];
```

You can find a particular record in the database with a statement such as

```
@Tools = @{$AllInvByNum{'35J912'}};
```

Of course, you can still use the associative array functions (keys, values, each, and exists), although you have to be a bit careful with how you handle anything that is a value, remembering that it is a list, not a scalar. For instance, to print a list of locations sorted by part number, you would use

```
foreach $Part (sort(keys(%AllInvByNum))) {
    print "Key $Part is found at location " .
        "$AllInvByNum{$Part}[0]\n";
}
```

However, if you want to print out the full records, you would use

```
foreach $Part (sort(keys(%AllInvByNum))) {
    print "Key $Part:  ",
        join("—", @{$AllInvByNum{$Part}}), "\n";
}
```

Beyond two dimensions

Lists of lists of lists of . . . well, you get the picture. Perl does not restrict you to having just two dimensions. In fact, many programs have multidimensional lists with three or more dimensions. For example, in our inventory example, imagine if @AllInv was really meant to be the inventory at *all* the locations in your company, not just one. The location and amount fields would then have more than one entry in them.

You can specify lists in lists in lists just as easily as you can lists in lists. For example, your new multilocation inventory list might now look like this:

```
@AllInv = (
    [['New York Shelf 17B', 'Ohio Slot 135'] , '35J912',
        'Tool chest, black', [11, 13]],
    [['New York Shelf 19A', 'Ohio Slot 142'], '20N14',
        'Crescent wrench set', [47, 12]]
);
```

This indicates that there are 11 tool chests at "New York Shelf 17B" and 13 tool chests at "Ohio Slot 135," and so on. To access this information directly, you would use a third subscript:

```
$OhioQuant = $AllInv[0][3][1];
```

Lists within Lists and Files

If you want to keep your data that will be handled in lists of lists in a file on disk, you need to be careful how you read it and write it. Actually, reading is not so difficult, but writing data that is in a multidimensional list is not as straightforward as if it were in a simple list.

In general, I always use tab-delimited files for all my data storage. Each line in the text file is an element of the top-level list. This makes it easy to read and write, and I can look at the files with a text editor if I need to figure out if something went wrong. The examples here are for tab-delimited files, but you can certainly use whatever kind of file you want.

Text files for two-dimensional lists of lists

For a two-dimensional list, you might use something like the following to write your data to a text file:

```
# Format is location, part number, description, quantity
open(INVOUT, ">inventory.txt") or
    die "Couldn't write to inventory.txt.\n";
$NumItems = @AllInv;
for($i = 0; $i < $NumItems; $i += 1)
    { print INVOUT "$AllInv[$i][0]\t$AllInv[$i][1]\t" .
        "$AllInv[$i][2]\t$AllInv[$i][3]\n" }
```

To read this database file, you would use something like this:

```
# Format is location, part number, description, quantity
@AllInv = ();
open(INVIN, "inventory.txt") or
    die "Couldn't read from inventory.txt.\n";
while(<INVIN>) {
    $TheRec = $_; chomp($TheRec);
    @NewItem = split(/\t/, $TheRec, 4);
    push(@AllInv, [ @NewItem ]);
}
```

Text files for more complicated lists of lists

If your list of lists has more than two dimensions, you have to be more careful when you write and read the text file on which it is based. When writing to a text file, you have to remember to pull out the items of the sublists. For example, in the extended @AllInv you just saw, you would use this:

```
# Format is New York location, Ohio location, part number,
#    description, New York quantity, Ohio quantity
open(INVOUT, ">inventory.txt") or
    die "Couldn't write to inventory.txt.\n";
$NumItems = @AllInv;
for($i = 0; $i < $NumItems; $i += 1) {
    print INVOUT "$AllInv[$i][0][0]\t$AllInv[$i][0][1]\t" .
        "$AllInv[$i][1]\t$AllInv[$i][2]\t" .
        "$AllInv[$i][3][0]\t$AllInv[$i][3][0]\n";
}
```

Note the additional items for the text file.

To read this database file, you would use something like the following:

```
# Format is New York location, Ohio location, part number,
#    description, New York quantity, Ohio quantity
@AllInv = ();
open(INVIN, "inventory.txt") or
    die "Couldn't read from inventory.txt.\n";
while(<INVIN>) {
    $TheRec = $_; chomp($TheRec);
    @NewItem = split(/\t/, $TheRec, 6);
    push(@AllInv, [ [ $NewItem[0], $NewItem[1] ],
        $NewItem[2], $NewItem[3],
        [ $NewItem[4], $NewItem[5] ] ] );
}
```

Chapter 17

Dancing with Databases

In This Chapter
▶ Storing data on disk
▶ Gaining quick access to keyed data

This is a very short chapter (you might be cheering now). Many people would expect that a chapter on databases would be long, involving lots of database commands and new ideas. Not so in a Perl book! Perl's interface to databases is amazingly simple.

When I was first learning Perl, I came to the section on how Perl accesses databases. I've used probably a dozen different database-management software packages in my life, and I've seen the good, the bad, and the just plain ugly. Perl was so amazingly simple that at first I couldn't believe that it would work. But, of course, it does. I remember laughing out loud about how easy it was.

It's All Done with Associative Arrays

In order to use Perl with database files, you need to understand associative arrays, as described Chapter 16. In fact, that's about *all* you need to understand. Beyond that, there are two Perl functions for opening and closing databases, and that's it.

How does Perl get away with not having dozens of different commands like most database-management programs? It binds an associative array to the database file so that any changes you make to the associative array are made to the database. When you look up a key in the associative array, Perl actually gets the value from the database.

Perl uses *DBM files* as its databases stored on disk. DBM is a Unix standard for simple key-value databases. There are many varieties of DBM files, and Perl knows about most of them. Perl prevents you from having to know how to program DBM directly. Other than associative arrays, you need only two functions: `dbmopen` and `dbmclose`. And yes, they do exactly like they sound like they would do.

The dbmopen function takes three arguments: the name of the associative array, the name of the database on disk, and a mode:

```
dbmopen(%AllInv, "/usr/general/inventory", 0600);
```

The mode is the numeric Unix file mode in which you want to open the file. If you aren't a Unixoid, or you are and you always get the file modes mixed up, the two modes you are most likely to use are 0600 if you want to read and write the database and 0400 if you just want to read it.

After you have used the dbmopen function, every time you access the associative array in the function, you actually access the database on disk. When you are done with the database, use the dbmclose function, whose argument is the name of the associative array:

```
dbmclose(%AllInv);
```

At the time I'm writing this, Perl-Win32 does not support dbmopen and dbmclose. Worse yet, it doesn't complain when you use them, making unwary users wonder what is going wrong because there are no error messages. Perl-Win32 may support these functions by the time you read this, and then again it may not. (By the way, MacPerl works just fine with dbmopen and dbmclose.)

Keeping It Small

The biggest advantage you receive from using Perl's database facilities instead of reading a text file from disk into an associative array is speed. Imagine if you had an inventory database as a text file with 10,000 lines. It would take a reasonable amount of time to read the entire file and parse it into an associative array. If you only want to look at one item, this would be a waste of time and computer resources.

Instead, you could use the Perl database functions to open a DBM file on disk. A program to look up the record for a key that is given in $ReqKey might look like the following:

```
# Open database for read-only
dbmopen(%AllInv, "/usr/general/inventory", 0400);
. . .
$TheRec = $AllInv{$ReqKey};
($Loc, $PartName, $Quant) = split(/\t/, $TheRec, 3);
. . .
dbmclose(%AllInv);
```

If you want to add a record to the database or change the value associated with a key that is already in the database, you might use something like this:

```
$AllInv{$MyKey} = join("\t", ($Loc, $PartName, $Quant));
```

Notes about Perl and Databases

Note that opening and closing a DBM database takes time (although not as much time as reading through a long text file), so you don't want to open and close it for each record. However, if you are accessing a database that others are also using, you should close the database as soon as you are finished.

You can't use associative arrays of lists with DBM files. The value written into the DBM file by an assignment must be a single value, not a list.

The dbmopen and dbmclose functions are special cases of Perl's tie and untie functions. tie and untie are well beyond a book like this, but they are useful ways to associate Perl variables with an action. In the case of dbmopen and dbmclose, they cause access to an associative array to be bound to a set of calls that reads and sets values in DBM databases.

As mentioned earlier, Perl understands how to use a variety of flavors of DBM files. At the time this is written, these include GDBM, BSD-DB, SDBM, NDBM, and ODBM. If you are on a Unix system, Perl uses NDBM as the default.

Chapter 18

Controlling Your Computer from Perl

● ●

In This Chapter

▶ Understanding Perl's system functions

▶ Using Perl to control PCs and Macintoshes

▶ Getting into Perl's Unix roots

● ●

*P*rograms can interact with a computer's operating system in many ways. You have already seen many ways that Perl interacts with you and your computer other than by simply calculating. For example, you saw in Chapters 12 and 13 that Perl can read and write files, both of which require interaction with the operating system.

This chapter explains some of the system-level things you can do with Perl. For instance, you can use Perl to run other programs or to monitor other programs that are running on your computer. This chapter also discusses the functions that help you control Windows and Mac systems.

Getting with the System

Perl makes it easy to run commands on your computer as if you had typed them on the command line. The system function executes a command. For example, on a Unix system, you might use the function to execute the ls command:

```
system('ls');
```

Of course, the program you name in the argument can have command-line arguments, such as

```
system('ls -la /var/spool');
```

The system function has had a mixed history in Perl-Win32. The version of Perl-Win32 that ships on the CD-ROM that comes with this book doesn't execute system functions the way you might expect. It cannot take as an argument MS-DOS internal commands (such as DIR and COPY); it can only run external commands that exist on your hard disk as .COM, .EXE, and .BAT files.

The system function causes Perl to run the named program and wait for that program to exit. That sounds logical, doesn't it? However, Perl has another function, exec, which doesn't wait. exec acts like system except that it causes the Perl program to immediately stop and run the program, never to return. The only way lines after the exec will ever be run is if the program wasn't found. Thus, the second line of this program will never be seen unless there is an error in finding the program you name:

```
exec('myprogram');
print "Hmmm, myprogram didn't seem to run.\n";
```

Getting output from a program

It is common to want to capture the output of a program in a variable and use that information. In this case, you should use Perl's ` operator, also called the *backtick operator*. The backtick operator around a program name causes the output to be returned. Here is an example:

```
$TheOutput = 'myprogram';
```

With the backtick operator in a scalar context, all output is written into the string variable. If you use the backtick operator in a list context, each line of the output is stored in a list item.

Using backticks takes the standard file output (described in Chapter 12) of the program and passes it into the variable. It does *not* cause the standard error output from the program to go into the variable, only the standard file output. This means that error messages might not appear in the variable.

Perl 5 has a new feature, qx//, which acts just like the backtick operator. It works like Perl's other quoting operators. Thus, you can use

```
$TheOutput = qx/myprogram/;
```

or

```
$TheOutput = qx(myprogram);
```

The venerable open *function*

The open function can also work somewhat like the backtick operator, except that instead of sending the output to a variable, it sends it to a file handle. To use open in this fashion, you use the command as the file name, followed by a vertical bar (|) character, sometimes called a *pipe* character:

```
open(THEOUT, "myprogram |");
```

You can then treat THEOUT like any other file handle that has input you want to read from. You do not need to use the close function to close programs that send output to Perl.

You can also use open in the opposite fashion: to pass data to the standard file input of the program. Here, you move the | in front of the program. You can then treat this file handle like any file that you are writing to. For instance, if your program takes data from the standard file input, you might have something like this:

```
open(THEPROG, "| myprog");
print THEPROG $a1, $a2, "\n";
close(THEPROG);
```

After the close, the program has all of its input and runs with it.

Using open to pass data to the standard file input of the program is much more common on Unix systems than on Windows, because MS-DOS programs rarely take much input from standard file input.

Running programs in MacPerl

Programs on the Macintosh do not work like programs on Unix or Windows. Thus, in MacPerl, system, exec, backticks, and open don't normally work. However, if you have a Mac program called ToolServer, available from Apple, you can use these programs. ToolServer comes as part of Apple's MPW development software and some other programming packages.

Having said that, I should point out that there are a few backtick commands that *do* work on the Mac. They are provided to help make porting some Unix-based Perl programs easier. Table 18-1 contains a list of the backtick commands that work on the Mac.

Table 18-1	Backtick Commands that Work on the Mac
Statement	*Returns*
`'pwd'`	The current folder, followed by a newline (you can also use `'Directory'` as well).
`'hostname'`	Name of the Macintosh.
`'glob <argument>'`	List of all files matching the argument. You can use `*` and `?`, such as `*.c`.

Controlling a Windows System with Perl-Win32

Although the user interface for Perl-Win32 is, to say the least, meager, it offers a fair number of Windows-specific functions and features. These let you follow what is going on with your system, change system parameters, and so on. Most are geared more toward Windows NT than Window 95, but some work fine on both platforms.

All the extensions that come with Perl-Win32 have the prefix `Win32::`. By the time you read this, there may be more in the most recent version of Perl-Win32. They fall into three categories: variables, functions, and modules. The following sections contain brief introductions to the features; the documentation that comes with Perl-Win32 goes into much more detail.

Perl-Win32 system variables

You can use these variables in your Perl-Win32 programs just like any other variable, although most of them are only useful for reading from. The system variables are shown in Table 18-2.

Table 18-2	Perl-Win32 System Variables
Variable	*Description*
`Win32::PerlVersion`	Version of Perl-Win32
`Win32::GetCwd`	The name of the current directory
`Win32::FsType`	Type of filesystem on the current drive
`Win32::LoginName`	Username of the process running Perl-Win32

Variable	Description
Win32::NodeName	Name of the machine's node (Microsoft Networks only)
Win32::DomainName	Domain name of the machine
Win32::GetLastError	Error value from a call to a Win32:: function

In addition, Win32::GetOSVersion returns a list containing the following operating system version information:

- A descriptive string
- The major version number (Humorously, Windows 95 shows up as "4," even though Microsoft insisted that it was *not* Windows 4.)
- The minor version number
- Microsoft's "build" number
- A signifying digit (0 for generic Win32, 1 for Windows 95, or 2 for Windows NT)

Perl-Win32 system functions

The functions built into Perl-Win32 are mostly for Windows NT, given their system administration nature. They are shown in Table 18-3.

Table 18-3	Perl-Win32 System Functions
Function	Description
Win32::Format Message(ERRORCODE)	Converts a Win32 error bitmap to a text string.
Win32::Spawn (COMMAND, ARGS, PID)	Spawns a new process with the command and arguments given. Perl puts the process id of the new process into the variable named in PID.
Win32::Lookup AccountName(SYSTEM, ACCOUNT, DOMAIN, SID, SIDTYPE)	Returns the domain name, the SID, and the SID type for a given user account on a particular system.

(continued)

Table 18-3 *(continued)*

Function	Description
Win32::LookupAccount SID(SYSTEM, SID, ACCOUNT, DOMAIN, SIDTYPE)	Returns the account name, domain name, and the SID type for a given SID on a particular system.
Win32::InitiateSystem Shutdown(MACHINE, MESSAGE, TIMEOUT, FORCECLOSE, REBOOT)	Causes the specified machine to shut down after the given timeout. Users are sent the message. If FORCECLOSE is true, all documents are closed first; if REBOOT is true, the machine is rebooted instead of shut down.
Win32::AbortSystem Shutdown(MACHINE)	Stops a shutdown that is in progress from continuing.

Perl-Win32 system modules

The Win32:: modules are mostly for advanced Windows NT programmers who need to do process-level communications, but a few of them are useful for all users, even those on Windows 95. Table 18-4 shows these modules.

Table 18-4	Perl-Win32 System Modules
Module	**Description**
Win32::Eventlog	Handles Windows NT eventlogs
Win32::Registry	Reads and writes the Windows Registry
Win32::NetAdmin	Creates and changes users on a net-worked machine
Win32::File	Looks at and changes file attributes
Win32::Service	Starts and stops Windows NT services
Win32::NetResource	Starts and stops Windows NT resources
Win32::Process, Win32:: Semaphore, Win32::Mutex, Win32::ChangeNotification	Process control (creating, suspending, killing) and interprocess communication

Controlling a Mac with MacPerl

The MacPerl package comes with many modules useful for controlling your Macintosh. Some of these are for advanced users only (such as the ones that control the network interfaces), but others are for all Perl programmers and give access to Macintosh user interface features. The modules are listed in Table 18-5.

Table 18-5	**MacPerl System Modules**
Module	*Description*
MacPerl::Answer	Displays a dialog box with buttons
MacPerl::Ask	Prompts the user for text in a dialog box
MacPerl::Pick	Prompts the user to pick one choice of many in a dialog box
MacPerl::SetFileInfo	Changes the file type and file creator of a file
MacPerl::GetFileInfo	Returns the file type and file creator
MacPerl::DoAppleScript	Runs an AppleScript program
MacPerl::Reply	Replies to AppleScript requests
MacPerl::Quit	Tells Perl when to quit
MacPerl::LoadExternals	Extends Perl with XCMD and XFCN programs written in other languages
MacPerl::DebugExternals	Allows you to debug XCMD and XFCN programs
MacPerl::Choose	Handles network sockets
MacPerl::MakeFSSpec	Creates a unique encoding for a file
MacPerl::MakePath Macaperl::MakeFSSpec	Turns an encoding from MacPerl::MakeFSSpec into a file name
MacPerl::Volumes MacPerl::MakeFSSpec	Returns the MacPerl::MakeFSSpec for the mounted volumes

Unix-only System Functions

Of course, Unix has its own set of system control functions. Most of them apply only to Unix systems, just like the ones shown earlier in this chapter apply only to Windows or the Macintosh. Usually only system administrators care about these functions because the functions do things like look at users and groups.

Users

The getpwent function reads the next record from the user database, which on Unix systems is usually the file /etc/passwd. It returns a list that contains the following items:

- User name
- Encrypted password (or an asterisk)
- User number
- Group number

- Quota field
- Comment field
- gcos field
- Home directory
- Default shell

Because getpwent gets the "next" record, it is common to use it in a loop like

```
while(@PWList = getpwent) { print "$PWList[0]\n" }
```

You can reset getpwent to the top of the database with the setpwent function and close the database with the endpwent function (although you don't have to). There is another pair of functions, getpwuid and getpwnam, which returns a list just like getpwent. However, these functions take a single argument (a userid or a username, respectively) and return the list for that argument. For instance, to get the list for user "phoffman", you would use

```
@PWList = getpwnam('phoffman');
```

The getlogin function returns the login name of the user running the program. You can obtain this name from the /usr/utmp file.

Groups

The getgrent function acts like the getpwent function, but it walks through the group database instead of the user database. getgrent returns

- Group name
- Encrypted password (or an asterisk)

- Group number
- String of member names

As you might expect, Perl also has the setgrent and endgrent functions. And, as you might also expect, you can use the getgrgid and getgrnam functions, both of which take a groupid as an argument and return a list like getgrent.

Chapter 19

Object-Oriented Perl

*T*he computer industry seems to be a magnet for fads. This is partly due to the fact that many people are afraid of computers and yet want to seem knowledgeable, so they repeat what they've heard is "cool." Sometimes the fads stick; sometimes they disappear within a year or two.

The programming world is much less prone to fads than the computer industry in general. Programming languages stick around forever, long after they probably should have died a quiet death. For instance, there is still a huge market for Cobol programmers.

Probably the only major fad to hit the programming world in the last decade is *object-oriented* programming. Like any fad, different people have different views of what it is and what it is good for. Clearly, however, object-oriented programming is here to stay, and Perl 5 has embraced it in a very Perl-like fashion. That is to say, you can use objects if you want to, but Perl doesn't force you to use them.

This chapter covers Perl's method of object-oriented programming so that you can use object-oriented programs written by other Perl programmers. Since Perl 5 came out, most Perl programmers who write programs that other people can use have written them using the object-oriented parts of Perl. Much of the CPAN library on the CD-ROM that comes with this book uses object-oriented Perl. Thus, it is useful for you to know how to use objects so you can use the wealth of prewritten Perl programs.

This chapter does *not* cover how to create your own objects in Perl modules. Learning the proper way to write your own programs with objects is well beyond the scope of this book. It requires some advanced Perl concepts like references that most beginners, and many intermediate users, find just too mind-boggling. Also, in order for object-oriented programming to work, you have to design your programs well, and just learning about this kind of design can take many chapters. Thus, to really learn how to create good object-oriented programs, you need an advanced book and lots of time and patience.

Why Objects Are Good

When people seriously began talking about object-oriented programming in the mid-1980s, many programmers were openly skeptical. The fact that its acronym is "OOP" didn't help, and was the basis for all too many jokes. However, over time, more and more programmers have become enamored with the promises that object-oriented programming holds, even though using it means more work and learning some new ideas.

The most important benefit of object-oriented programming is that you get more programs that can be reused in many ways. For example, if you write a program that does one particular task on the Internet, using object-oriented programming makes it easier for other people to use what you have done as part of their programs. Without object-oriented programming, this is still possible, but it is much more difficult.

Another significant benefit is that team programming projects are much easier to coordinate when the programmers are all using object-oriented programming. Because object-oriented programming forces programmers to use a consistent interface on the code that they write, each piece of the larger project can be more easily integrated. Given how often programmers come and go in many companies, this is a great boon to managers.

Object-oriented programming also makes it easier to use hierarchical programming, meaning programming that can be planned from general to specific specifications. Thus, if you are working on a project in which the customer knows in general what the program is supposed to do but won't know the specifics until you are well under way, you can begin general programming and then fill in details at different levels of the program as the customer provides more of the specifics and have those changes affect all levels of the program.

Using object-oriented programming is a good way to manage complexity on a programming project. Some of this complexity comes because projects are not well defined, some comes from fluctuations in programming staff, and some comes from the fact that programs always evolve as they are written. Big programs are inherently complex, just because they're doing a lot of stuff. The goal of object-oriented programming is to make it easier to make the process modular, thereby making it easier to perform one task at a time.

I want to make it clear that I'm not an object-oriented programming zealot, although I have some friends who are. I think writing programs using object-oriented programming techniques is great for large programs, and probably even for some medium-sized ones, but not for the kinds of small programs Perl is often used for. The fact that many Perl programmers use object-oriented programming is a boon for us all because it makes their programs more easily used by us. For most one-person projects, however, object-oriented programming is not necessary (unless those projects become successful and turn into multiperson projects).

An Overview of Object Orientation

In Perl programs, most of the action takes place in variables. You set this numeric variable here, you add items to this list variable here, you split this string variable into these other string variables, and so on. Variables are the things that hold information in a Perl program.

In an object-oriented program, there are still variables, but the main things that you use to hold information are *objects*. An object is much more than just a variable. It is a collection of variables combined with a collection of actions (called *methods*) that the object is capable of. You don't look at or change the variables in an object using the standard Perl commands you've learned up to now; instead, you use an object's methods to handle its variables.

You can think of an object as a black box that comes with an instruction list pasted on the side, a microphone for giving it directions, and a slot where things might come out. You don't know what's in the box or how its innards work, and you don't even know if the instructions are complete. You just know that you will give the instructions to the object and possibly receive some result.

For example, imagine that you have a "bicycle" object. However, it doesn't look like a bicycle as we know it; instead, it is a black box. The instructions on the side of the box has a list of methods that apply to this object, including "TellColor," "GoForwards," "FallOver," and so on. You say "TellColor" into the microphone, and out comes a slip of paper saying "blue." You say "GoForwards 7" into the microphone, and the box jumps forward seven inches. Some methods have arguments, some don't; some return a value, others just do something.

Objects might seem a bit confusing because they are so unlike variables. The differences at first are a bit frustrating, but they are valuable for making object-oriented programs help manage complexity. If you could just stick your hand inside an object and change some of the variables in many different fashions, it would be almost impossible to write the programs for objects in ways that are predictable. Forcing everyone to use only the methods associated with an object prevents surprising results.

Using methods has another advantage: You can later change how a method works in an object without changing all the programs that use an object. Using your bike example, assume that a few people are using this object in their programs. You later discover a much faster way to implement the "GoForwards" method. You can change that method without forcing people who are already using your object to change anything they are doing.

Objects don't just appear out of nowhere. Instead, they are created from *classes*. "Created from" isn't really correct, but I can't think of a good English way of saying what happens. The technical jargon for this is to say "an object is instantiated from a class" or "an object is an instantiation of a class." Think of a class as a cookie cutter from which you stamp out identical objects. The cookie cutter and the resulting cookie are very different things.

Perl's Objects Made Easy

Okay, if you got through all that (and maybe even if you didn't), you probably want to know, "So how do I use Perl's object-oriented features?" Fortunately, the answer is, "Very easily."

In case you skipped all that introductory information about object-oriented programs, you should understand three important things:

- ✔ Classes
- ✔ Methods
- ✔ Objects

In Perl 5, a class is just a package. (And, in case you've forgotten about packages, they are described in Chapter 10.) Inside a package that is a class, there are definitions of the various methods of that class. These methods are, in fact, just subroutines (which are also described in Chapter 10).

The only tricky part of using Perl's object-oriented features is creating the objects themselves. It isn't all that tricky, but it involves a part of Perl that is not covered in this book, namely references. Fortunately, you can use references with objects without understanding what's behind them.

The rest of this chapter uses the object-oriented interface of the libwww-perl library described in Chapter 15. You can follow along with the discussion without using the library, or you can use the library on your system (assuming that it has been installed).

Using use

Before you create objects, you have to open the Perl 5 module that contains the classes you want. To open a Perl 5 module, you use the use function. You normally have only one argument, the module name. Module names are not put in quotation marks, and you may leave off the ".pm" part of the file name. For example, you might have

```
use(LWP::UserAgent);
```

However, you will see the use function more frequently without the parentheses:

```
use LWP::UserAgent;
```

You can also include additional arguments in the use statement if there are particular variables you want from the module. Don't worry about this, it is rarely used.

Making new objects

After you have specified one or more modules for Perl to open, you are ready to create objects. Remember that each object comes with methods, and therefore you have to create an object before you use its methods. In Perl, you almost always use the new subroutine of a packages to create a new object:

```
$TheAgent = new LWP::UserAgent;
```

This creates a new object from the LWP::UserAgent class and makes $TheAgent a reference to the new object.

Okay, time for a bit of technical talk. I keep talking about "references" without explaining what they are. In the previous paragraph, I said that $TheAgent is a reference to the new object. Believe it or not, you *still* don't need to know what a reference is or what it does. Just use the notation for objects shown in this chapter, and you'll be fine.

The trick is to not think of $TheAgent as "the object" but as "something that points to the object." You might even mix them up in your head, in the same way that people say to me "You are Paul Hoffman" instead of saying "You are the person who is named Paul Hoffman." I am really the person, not the name, but it is easier to just think of me by name.

The new subroutine of a package can sometimes require arguments. These are listed after the name, such as

```
$Req = new HTTP::Request 'GET', 'http://www.scruz.net/';
```

However, most Perl object libraries let you invoke the new subroutine with no arguments and supply what would have been the arguments through methods. Here is an example of a new subroutine with no arguments:

```
$Req = new HTTP::Request;
```

With objects come methods

Once you have created an object, you can use its methods. You invoke Perl methods with the following format:

```
$OBJECTREF->METHODNAME(ARGUMENTS);
```

For example, in the preceding section you saw an example of creating an HTTP::Request object pointed to by the name $Req. All HTTP::Request objects have a method called url. You might invoke this method with

```
$Req->url('http://www.scruz.net/');
```

Note that to the left of the -> is the reference to the object whose method you want to invoke, and to the right of the -> is the method name. Some methods take arguments (in parentheses, of course), and others are just bare:

```
$Req->url;
```

Real-World Objects

The libwww-perl set of modules is a good example of an object-oriented Perl program that does real work. As described in Chapter 15, it allows you to create Perl programs that act like Web clients. This section shows you just a hint of what you can do with `LWP::UserAgent`; see the "pod" documentation that comes with the module for a complete list of methods.

There are three types of objects used in simple `LWP::UserAgent` programs:

- ✔ HTTP user agents, created with `new LWP::UserAgent`
- ✔ HTTP requests, created with `new HTTP::Request`
- ✔ Responses from requests, which are returned from calls to the `request` method used on HTTP user agents

Therefore, you have three different kinds of objects, and each kind of object has its own methods. Table 19-1 contains some of the methods.

Table 19-1	Examples of Methods
Object	*Sample Methods*
`LWP::UserAgent`	request, time-out, proxy
`HTTP::Request`	method, url
`HTTP::Response`	content, is_success, is_error, code

To start a libwww-perl program that will act as an Web client, you create an agent object and a request object:

```
use LWP::UserAgent;
$TheAgent = new LWP::UserAgent;
$Req = new HTTP::Request;
```

In this case, `$TheAgent` points to the agent object and `$Req` points to the request object.

The request object has methods that specify the HTTP request method and the URL to which you want to make the method. These methods are called `method` and `url`, respectively. If you just want to get the contents of a Web page, you use the HTTP "GET" method. For instance, your program might have these two lines:

```
$Req->method('GET');
$Req->url('http://www.scruz.net/');
```

These two lines assign the kind of method and URL you want to use. You are now ready to make the request over the Web. For this, you tell your agent the request that it should use with the `request` method. Perl returns the Web page as a response object:

```
$TheResp = $TheAgent->request($Req);
```

This means that you have created a response object that is pointed to by the `$TheResp` variable.

Of course, once you have a Web page, you want to look at it. However, remember that `$TheResp` points to a response object, not to the content itself. However, response objects have a method that lets you look at the content, namely `content`. Thus, you might have these lines:

```
$TheRespContent = $TheResp->content;
$TheRespContent is now a string that contains the content.
```

Response objects have other interesting methods that can tell you more about the response you got from the Web server. For example, `is_success` and `is_error` tell you whether or not your Web request was successful. Instead of assuming that there is content, you might want to check first:

```
if($TheResp->is_success)
    { $TheRespContent = $TheResp->content }
```

If you get an error, the response object can format the error message for you as an HTML document using the `error_as_HTML` method:

```
if($TheResp->is_success)
    { $TheRespContent = $TheResp->content }

else { $TheRespContent = $TheResp->error_as_HTML }
```

Again, there are lots of different methods for these objects, and the best way to find out more is to look in their documentation.

Programming with Pragmas

The standard Perl distribution comes with many modules, most of which are for advanced programmers. A few of the built-in modules, called *pragmas,* affect the way the way that Perl compiles your program before it executes the program. These can sometimes be useful to you in debugging your code or as a way to force you to program better (you can make the Perl compiler complain more).

You turn on Perl's pragmas using the use function, just like you do with other modules. Pragmas usually only apply to the current block in which they are set. Thus, you can turn one on in a block, and at the end of the block, Perl will return to its normal mode of operation. For example, to start using the diagnostics pragma, you would say the following in your program:

```
use diagnostics;
```

Table 19-2 contains the most useful built-in pragmas.

Table 19-2	Useful Pragmas
Pragma	*Description*
diagnostics	Causes Perl to give longer and more descriptive error messages
English	Allows you to use easier-to-read names for built-in variables
integer	Forces integer arithmetic on calculations
strict	Causes compile errors for some possibly unsafe programming practices

The strict pragma checks for symbolic references, variables that weren't declared with my, and subroutine names as bare words unless they are defined. It helps find some subtle programming mistakes.

After you turn on a pragma, you can turn it off with the no function. It acts just like the opposite of use:

```
no diagnostics;
```

You can use use and no in your program to turn on and off a pragma.

Chapter 20

Programming in Style

● ●

In This Chapter
▶ Reading about programming style
▶ Making your programs easier to maintain

● ●

*T*hroughout this book, I've mentioned little things about programming style. Every programming language has its own hard-and-fast rules for how you must program, as well as many completely optional rules about how you should program. Perl certainly has plenty of both. For example, a "must" rule in Perl is, "You must use correct capitalization for function names." The following generates a Perl error:

```
Print $SomeVariable;
```

If you violate the "should" rules for Perl programming, you will not get an error message, and your program will work just fine. When you follow the "should" rules, you make your programs easier to read by you and others and make maintaining your programs easier.

Programming Style Is Relative, But Important

Over time, programmers using a particular language create style rules that they think make programs more readable. These rules involve things like

✔ Formatting programs (indentation, blank lines)
✔ Choosing between equivalent operators
✔ Wording comments
✔ Placement of short comments on lines

If lots of early adopters of a language agree to particular rules, then they become part of the culture of the programming language.

Nice formatting

In the case of Perl, Larry Wall, Perl's originator, laid down some of his style preferences early on in Perl's life. Many programmers take these as gospel, while others generally follow them but feel free to make changes for their own tastes. I'm in the latter group.

The Perl documentation has a very useful list of style guidelines. Here is the main list of style guidelines from the documentation:

- 4-column indent.
- Opening curly on same line as keyword, if possible, otherwise line up.
- Space before the opening curly of a multiline BLOCK.
- One-line BLOCK may be put on one line, including curlies.
- No space before the semicolon.
- Semicolon omitted in "short" one-line BLOCK.
- Space around most operators.
- Space around a "complex" subscript (inside brackets).
- Blank lines between chunks that do different things.
- Uncuddled elses.
- No space between function name and its opening paren.
- Space after each comma.
- Long lines broken after an operator (except "and" and "or").
- Space after last paren matching on current line.
- Line up corresponding items vertically.
- Omit redundant punctuation as long as clarity doesn't suffer.

Most of these make very good sense, even the ones that conflict with each other. The conflict isn't bad: It just means that you should use your best judgment. These are guidelines, not laws.

A great example of letting you choose what you want is one-line blocks. The second rule would have you do something like

```
if($Num < 10) {
    print "$Num is too small.\n";
}
```

However, the fourth rule makes more sense to me:

```
if($Num < 10)
    { print "$Num is too small.\n" }
```

In cases like this, I will even do this:

```
if($Num < 10) { print "$Num is too small.\n" }
```

Choose your operator

The preceding rules cover the look of your program, not the actual programming constructs you use. Perl's wealth of operators often gives you a choice between two equivalent operators for the same task. In these cases, I always recommend that you choose the operator that will make the most sense when you later read the program.

For example, should you use the ++ or += 1 operator after a variable? Compare the following:

```
if($Done) { $Count++ }
if($Done) { $Count += 1 }
```

In my mind, the latter more clearly looks like "add 1 to $Count". However, most Perl programmers use $Count++ instead. They both do the same thing, and I can certainly recognize that $Count++ means "add 1 to $Count", but somehow I prefer to see the 1 in the program.

The previous example brings up another interesting stylistic difference: Should you use the assignment operators like += and .= or specify the actual assignment? Compare the following:

```
if($Done) { $Count += 1 }
if($Done) { $Count = $Count + 1 }
```

The latter is clearer, but using $Count twice on the same line seems redundant to me; thus, I almost always prefer using the assignment operator +=. Some folks prefer to be more explicit.

Parentheses are your friends

In many cases, parentheses are optional in Perl programs. In mathematical equations, you can omit the parentheses if you are sure you understand the order in which the operators will be evaluated. However, it is safer to include them.

You can also omit the parentheses around functions, but doing so makes many Perl statements hard to read. For example, the following two statements are the same:

```
mkdir("/usr/home/paul/Temp", 0700);
mkdir "/usr/home/paul/Temp", 0700;
```

To me, the first is much more readable than the second because you can see the arguments grouped together in the parentheses. To other Perl programmers, the parentheses just get in the way and don't add anything to the program.

Of course, sometimes even I don't use parentheses, namely in the print function. You'll notice that throughout the book I use statements like

```
print "The name is $Name\n";
```

instead of

```
print("The name is $Name\n");
```

I don't know why I started using print without the parentheses, but once I started that way, I kept it up. Every Perl programmer I know uses print without parentheses, so I guess I'm in good company.

Flexible order for conditionals

In this book, I have always written conditional statements (if and unless) with the condition first:

```
if($Done) { $Count += 1 }
```

If the block that follows the conditional has exactly one statement in it, such as the preceding one, you can put the statement first, followed by the conditional. You can even pull the expression outside the parentheses, if you wish. You could replace the preceding example with either of the following:

```
$Count += 1 if($Done);
$Count += 1 if $Done;
```

To some people, this is more natural, sounding a bit like English: "Do this if that is true." However, I find this confusing, because it violates the visual left-to-right reading that we are all used to. The left part will only get executed if the right part is true, so you have to read from right to left on lines like these. Also, seeing the conditional test outside of the parentheses just bugs me, because you can't have it that way if the conditional comes first.

You can even use the "statement first" form for `while` and `until` as long as there is only a single statement. For example, the following is perfectly legal:

```
&MySub while $Count < 0;
```

This statement will cause the &MySub subroutine to be executed repeatedly until $Count is greater than or equal to 0. This statement is equivalent to the following statement that you learned earlier in the book:

```
while($Count < 0) { &MySub }
```

Just because I always put the conditional first doesn't mean you have to. In fact, you'll find lots of examples of Perl programs written by very good programmers that have the conditional second. Because it always makes me stop and stare when I come across this form, I choose not to use it.

Many Comments about Comments

Programming style is all well and good, but a program without comments is often worthless. Yes, that's a strong statement. Yes, I sometimes violate this rule myself. Yes, I really mean it.

Unless a program is five lines or shorter, you should always start it with at least one line of comments. In fact, even on those little three-line programs that you may have written by now, adding one line of comments may take you all of 15 seconds and will make the program much more useful in the future.

Chapters 3 and 4 talk a fair amount about comments, so I won't rehash that again. However, there are some stylistic points that are appropriate here.

For multiline comments, I usually indent the second line a few extra spaces so it is clear that it is a continuation of the previous line:

```
# empdata1.pl: a very simple employee database application.
#     This program reads a text file that is an employee
#     database and lets you query it by ID number.
```

Other programmers don't indent:

```
# empdata1.pl: a very simple employee database application.
# This program reads a text file that is an employee
# database and lets you query it by ID number.
```

Making lines

Some folks like to embellish the comments at the beginning of programs (and sometimes at the beginning of subroutines) with long lines of characters to make them stick out more:

```
###############################################################
# empdata1.pl: a very simple employee database application.
###############################################################
```

As long as the line starts with a # character, it is a comment. Some people, however, get a bit carried away:

```
#-*-*-*-*-*-*-*-*-*-*-*-*-*-*-*-*-*-*-*-*-*-*-*-*-*#
# empdata1.pl: a very simple employee database application.
#-*-*-*-*-*-*-*-*-*-*-*-*-*-*-*-*-*-*-*-*-*-*-*-*-*#
```

Here's one I came across years ago for another language. It has a nice, useless art deco feeling to it.

```
#_____.__...—~~~~****\/\/||||\/\/****~~~~—...._____
# empdata1.pl: a very simple employee database application.
#_____....—~~~~****\/\/||||\/\/****~~~~—...._____
```

If this kind of artistry makes it more likely that you will write many clear comments, by all means use it.

Comments on the same line

As if we didn't have enough to argue about, there is also a bit of disagreement about which of the following is better:

```
if($Signature ne 'Dave') { next }  # Wasn't what we wanted
```

or

```
# Check if signature is correct
if($Signature ne 'Dave') { next }
```

I'll admit that I go both ways on this. Sometimes I put my short comment on the same line as the test, sometimes before it. Other folks insist that you should never put a comment on the same line as Perl code because it's harder to read. My suggestion is try both and see which suits you best.

Naming your variables

Another very common way to "comment" a program is to use descriptive names for your variables. You have no doubt noticed that throughout the book, the variable names, even in the short snippets, often have mnemonic names like `$Count`, `$TheLine`, and so on.

The longer the program, the more variables you will generally have. The more variables you have, the more important it is for you to know what each variable does. Thus, the more important the variable names.

The beauty of blank lines

The lowly blank line is one of the most neglected kinds of comments. It doesn't have anything in it, so why pay any attention to it? To me, a blank line is one of the more important kinds of comments, particularly when I'm reading a program by an author who doesn't use real comments very much.

A blank line tells you where one thing starts and another begins. You might be able to figure this out by reading the statements in the program, but it is very useful to be able to scan a long program vertically and see where the programmer thought that the "sections" were.

Having said that, I rarely use two blank lines together. One is enough to break the visual flow of a program; two seem like a chasm.

There is a long history of programmers using short, unmnemonic names like $i, $j, $x, and the venerable $foo and $bar. This is fine if you never have to look at the program again after you write it and you remember what each of these poorly named variables is for. In other words, it's a bad idea.

By the way, you may have noticed that I use $i and $j. It is okay to use short names like these only in places where the variable will be used only for one or two lines, such as in a short for statement. In fact, I think it is a good practice because it tells you visually "this is a short-lived variable." However, if the variable will be "alive" for more than four or five lines, I give it a useful name.

Another area of controversy among programmers is capitalization in variable names. In Perl, capitalization counts, so that the variable $OldFileHandle is different than $OldfileHandle (note the "f"). Some folks like to use mixed case in a variable name because it is visually clearer what this jumble of characters is; others don't like using mixed case because it is prone to typing errors. People in the latter group usually like all lower-case (such as $oldfilehandle), or just an initial capital (such as $Oldfilehandle).

As you can see in this book, I like having internal capitals (the dweebspeak term for these is *intercaps*). However, I have to agree with the people who say that intercaps are prone to typing errors. These kinds of errors are often hard to find in Perl programs because you don't have to predeclare your variables.

This is a good place to remind you about Perl's -w command-line switch. Running Perl from the command line with the -w switch causes Perl to scan your program and print warnings about common errors you might have made before it runs the program. If you are using Unix, you can also put the -w switch on the first line of your program, after the #!/usr/bin/perl invocation.

The -w switch on the Perl command line is a good way to avoid many common errors, but it is not perfect. It is often good at finding mistyped variable names, for example, but if you make the same typo twice, it will probably miss the error.

Some programmers avoid intercaps by using all lowercase letters and underscore (_) characters between the parts of the name. These folks might have a variable called $old_file_handle, for example. I have a hard time with this because you have to use the Shift key on your keyboard to get the underscore, and you might as well make a capital letter. Also, it just doesn't look as "right" to me as intercaps. Clearly, you can make your own choices about this.

Part V
The Part of Tens

In this part . . .

People love lists, and the chapters in this part are laid out as lists of ten items. There's a lot of good, quick information in these chapters; so spend a bit of time before you finish the book!

Chapter 21

Ten Even More Advanced Perl Topics, Covered Lightly

- -

In This Chapter

▶ Looking at what you didn't learn

▶ Finding out just a bit about some pretty advanced topics

- -

A book for novices can't cover every topic. Novice programmers might find some of the advanced material presented interesting but not useful in the learning process. Thus, I've skipped some topics in this book so as to give more space to the topics of greater interest to typical novice and intermediate users.

This chapter gives a very brief introduction to some larger Perl topics skipped in this book. Note that many of the Perl features in this chapter are not yet supported in the non-Unix implementations of Perl.

Compiled Perl

The early chapters of this book describe how Perl is an *interpreter*. This means that each time you run a program, Perl interprets the source code of the program and turns it into instructions the CPU can use. Although this process is fast, it is not as fast as *compiling* the program once and saving the instructions for the CPU on disk so you can just run them directly.

Until recently, there was no way to compile Perl. As this book is being written, there is a project led by Malcolm Beattie to create a solid, useful Perl compiler. By the time you read this, the compiler may be fully (or reasonably) functional. You can look at an early, but useful, version of the compiler in the CPAN library on the CD-ROM that comes with this book.

Formats

If you try to write text files that are supposed to be printed on a page, you can drive yourself crazy trying to keep track of the number of lines you have put on a page. It gets even harder if you want to put a standard heading at the top of each page, keep field widths constant, and so on. These kinds of reports are the bane of a programmer's existence.

Perl's format function lets you describe how to lay out a page, which is then written out with the write function. format has many ways of letting you describe what you want where, what to do at page breaks, and so on.

The following functions deal with formats:

- ✔ format
- ✔ formline
- ✔ write

Data Packing

If you deal with binary data much, you know how hard it is to convert back and forth between regular numbers and the various kinds of binary encodings. Perl can help here with its pack and unpack functions, which have templates (much like printf) that describe how to convert between regular numbers and their binary equivalents. A related function, vec, lets you quickly create a binary array and pick values out of it.

These functions deal with data packing:

- ✔ pack
- ✔ unpack
- ✔ vec

Debugging

After you have written a program, you test it. It always works just fine the first time, right? Right? Er, no. Rarely have I written a program of over 25 lines that worked exactly as I expected the first time. When your program does not work as planned, you have to read your program carefully to try to figure out what went wrong. Another common step is to add lots of print statements in the program to see what is happening. This incremental fix-test-fix-test process is called *debugging*.

Perl also has a built-in debugging mode that lets you look inside your program using debugging commands. To start Perl in debugging mode, you add -d to the command line. Perl lets you step through your program, one line at a time, to see what each variable has in it.

Handling System Processes

Perl programs can create their own processes, allowing Perl programs to run as *daemons,* programs that run all the time in the background. You can also look at and change processes. These kinds of tasks require a deep understanding of the innards of your operating system and are thus beyond the scope of this book.

These functions deal with system processes:

- ✔ alarm
- ✔ chroot
- ✔ fork
- ✔ getpgrp
- ✔ getppid
- ✔ getpriority
- ✔ kill
- ✔ pipe
- ✔ setpgrp
- ✔ setpriority
- ✔ times
- ✔ umask
- ✔ wait
- ✔ waitpid

Advanced File Functions

Perl has many functions for reading and writing directly to your disk, bypassing the normal operating system methods. These functions are convenient if you know what you are doing and *very* dangerous if you don't. The functions in this section mostly match exactly what is available to Unix system programmers.

The following functions deal with advanced file handling:

- ✔ fcntl
- ✔ fileno
- ✔ flock
- ✔ ioctl
- ✔ select
- ✔ sysopen
- ✔ sysread
- ✔ syswrite

Advanced Internet Functions

Chapters 11 and 15 cover many topics relating to Perl and the Internet. Perl has many more Internet-related functions, mostly emulating the standard Unix system calls for Internet names and addresses. These functions are useful only on Unix hosts connected to the Internet.

These functions deal with advanced Internet handling:

- endhostent
- endnetent
- endprotoent
- endservent
- gethostbyaddr
- gethostbyname
- gethostent
- getnetbyaddr
- getnetbyname
- getnetent
- getprotobyname
- getprotobynumber
- getprotoent
- getservbyname
- getservbyport
- getservent
- sethostent
- setnetent
- setprotoent
- setservent

Advanced Programmer Aids

Perl has a wide variety of functions that are mostly valuable only to advanced programmers. These functions are a mishmash, covering topics like creating object-oriented programs and looking inside Perl's variables. There is also one operator, \, that falls into this category, because it is used with references.

These functions are used as advanced programmer aids:

- bless
- dump
- import
- ref
- study
- tie
- tied
- undef
- untie
- wantarray

Sockets and Other Communications

All Unix networking is based on the concept of a *socket,* an electronic data pipe between two computers. Sockets have nothing to do with hardware: They are software metaphors for physical sockets. Other operating systems use sockets or socketlike ideas as well.

If you are creating programs that do any network communications, you use sockets. Fortunately, the Internet-related functions covered earlier in this book hide all the socket-related functions so you don't have to learn about the intricacies of setting up and using them.

Perl also has support for other communications concepts that are common in Unix systems. For example, processes can communicate through *messages* and *semaphores,* and you can use Perl functions to create these kinds of communications.

The following functions are used for sockets and other communications:

- accept
- bind
- connect
- getpeername
- getsockname
- getsockopt
- listen
- msgctl
- msgget
- msgrcv
- msgsnd
- recv

- semctl
- semget
- semop
- send
- setsockopt
- shmctl
- shmget
- shmread
- shmwrite
- shutdown
- socket
- socketpair

These Didn't Fit Anywhere

Don't you just hate it when you are putting things into nice, neat little categories, and there are one or two things that don't fit? You would really rather throw them out, or pretend that they got "lost," but you're too honest for that (usually).

The end result is that you give them more attention than they are due. In this case, there are two Perl functions that don't fit anywhere else in the book. crypt is used for checking Unix passwords; it's a one-way encryption function. The syscall function lets Unix programmers make operating system calls directly from Perl.

These functions defy categorization:

- ✔ crypt
- ✔ syscall

Chapter 22

Ten Really Short, Really Useful Perl Programs

• •

In This Chapter

▶ Seeing how short a good Perl program can be

▶ Printing, sorting, and listing files and directories

▶ Working with passwords and calculators

• •

*Y*ou've seen both long and short programs throughout this book. Some people don't believe that short programs can do very much, but that's not true for Perl. A couple of lines of Perl code can go a long way. This chapter lists some of my favorite teeny Perl programs.

Collecting Unique Lines

If your text file has a lot of lines that are duplicates and you only want to see the unique lines, you can collect them into an array (in this case called @Unique) with the following:

```
open(IN, "somefile.txt"); @Unique=();
while(<IN>) { unless($i{$_}++) { push(@Unique, $_) } }
```

The trick here is that $i{$_}++ will return 0 the first time you create a key-value pair with $_ as the key, and some nonzero value after that.

Getting Rid of Multiple Blank Lines

Some text files have multiple consecutive blank lines, which make them hard to read, particularly on smaller screens. The following program prints a text file, compressing all instances of two or more blank lines into a single blank line. Note that a "blank line" can have whitespace characters on it, such as spaces and tabs, but no displayable characters.

```
open(IN, "somefile.txt"); $PrevBlank = 0;
while(<IN>) {
    if(/\S/ or !$PrevBlank) { print $_ }
    $PrevBlank = /^\s*$/;
}
```

The if statement is true if there are nonblank characters on the line or if the previous line was not blank. The $PrevBlank assignment tells whether the current line is blank, meaning that it has zero or more whitespace characters and nothing else.

Printing Lines from a File in Sorted Order

It's easy to forget how useful Perl's sort function is. This program reads the entire file into an array, sorts the array, and prints the result. Short and sweet, and pretty efficient to boot.

```
open(IN, "somefile.txt");
print sort(<IN>);
```

Printing a Range of Lines from a File

Have you ever wanted to read just a few lines from a file, not the whole thing? The following program prints just a range of lines. You run the program with two arguments: the range you want and the file name. For instance, if you name your program "showline," and you want to see lines 10 through 20 of the somefile.txt file, you would give this command line:

```
showline 10-20 somefile.txt
```

Here is the program to print a range of lines:

```
open(IN, $ARGV[1]) or die "Could not read $File.\n";
($Start, $Stop) = split(/-/, $ARGV[0]);
for($i=1; $i<=$Stop; $i += 1)
    { $Line = <IN>; if($i>=$Start) { print $Line } }
```

Listing Only Files in a Directory

Sometimes you know that there are subdirectories in a directory, but you only care about the files. You can use the -f file test to list all the files in a directory.

```
foreach $f (<*>) { if(-f $f) { print "$f\n" } }
```

Listing a Directory by Size

To get a directory listing sorted by anything other than the file name, you have to keep a list of names and the other items. Associative arrays are great for this. The following program makes an associative array with the sizes and then sorts the items for output. You can easily modify this program to sort by date.

```
foreach $f (<*>) { $i{$f} = -s $f };
foreach $k (sort{ $i{$b} <=> $i{$a} } keys %i)
    { printf "%8d %s\n", $i{$k}, $k }
```

Sorting Directories by Extension

Sorting by part of the file name is a bit more difficult than sorting by size or date. The following program breaks the file name into two and sorts by the second part. If you are running on a Unix or Macintosh system, this program only works predictably if the file names only have zero or one period.

```
foreach $FullName (<*>) {
    ($Name, $Ext) = split(/\./, $FullName, 2);
    push(@Temp, "$Ext\t$FullName");
}
foreach $Val (sort(@Temp)) {
    ($Ext, $FullName) = split(/\t/, $Val);
    print "$FullName\n";
}
```

A Very Simple Calculator

Ever wanted a quick-and-dirty calculator? Let Perl do all the work. This program just uses Perl's `eval` function to print out the answers to each equation you enter. To end the program, enter a blank line. For example, you can enter something like

```
((2**8) + (3**8))
```

and receive the answer

```
Answer = 6817
```

Here is the program for the calculator:

```
while(<STDIN>) {
    $i = $_; chomp($i); unless($i) { last }
    $o = eval($i); print "Answer = $o\n";
}
```

Randomizing a List

It's easy enough in Perl to generate random numbers, but randomizing the order of an array isn't quite as easy. However, you can use the `splice` function to pull a random element from the array and then place the element in another array. The following program randomizes the list `@MyList`.

```
my @TempList = ();
while(@MyList)
    { push(@TempList, splice(@MyList, rand(@MyList), 1)) }
@MyList = @TempList;
```

The trick here is that `rand(@MyList)` picks a number between 0 and the number of elements in `@MyList`, and `splice` changes this into an integer.

Generating Random Mnemonic Passwords

Security is a tricky thing, mostly because it is hard to get computer users to pay any attention to it. Trying to convince people to use good, unguessable passwords is by far one of the hardest jobs for a system administrator.

The following program generates random passwords. Instead of a jumble of hard-to-remember letters, however, the passwords have a mnemonic quality of being pairs of consonants and vowels. By stringing together these humorous-sounding syllables, you can generate easy-to-remember nonsense phrases. Each syllable can represent one of 100 numbers, so a single four-syllable password like "votahubo" is one of 100 million (that is, 100 to the fourth power) possible passwords generated by the program. This should give you much more security than letting your users pick their own passwords.

```
print "Enter a seed number: "; $s=<STDIN>;
srand($s ^ time);
@c=split(/ */, "bcdfghjklmnprstvwxyz");
@v=split(/ */, "aeiou");
for($i = 1; $i <=4; $i += 1)
    { print $c[int(rand(20))], $v[int(rand(5))] }
```

The first two lines initialize the seed for the random numbers, and the next two lines create lists containing the 20 consonants (minus "q") and the 5 vowels. The for loop simply prints the four syllables.

Chapter 23

Ten Great Perl Sites on the Web

*I*f you want to go further with Perl than this book has taken you (and I sincerely hope that you do!), the best way to find out more is to look around the World Wide Web for Perl resources. The Perl community has contributed thousands of hours of work, mostly for free, and most of it is available on the Web. Happy hunting!

The Perl Institute

```
http://www.perl.org/
```

Until recently, there was no single, easy-to-reach, group of people who were dedicated to helping Perl thrive. The Perl Institute is now that group. Their own blurb describes it best:

"The Perl Institute is dedicated to making Perl more useful for everyone. We are a non-profit organization, established to support the community of people who use Perl and to support the development of Perl as a language. The Institute acts as a coordinating and communication center to connect people, information, ideas and resources."

This is a great resource for finding Perl professionals, particularly trainers and programmers.

Perl Language Home Page

```
http://www.perl.com/perl/
```

Another excellent general resource for Perl is the Perl Language Home Page. It is a collection of a wealth of information about Perl and the people supporting it. This is a great place to look if you want a feeling about the breadth and depth of the Perl world. The Perl Language Home Page is a great example of dweeb advocacy. It is fiercely (although not completely) pro-Perl and exhibits a boosterism that makes you think that it is supporting a political candidate or a contestant for homecoming queen. However, instead of just talking about how wonderful Perl is, the site makes its point by providing lots and lots of information.

CPAN, the Comprehensive Perl Archive Network

```
http://www.perl.com/CPAN/README.html
```

The vast majority of the CD-ROM that comes with this book consists of the CPAN library. CPAN is a huge network of volunteers who contribute Perl software and organize it in an accessible fashion. The Web link for CPAN doesn't actually lead to a Web page but to one of the many FTP sites that replicate CPAN. As you can see from the CD-ROM, there's an incredible amount of useful material in the CPAN library. If you become a serious Perl programmer, you should certainly consider contributing to CPAN. Even if you don't become serious, you should visit one of the CPAN sites so you can get the latest versions of programs found on the CD-ROM.

The Perl Journal

```
http://orwant.www.media.mit.edu/the_perl_journal/
```

This site is the Web presence for the (at the time of this writing) only magazine that covers Perl exclusively. Although the magazine is just starting, it has already run many interesting articles that would-be Perl programmers will find fascinating. Although the content of the magazine isn't available online (they have to make money somehow!), the Web site has copies of the programs covered in the magazine. There are also tables of contents for previous issues in case you want to order issues one at a time.

MacPerl

```
http://www.iis.ee.ethz.ch/~neeri/macintosh/perl.html
```

MacPerl's author, Matthias Neeracher, hosts a useful MacPerl resource. This page has many links to other MacPerl resources, such as sample programs, hint documents, and so on.

Even if you are a Windows user, I suggest that you take a look at the MacPerl home page. MacPerl is much better integrated into the Mac than Perl-Win32 is into Windows 95 or Windows NT, and this page is a good example of how Mac users try harder than their Windows-based compatriots. If you are a Perl-Win32 user and have a friend with a Mac, you may want to have them go to this site and take a look at MacPerl.

Perl-Win32

```
http://www.perl.hip.com/
```

Most readers of this book will be Windows users, so being able to find out more about Perl-Win32 will be quite important. This Web site, maintained by the people who wrote Perl-Win32, is a good place to find the latest version of the software as well as to find related material. At the time this book was written, the site didn't have many links to other sites covering Perl-Win32. It appears that the people who wrote Perl-Win32 aren't supporting or promoting it nearly as much as the MacPerl folks. Hopefully, the situation has changed by the time you read this and there is more support for the program.

libwww-perl

```
http://www.ics.uci.edu/pub/websoft/libwww-perl/
```

If you are doing anything with making a Web client in Perl, or even just doing HTTP or FTP access, you should definitely check out libwww-perl, which is short for "Library of WWW functions, written in Perl" (or something like that). Chapter 15 contains a few examples of using libwww-perl, but the library goes much beyond what is shown there. The library gives you very precise control over how you access Web and FTP servers on the Internet. The Web page is still maintained by Roy Fielding, who wrote the Perl 4 version of libwww-perl.

Earl Hood's Home Page

```
http://www.oac.uci.edu/indiv/ehood/
```

This page is a great example of what individual Perl programmers do to make their work available to the public. The page is simple and to the point and contains a handful of useful Perl programs, some of which are also available on CPAN and the CD-ROM that comes with this book. The programs on this site are excellent examples of what Perl can be used for if you're willing to throw some time into it. Hood has written programs that make mailing list archives, handle HTML and SGML documents, and perform other kinds of conversions.

Jeffrey Friedl's Home Page

```
http://enterprise.ic.gc.ca/~jfriedl/perl/
```

Here's another example of a serious Perl hacker who gives away lots of good code. Jeffrey's page has full-featured programs for doing things like Web access and translating Japanese characters. The programs here can be very useful even if you don't know Perl. For example, `search` lets you look for particular text in a whole directory and all its subdirectories in a single command. There are also programs for creating transparent GIF image files, converting text files to Postscript, and doing many other things.

Malcolm Beattie's Work on Perl5

```
http://users.ox.ac.uk/~mbeattie/perl.html
```

This site is probably of more interest to intermediate and advanced Perl programmers, but it is a good representative of where Perl is going. Malcolm has produced some excellent tools for serious Perl programmers, including libraries that link Perl to the popular Tcl/Tk programming framework. This page also has links to Safe CGI Perl, which allows system administrators to let system users write CGI programs in Perl without worrying as much about the security of the resulting programs.

Chapter 24

Ten Differences Between Perl 4 and Perl 5

. . . .

In This Chapter

▶ Understanding what is new in Perl 5

▶ Comparing Perl 4 and Perl 5

. . . .

M any people who learned to program Perl using Perl version 4 don't see what all the fuss is about with Perl 5. Almost everything done in Perl 5 can be done in Perl 4, and Perl 5 doesn't do it any faster.

Some of the differences between Perl 4 and Perl 5, however, are quite important. They allow intermediate and advanced Perl programmers to make better programs — in particular, programs that other people can use more easily. Of course, there are a few small changes that are mostly for convenience, but the big ones (which are listed first here) make Perl 5 a much more robust and useful language.

Multidimensional Lists

This feature, described in Chapter 16, lets you create lists that are more than a single set of items. Multidimensional lists allow you to have lists of records for a database, for example.

Better Error Messages

Not that Perl 4's error messages were all that bad, but Perl 5 error messages are much more informative about what went wrong in your program. Of course, this makes finding the errors and fixing them all that much easier.

Objects

Perl's new object-oriented features, described in Chapter 19, allow you to use parts of programs created by other people using a standardized programming interface. Although creating objects is beyond the scope of this book, using them is quite simple and lets you have access to the hundreds of modules available on the CD-ROM.

Modules

Even without using object-oriented programming, Perl's new module approach lets you compartmentalize your programs so that variables are not seen outside of a particular module. This is useful if you are sharing code with other programmers and don't want their variables messing with yours except in a controlled fashion.

Interactions with C Programs

For advanced programmers, Perl can now be linked with programs written in C. Perl programs can have parts written in C, and vice versa. This feature allows programmers to use C for what it is best for and Perl for what it is best for.

POSIX

Perl 5 includes a library that allows programmers to access essentially all of the identifiers in POSIX version 1003.1. In short, this means that companies and government agencies that have specified that all programs they use must be "POSIX compliant" can use Perl 5 programs that use the POSIX library. It turns out that this is a pretty large market, and thus a boon for Perl programmers.

Case-changing Functions

The lc, lcfirst, uc, and ucfirst functions in Perl 5 make it a bit easier to change the case of letters in strings. You could do this in Perl 4, but the new functions make more sense.

map

The new map function is a useful feature for people who process lists a lot. It returns a single list that is the result of repeatedly running an expression or a block on another list.

chomp

Okay, so this one is pretty trivial, but I use it all the time. chomp does what chop is mostly used for, namely to remove the end-of-line character or characters from a string. Because some operating systems, notably MS-DOS and Windows, have two end-of-line characters instead of one, this is pretty handy.

More Programmers! More Free Stuff!

Although the Perl community was constantly growing even before Perl 5 was developed, Perl 5 has caused even more people to get interested in Perl. The community has been enriched with much more freely accessible code, particularly through CPAN, partially due to the modular and object-oriented features in Perl 5.

Chapter 25

Ten Reasons Why Perl Is Better Than Java

In This Chapter

▶ Comparing the most overhyped language with the most useful one

▶ Understanding the benefits of Perl

*O*kay, okay, so this is a pretty provocative title. Some folks just love Perl, and many of us are getting pretty tired of hearing "Java, Java, Java" as if it were the only valuable programming language on earth.

More than a year after its release, Java has still to prove its worth. The wonderful programs that are being promised are still vaporware as this book is being written. Perl, on the other hand, runs the Internet day in and day out.

By the way, please don't interpret this chapter as meaning "Perl is better than Java in every way." It isn't. There are many useful features of Java that Perl can't match. They are designed for different tasks, and Java excels at some of the tasks for which it is designed. Still, Perl can hold its own on many counts.

Java requires predeclaration of variables

If you're trying to whip together a quick program, nothing gets in the way more than having to tell the programming language ahead of time the name of every variable you are going to use and the type of variable it is. Some programmers have no problems with predeclaration, but most folks find it tedious and the cause of many error messages when testing their programs.

Java forces you to use an object model; Perl makes objects an option

Object-oriented programming, described in Chapter 19, is useful in some cases but overkill in others. With Java, almost everything is a class, and you can't even put out simple messages on the screen without using object-oriented syntax. Perl is much more flexible: Use objects if you want, ignore them if you want.

Strings in Java are much harder to handle than strings in Perl

Java has the same problems with text as most other programming languages do: few functions and clunky handling of string variables. You have to create all your own string-handling features in Java. It's as if the people writing Java forgot how much people like using text.

Perl handles lists with ease

The Java model says that less is more, and there is certainly not much in the way of list handling built into Java. As with strings, Java provides almost nothing for handing lists. Perl, of course, gives you lots to work with.

Perl can do many more system-level tasks

Because Java is meant to be secure, it has very few built-in features for handing system-level functions like process handling, file manipulation, and so on. Again, you have to build your own or use one of the many third-party libraries.

Perl is always free

Most usable implementations of Java cost money, sometimes a lot of money. Dozens of companies are willing to sell you Java programming environments, class libraries, debuggers, and so on. Almost everything in the Perl world, and certainly the main language systems, is free.

You can't write many useful one-line Java programs

If you want to do a quickie little single-function program in Java, you still have to write about a dozen lines. Most of this is due to Java's forcing you into object-orientated programming even when it makes little sense.

Most sample Perl programs do a lot more than put animated pictures in a Web browser

As I write this, Java has been out more than a year, and most of the sample Java programs that you can find are for cute little Web applets. Animated balls bouncing around are all well and good, but where's the serious Internet code, the serious conversion programs, and so on that have been available to Perl programmers for so many years?

Perl programmers didn't immediately come up with dozens of dumb oyster jokes

This is more of a criticism of the marketing departments of Java companies and the bored headline writers of the trade press. Many industry pundits have called for a moratorium on cloying names that are related to coffee, but to no avail. Sure, caffeine is the most frequently used stimulant in the world, but that's no reason to extend the joke as far as it has gone.

Perl isn't named after the capital island of a government that has killed hundreds of thousands of people in a forced takeover of another country

The 1996 Nobel Peace Prize went to Carlos Felipe Ximenes Belo and Jose Ramos-Horta for their work in continuing to remind the world about the plight of East Timor, a country that was invaded by Indonesia in 1975. In the past 20 years, the government of Indonesia, headquartered on the island of Java, has killed over 200,000 people who have resisted the bloody takeover.

Appendix A
What's on the CD-ROM

• •

*T*he CD-ROM that comes with this book contains copies of Perl for various computers, many of the programs from the earlier chapters, and the CPAN library of all things Perl. There isn't much of an "interface" to the CD-ROM, you just pop it in your computer and it looks like another disk.

Because of the differences between the two operating systems, Windows 95 users and Macintosh users each only see about half of the full CD-ROM. However, that half is enough, given how much space there is on the CD-ROM. Windows 95 (and Windows NT) users won't see any of the Macintosh files, and vice versa.

The instructions for installing Perl on Windows, Mac, and Unix, are all in Chapter 2. This appendix mostly talks about the CPAN library and how you can access it from the CD-ROM.

The CPAN Library

You've heard a fair amount about the CPAN library in different chapters in the book. Basically, it's everything that is freely available about Perl, including the Perl program itself. It is constantly being updated, and the CD-ROM has a snapshot of much of the library from mid-December 1996.

The best way to describe CPAN is to let the person who put it together, Jarkko Hietaniemi, describe it himself. From the README file:

> The basic principle of CPAN is being distributed. It would be quite frankly impossible to coordinate the numerous resources so that all the people contributing Perl material would enter their contributions into some central site. Therefore, most of the contents of the CPAN will be mirrored from other sites, CPAN will just pull all the various resources together and layer them together into a (hopefully) coherent whole.

This modest statement makes it sound like CPAN is a smallish set of files mirrored from other sites: nothing could be further from the truth. The archive is well over 200 megabytes and comes from dozens (maybe hundreds) of FTP sites all over the world and processed before being put out on the main CPAN directory in Finland. As you might imagine, that task is performed with Perl.

Files in the Library

There is no way to sensibly list all the files in the archive here: most are of no interest to most readers of this book. However, it is good to understand the general structure of the archive so you can move around the CD-ROM easily. Or, if you have access to an FTP client and the Internet, you can use this guide as you move around the directory on a local FTP site.

The files of general interest at the top level of the library are:

File	Description
CPAN.TXT	Where you can find the local CPAN mirror FTP site
ENDINGS.TXT	Description of all the file name endings (extensions) and what they mean
README.TXT	General introduction to the CPAN library
ROADMAP.TXT	Overview of the directory structure

The main directories at the top level of the library are:

Directory	Description
authors	The contributed files, arranged by the author's name (actually, by an abbreviation of the author's name)
clpa	Archive of the messages that were posted in the comp.lang.perl.announce newsgroup on Usenet
doc	Perl documentation in various formats (text, pod, HTML, and so on)
indices	Lists of all the files in the library

Directory	Description
misc	Files that are hard to categorize
modules	Modules and extensions, mostly for Perl 5
other-archives	An archaic collection of really old Perl stuff
ports	Perl for non-Unix operating systems
scripts	Full Perl programs
src	Source code for Perl for Unix

Remember that the snapshot of the library on the CD-ROM is a snapshot from mid-December, and that it is likely that hundreds of the files have been updated by the time you read this. Thus, you may want to check the most local CPAN mirror when you use files from the CD-ROM.

CPAN on the CD-ROM

Due to space limitations and some pretty daunting restrictions on how CD-ROMs are made, the CD-ROM that comes with this book doesn't have all the files from CPAN. For example, the "authors" directory is missing, although all the files that were there are included in the other directories.

However, there is a worse problem with putting together the CD-ROM, one that I'm pretty embarrassed about. Due to a combination of poorly-written CD-ROM driver software, incompatible naming schemes, and other bad dweeb stuff, we couldn't just copy the CPAN library file-for-file to the CD-ROM: most of the readers of this book wouldn't have been able to use it. What we did was an ugly kludge, but the end result is that you can still get at the files.

That kludge is an old (really, *really* old) Unix program called *tar*. A tar archive is a collection of files put into a single package. In order to get at the files, you have to open the package and pick the ones you want. Fortunately, that's pretty easy for both Windows and Mac users. Unfortunately, we had to use ugly MS-DOS compatible names for everything.

Each of the smaller directories from CPAN was turned into a tar archive. If the directory was too large, only the directories beneath it was turned into a tar archive. The following shows the archive names and their equivalence with the CPAN library.

CD-ROM archive	*CPAN directory*
CLPA.TAR	clpa
DOC.TAR	doc
INDICES.TAR	indices
MISC.TAR	misc
MODULES	modules
OTHERARC.TAR	other-archives
PORTS	ports
SCRIPTS.TAR	scripts
SRC	src

Note that MODULES, PORTS, and SRC each have a structure under them. The structure under each is pretty much the same as it is in CPAN, but some of the names have been changed to fit the grukky old MS-DOS naming scheme.

The rest of this appendix shows you how you can investigate what's in the tar archives and copy individual files out of the archives and onto your hard disk.

Getting at the files on Windows 95

To get into the tar archives, you use the *WinZip* program that is provided on the CD-ROM. You'll remember WinZip from Chapter 2, because you needed it to extract Perl-Win32 from its .ZIP file. Here, WinZip performs yet another great task: it lets you open tar archives. In this section, all we really care about here is getting at the files from the archives on the CD-ROM onto your hard disk. Remember that WinZip is shareware, and in my opinion one of the best shareware deals available anywhere.

To view a tar archive, choose the "Open Archive" command from the File menu. In the dialog box, choose the "all archives" option in the "Files of type:" choice so that WinZip will show you tar archives in the main list. Then simply choose the archive you want and click the "Open" button. Because WinZip shows many columns of information, you should expand WinZip's window to its fullest width. Also, note that you can sort the list you see by any of the columns by clicking on the column names near the top of the window.

To extract one file, simply select it by clicking on it, and then click the "Extract" button. To extract more than one file at a time, click the first file, then hold down the Ctrl key and click the next file, and so on. If you want to select a set of files that are next to each other in the list, holding down the Shift key when you click on the second file causes WinZip to select all the files between the first and second file. When you've selected what you want, click the "Extract" button.

When WinZip extracts files to your hard disk, it recreates the directory structure of the tar archive. Thus, if you've chosen to extract a file that is listed as being "FAQs/META/metaFAQ.txt", WinZip will create a folder called "FAQs" and put a folder called "META" inside of it, and then extract the file you want inside of that inner folder.

Getting at the files on a Mac

To get into the tar archives, you use the *suntar* program that is provided on the CD-ROM. suntar lets you open archives, create new ones, and a host of other features, but all we really care about here is getting at the files from the archives on the CD-ROM onto your hard disk.

suntar's interface isn't exactly Mac-like, but it isn't hard either. The trick to using suntar to read existing tar archives is knowing that you have to first use the "Open file/decode" command from the File menu and specify the archive you want to look into. Giving this command opens a window that only tells you that you opened the archive, not what was in the archive.

The second, and more interesting step, is to use the "Extract selected files" command from the File menu. This command puts up a list of the files in the archive that you opened in the previous step. Since the archives are fairly large, and CD-ROMs are notoriously slow, this step can take some time. After suntar has listed all the files in the archive, the rest is pretty easy.

To extract one file, simply select it by clicking on it, and then click the "Extract" button. To extract more than one file at a time, click the first file, then hold down the Command key and click the next file, and so on. If you want to select a set of files that are next to each other in the list, holding down the Shift key when you click on the second file causes suntar to select all the files between the first and second file. When you've selected what you want, click the "Extract" button.

When suntar extracts files to your hard disk, it recreates the directory structure of the tar archive. Thus, if you've chosen to extract a file that is listed as being "FAQs/mac/MacPerlFAQ.txt", suntar will create a folder called "FAQs" and then put a folder called "mac" inside of it, and then extract the file you want inside of that inner folder.

Appendix B
The Great Perl Reference

● ●

Perl Operators

The following is a list of Perl's operators. Note that some Perl books call some features "operators," while other Perl books call the same features "functions." Perl's flexibility (and overall looseness) makes it much less clear what is an operator and what is a function.

Operator	Description	Chapter
x	Character repeat and list repeat.	5
.	String concatenation.	5
=	Assignment.	6
+	Add.	6
-	Subtract.	6
*	Multiply.	6
/	Divide.	6
%	Modulo divide.	6
-	Unary negation: negates the number it precedes.	6
+	Unary plus: does nothing.	6
*	Raise to the power.	6
++	Unary increment; can be used before or after a variable to increment before or after the variable is evaluated. Thus, if $a is 5, $a++ is 5 until it is evaluated, and then $a becomes 6; ++$a is 6 when it is evaluated.	6
- -	Unary decrement; can be used before or after a variable to decrement before or after the variable is evaluated. Thus, if $a is 5, $a- - is 5 until it is evaluated, and then $a becomes 4; - -$a is 4 when it is evaluated.	6
+= .= etc.	Assignment after operation. For example, $a += 3 means to add 3 to $a and store that value in $a.	6
,	List separator.	7

Operator	Description	Chapter
..	Range.	7
< > <= >= == != <=>	Numeric comparisons: less than, greater than, less than or equal to, greater than or equal to, equal to, not equal to, comparison.	8
eq ne cmp lt gt le ge	String to comparisons: less than, greater than, less than or equal to, greater than or equal to, equal to, not equal to, comparison.	8
not	Logical not. Can also be !.	8
and	Logical and. Can also be &&.	8
or	Logical or. Can also be ||.	8
xor	Logical xor.	8
?:	Conditional comparison: TEST ? IFTRUE : IFFALSE	8
~	Bitwise logical not.	9
&	Bitwise logical and.	9
|	Bitwise logical or.	9
^	Bitwise logical xor.	9
<< >>	Bit shift to the left and to the right.	9
<>	I/O operator, such as <STDIN>.	12
=~ !~	Binds a scalar on the left to a pattern match, substitution, or translation on the right. !~ returns the inverse of the bound value.	14
m/PATTERN/ MODIFIERS	Searches for the pattern and returns true if found. Can also be specified without the m.	14
s/PATTERN/ REPLACEMENT/ MODIFIERS	Searches for the pattern and replaces it with the specified text.	14
tr/FROMRANGE/ TORANGE/	Returns a string with letters translated from one range to another. The tr with y operators are identical.	14
=>	List separator; same as comma.	16
` (backtick)	Runs the command between the two backticks and returns the STDOUT.	18
->	Dereference. Usually used with object-oriented programs as CLASS->METHOD.	19
\	Reference.	21

Operator Precedence

Although it is always safer to use parentheses to group your operations, some programmers like to trust Perl's rules for deciding which operators will be evaluated first. The following table lists the operators from most precedence (meaning that they will be evaluated first) to least precedence. If operators have equal precedence (they are on the same line in the table below), Perl evaluates them left to right.

For instance, this statement

```
$a = 3 / 4 ** 2;
```

would be interpreted as

```
$a = 3 / (4 ** 2);
```

because ** has higher precedence than / and is therefore evaluated first.

Here is the order of precedence:

```
->
++ --
**
! ~ \ {unary +} {unary -}
=~ !~
* / % x
+ - .
<< >>
< > <= >= lt gt le ge
== != <=> eq ne cmp
&
| ^
&&
||
.
?:
= += -= *= etc.
, =>
not
and
or xor
```

Perl's Functions and Statements

The following lengthy table shows all Perl's functions and statements, arranged in alphabetical order.

Name	*Brief Description*	*Chapter*	*New in Perl 5*
abs(NUMBER)	Takes the absolute value of the argument (that is, negative numbers are simply turned positive).	6	
accept (NEWSOCKETHANDLE, GENERICSOCKETHANDLE)	Accepts a connection on a socket.	21	
alarm(TIME)	Sends the SIGALRM signal to this program after the specified number of seconds.	21	
atan2(Y, X)	Returns the arctangent of Y/X.	6	
bind(SOCKET, NAME	Assigns a name to an existing open socket.	21	
binmode (FILEHANDLE)	Tells Perl to treat the file as a binary file. It has no function under Unix or MacOS.	13	
bless(REFERENCE, PACKAGE)	Tells the item that is referred to in the reference that it is an object in the specified package. If the package is not specified, Perl uses the current package.	21	
caller (NUMBEROFSTACKS)	Tells about the stack of subroutine calls. The argument is the number of subroutine calls to unnest. With an argument, it returns a list with the package name, file name, line number, subroutine name, whether or not the subroutine has arguments, and whether or not the subroutine wants an array as its argument. Without an argument, this returns just the first three list items, referring to the current subroutine.	10	
chdir(DIRNAME)	Changes the working directory of the program to the specified directory or, with no argument, changes to the home directory of the user. Returns true if successful, false if not (such as if the directory doesn't exist).	12	
chmod(NUMMODE, LISTOFFILES)	Changes the access permissions on one or more files. The first argument must be a octal file mode, such as 0777. The function returns the number of files successfully changed.	13	

Name	Brief Description	Chapter	New in Perl 5
chomp(STRINGVAR)	Removes the line ending from the end of the string variable, returning the number of characters deleted. If the last character is not a line-ending character, as defined in the special variable $/, nothing is removed. If $/ is two characters, both are removed. Note that this function changes the value of the variable. You can also use chomp(LIST), in which case the line ending from the end of each of the list items is removed.	5	New
chop(STRINGVAR)	Removes the last character from the end of the string variable, returning the character deleted. Note that this function changes the value of the variable.	5	
chown(USERID, GROUPID, LISTOFFILES)	Changes the user and group ownership of one or more files. The userid and groupid must be numbers, not names. The function returns the number of files successfully changed.	13	
chr(NUMBER)	Returns the character represented by the argument.	5	
chroot(DIRECTORY)	Changes the root directory available to a program to the one specified. This means that the named directory now becomes "/" to the program and the program cannot modify or even see other directories above this one in the directory hierarchy.	18	
close(FILEHANDLE)	Closes a file opened with the open function.	12	
closedir (DIRHANDLE)	Closes a directory opened by the opendir function.	13	
connect(SOCKET, NETADDRESS)	Connects to another process using the specified socket.	21	
continue { BLOCK }	Executes the block. The real use of the continue statement is following other blocks, because it is executed when other blocks exit.	8	
cos(NUMBER)	Returns the cosine of the number, expressed in radians.	6	
crypt (PLAINTEXT, SALT)	Encrypts the first argument using the salt. This function is highly system dependent, meaning that you can get very different results on different operating systems.	21	

Name	Brief Description	Chapter	New in Perl 5
dbmclose(ARRAY)	Breaks the binding between the array and the DBM file that was associated with it by an earlier dbmopen function.	17	
dbmopen(ARRAY, FILENAME, MODE)	Begins associating an associative array with the named database. The mode is the octal file mode with which to open the database. This function clears out any values already in the associative array.	17	
defined(VARIABLE)	Returns true if the variable has been defined, meaning if it has a valid string, numeric, or reference value. This is useful for testing the return value from a function that returns undefined values in error conditions.	9	
delete($ARRAY{KEY})	Removes a key and its value from an associative array.	16	
die(TEXT)	Prints the text to the standard error output and terminates the Perl program. The program returns the value that was in the $! special variable.	10	
do { BLOCK }	Executes the block and returns the value of the last expression in the block.	21	
do(FILENAME)	Executes the statements in the file and returns the value of the last expression in the file.	21	
dump	Causes a core dump, if the operating system supports it. You can also specify a label, which the program will start from if you somehow re-create the core from the dump.	21	
each(ARRAY)	Returns a two-item list of the key and value for the next value in the array.	16	
endgrent	Resets the cycling through the group list started by the getgrent function.	18	
endhostent	Resets the cycling through the host list started by the gethostent function.	21	
endnetent	Resets the cycling through the network list started by the getnetent function.	21	
endprotoent	Resets the cycling through the protocol list started by the getprotoent function.	21	
endpwent	Resets the cycling through the password list started by the getpwent function.	18	

Name	Brief Description	Chapter	New in Perl 5
endservent	Resets the cycling through the server list started by the getservent function.	21	
eof(FILEHANDLE)	Returns true if the next read on the file handle would read off the end of the file.	13	
eval(EXPRESSION)	Perl executes the expression as though it were a Perl program. The expression can be one or more statements.	10	
exec(PROGRAM)	Causes the Perl program to stop and the program named in the argument to be run. The argument can be a list, in which case each item is passed as elements of the command line to be executed.	18	
exists ($ARRAY{$KEY})	Returns true if the specified key exists in the specified array.	16	
exit(NUMBER)	Stops the program. The argument is used as the return value for the program.	10	
exp(NUMBER)	Returns e raised to the power of the argument.	6	
fcntl(FILEHANDLE, FUNCTION, SCALAR)	Executes Unix's fctl function for performing low-level file control.	21	
File tests: -X FILENAME	Returns values based on the file. File tests include tests of whether or not the file exists, how many bytes are in the file, and so on.	12	
fileno(FILEHANDLE)	Returns the numeric file descriptor of the handle given, or the undef value if the file is not open.	21	
flock(FILEHANDLE, OPERATION)	Performs low-level file locking in Unix.	21	
for (INITEXPR; TESTEXPR; ENDEXPR) { BLOCK }	Executes the block repeatedly. The initial expression is evaluated first, followed by the test expression. If the test expression is true, the block is executed, and the end expression is evaluated. The test expression is then evaluated, and the loop continues.	8	
foreach VARIABLE (LIST) { BLOCK }	Executes the block repeatedly. For each item in the list, the variable is set to the items' value and the block is executed.	8	
fork	Starts a child process and returns the child processes' process ID number.	21	

Name	*Brief Description*	*Chapter*	*New in Perl 5*
`format NAME=` `FORMATLIST .`	Creates a format that can be used by the `write` function. The format list consists of lines that contain picture formats, lists of arguments, or comments.	21	
`formline(PICTURE,` `LIST)`	Formats a list of values according to the picture.	21	
`getc(FILEHANDLE)`	Returns the next byte from the file, or a null string if you are at the end of the file. If called without an argument, it returns the next byte from the standard file input.	13	
`getgrent`	Returns Unix group information from the next line of the /etc/group file. The list returned has four items: the group name, the group password (encrypted), the group number, and a string of all the members' names.	18	
`getgrgid(GROUPID)`	Returns information about the group, based on the group ID number. The list returned has four items: the group name, the group password (encrypted), the group number, and a string of all the members' names.	18	
`getgrnam` `(GROUPNAME)`	Returns information about the group, based on the group's name. The list returned has four items: the group name, the group password (encrypted), the group number, and a string of all the members' names.	18	

`gethostbyaddr`
`(PACKEDADDR,`
`ADDRTYPE)`
	Returns information about the host based on its address. The address argument is packed, probably with the `pack('C4')` function, and the address type is always 2 for Internet addresses. In scalar context, `gethostbyaddr` returns the host name; in list context it returns the host name, a string of aliases, the address type, the length of the returned list of packed addresses, and a list of packed addresses.	21	

`gethostbyname` `(DOMAINNAME)`	Returns information about the host based on its domain name. In scalar context, `gethostbyname` returns the IP address, packed; in list context it returns the host name, a string of aliases, the address type, the length of the returned list of packed addresses, and a list of packed addresses. You can unpack the IP address with the `unpack('C4')` function.	21	

Name	Brief Description	Chapter	New in Perl 5
gethostent	Returns the next record from the /etc/ hosts file. It returns the host name, a string of aliases, the address type, the length of the returned list of packed addresses, and a list of packed addresses.	21	
getlogin	Returns the current login name by querying the /etc/utmp file.	18	
getnetbyaddr (PACKEDADDR, ADDRTYPE)	Returns information about the network based on its address from the /etc/ networks file. The address argument is packed, probably with the pack('C4') function, and the address type is always 2 for Internet addresses. In scalar context, getnetbyaddr returns the network name; in list context it returns the network name, a string of aliases, the address type, and the packed address.	21	
getnetbyname (DOMAINNAME)	Returns information about the network based on its name from the /etc/networks file. In scalar context, getnetbyaddr returns the network name; in list context it returns the network name, a string of aliases, the address type, and the packed address.	21	
getnetent	Returns information from the next line in the /etc/networks file. In scalar context, getnetbyaddr returns the network name; in list context it returns the network name, a string of aliases, the address type, and the packed address.	21	
getpeername(SOCKET)	Returns the socket address of the other end of a connection. The address returned is packed.	21	
getpgrp(PROCESSID)	Returns the process group number for the given process number. Use an argument of 0 to indicate the current process.	18	
getppid	Returns the process number of the parent process.	18	
getpriority (PROCESSKIND, WHO)	Returns the priority of a process.	18	
getprotobyname (PROTONAME)	Returns information about a protocol based on its name. In scalar context, the protocol number is returned. In list context, the items in the list returned are the protocol name, aliases for the name, and the protocol number.	21	

Name	Brief Description	Chapter	New in Perl 5
getprotobynumber (PROTONUMBER)	Returns information about a protocol based on its number. In scalar context, the protocol name is returned. In list context, the items in the list returned are the protocol name, aliases for the name, and the protocol number.	21	
getprotoent	Returns the next record from the /etc/ protocols file. In scalar context, the protocol name is returned. In list context, the items in the list returned are the protocol name, aliases for the name, and the protocol number.	21	
getpwent	Returns user information from the next line of the /etc/passwd file. The list returned has nine items: the user name, the password (encrypted), the user number, the group number, the quota field, the comment field, the gcos field, the home directory, and the default shell. In scalar context, only the user name is returned.	18	
getpwnam(USERNAME)	Returns user information for the specified user name. The list returned has nine items: the user name, the password (encrypted), the user number, the group number, the quota field, the comment field, the gcos field, the home directory, and the default shell. In scalar context, only the user number is returned.	18	
getpwuid(USERID)	Returns user information for the specified user number. The list returned has nine items: the user name, the password (encrypted), the user number, the group number, the quota field, the comment field, the gcos field, the home directory, and the default shell. In scalar context, only the user name is returned.	18	
getservbyname (SERVICENAME, PROTO)	Returns information about a service based on its name. In scalar context, the port number is returned. In list context, the items in the list returned are the service name, aliases for the name, port number, and protocol name.	21	
getservbyport (PORT, PROTO)	Returns information about a service based on its port number. In scalar context, the service name is returned. In list context, the items in the list returned are the service name, aliases for the name, port number, and protocol name.	21	

Name	*Brief Description*	*Chapter*	*New in Perl 5*
getservent	Returns information from the next record in the /etc/services file. In scalar context, the service name is returned. In list context, the items in the list returned are the service name, aliases for the name, port number, and protocol name.	21	
getsockname (SOCKET)	Returns the socket address of this end of a connection. The address returned is packed.	21	
getsockopt (SOCKET, LEVEL, OPTIONNAME)	Returns the socket option specified.	21	
glob(STRING)	Returns a list of files matching the argument, which may have wildcard characters.	13	New
gmtime(TIME)	Converts the given time into Greenwich Mean Time. In scalar context, this returns a string somewhat like Sat Nov 23 20:07:47 1996 (in Perl 5 only); in list context, the items are: second, minute, hour, day of month, month (January = 0, February = 1, . . .), year, weekday (Sunday = 0, Monday = 1, . . .), day of the year (January 1 = 0, January 2 = 1, . . .), and daylight standard time (true or false). With no argument, the function assumes the current time.	9	New
goto LABEL	Jumps to the named label. You can use an expression instead of a label name, and Perl will interpret that expression into a label name.	8	
grep(BLOCK, LIST)	Evaluates the block in Boolean context on each item of the list. In scalar context, it returns the number of times that the block evaluated true; in list context, it returns the list of items matched.	14	
grep(REGEXP, LIST)	Searches for the regular expression in each item of the list. In scalar context, returns the number of times that the regular expression was found; in list context, returns the list of items matched.	14	
hex(STRING)	Returns the number that is the interpretation of the string as hexadecimal digits.	6	

Name	Brief Description	Chapter	New in Perl 5
`if(TEST) { BLOCK1 }`	Executes the block if the test is true. The first block may be followed by `else { BLOCK2 }`. In this case, if the test is false, the second block is executed. The first block may also be followed by one or more instances of `elsif { BLOCKn }`, which acts the same as `else if`.	8	
`import(CLASSNAME)`	This class method exports the class name to the current module.	21	
`index(STRING, SUBSTRING, POSITION)`	Returns the position of the first occurrence substring in the string, or -1 if the substring isn't found. If the position is specified, Perl starts looking from that position instead of from the beginning of the string.	9	
`int(NUMBER)`	Returns the integer portion of the number.	6	
`ioctl(FILEHANDLE, FUNCTION, SCALAR)`	Executes Unix's `ioctl` function for performing low-level input and output.	21	
`join(SEPARATOR, LIST)`	Returns a string that consists of the items of the list with the separator between each item. The separator is not added to the beginning or end of the resulting string.	9	
`keys(ARRAY)`	Normally used to return a list of all the keys in the associative array. In scalar context, it returns the number of elements in the associative array.	16	
`kill(SIGNAL, LIST)`	Sends the signal to the list of processes IDs. The signal is either the signal number or the name of the signal, such as "HUP". The function returns the number of processes signaled.	21	
`last`	Exits the innermost loop that is executing. You can also give an argument of a label, in which case the Perl exits out to the loop with that label.	8	
`lc(STRING)`	Returns the string in all lowercase.	5	New
`lcfirst(STRING)`	Returns the string with the first character changed to lowercase.	5	New
`length(STRING)`	Returns the length of the string.	5	
`link(OLDFILE, NEWFILE)`	Creates a new file that has a hard link to the old file. Returns true if successful.	13	

Name	Brief Description	Chapter	New in Perl 5
`listen (SOCKET, MAXCONN)`	Causes the system to allow connections on the socket. The system queues up to the number of connections specified.	21	
`local(VARIABLES)`	Makes one or more variable local to the current block, subroutine, `eval` function, or file.	10	
`localtime(TIME)`	Converts the given time into the local time. In scalar context, this returns a string somewhat like `Sat Nov 23 20:07:47 1996` (in Perl 5 only); in list context, the items are: second, minute, hour, day of month, month (January = 0, February = 1, . . .), year, weekday (Sunday = 0, Monday = 1, . . .), day of the year (January 1 = 0, January 2 = 1, . . .), and daylight standard time (true or false). With no argument, the function assumes the current time.	9	
`log(NUMBER)`	Returns the natural logarithm (base e) of the number.	6	
`lstat(FILE)`	Returns information about the file. The argument can be either a file handle or a string with the file's name. If the file is a symbolic link, the information is about the file linked to, not the link itself. These items in the list are returned: device number of the filesystem, inode number, file permissions (number), number of hard links to the file, user number of file's owner, group number of the file's owner, device identifier for special files, size of file, last access time, last modify time, last inode change time, preferred block size, number of blocks allocated.	13	
`map { BLOCK } LIST`	Returns a list of the block evaluated in list context for each item in the list. During evaluation, `$_` is set to the list item being evaluated.	8	New
`map(EXPRESSION, LIST)`	Returns a list of the expression evaluated in list context for each item in the list. During evaluation, `$_` is set to the list item being evaluated.	8	New
`mkdir(DIRNAME, PERMISSION)`	Creates a directory with the specified permissions (in octal). Returns true if successful.	13	
`msgctl(ID, COMMAND, ARGUMENT)`	Sends a low-level message using Unix's `mesgctl` function.	21	

Name	Brief Description	Chapter	New in Perl 5
msgget(KEY, FLAGS)	Returns the message ID for System V IPC messages.	21	
msgrcv(ID, VARIABLE, SIZE, TYPE, FLAGS)	Receives a message with the message ID.	21	
msgsnd(ID, MESSAGE, FLAGS)	Sends a message with the message ID.	21	
my(VARIABLES)	Makes one or more variable local the current block, subroutine, eval function, or file.	10	
new(CLASSNAME)	Constructs a object from the class. You can also specify a list after the class name as arguments passed to the constructor.	21	
next	Causes the innermost loop to start again from the beginning of the loop. You can also include a label with the function, in which case Perl jumps to the beginning of the loop with that label.	8	
no MODULE	Removes semantics that were imported by the use function with the same module name.	19	New
oct(STRING)	Returns the number that is the string interpreted as an octal value.	6	
open(FILEHANDLE, NAME)	Opens the named file or command and associates it with the given file handle. The characters at the beginning of the name determine whether the file is opened for input, output, or appending. In the case of a command, the location of the vertical bar determines whether the file handle is for reading or writing. The function returns true if the file or command was opened successfully.	12	
opendir(DIRHANDLE, DIRNAME)	Opens the directory for reading and associates the directory handle with that directory.	13	
ord(STRING)	Returns the ASCII value of the first character of the string.	5	
pack(TEMPLATE, LIST)	Returns a string containing the items from the list put together using the template.	21	
package NAME	Declares that the rest of the innermost block, subroutine, eval function, or file belongs to the specified package name.	10	New
pipe(READHANDLE, WRITEHANDLE)	Opens a pair of pipes for use by other functions.	21	

Name	Brief Description	Chapter	New in Perl 5
pop(LISTNAME)	Shortens the list by removing the last item, and returns that item. If the list is empty, it returns the undefined value. Note that the argument must be the name of a list, not an actual list.	7	
pos(VARIABLE)	Returns the position in the variable where the last m//g associated with that variable left off.	14	
print(FILEHANDLE, LIST)	Sends the list to the file specified by the file handle and returns true if successful. Note that the argument is a list, not a scalar; thus, variables that are arguments to print are evaluated in list context. It is more common to see the print function without the parentheses.	12	
print(LIST)	Sends the list to the standard file output and returns true if successful. Note that the argument is a list, not a scalar; thus, variables that are arguments to print are evaluated in list context. It is more common to see the print function without the parentheses.	12	
printf(FILEHANDLE FORMAT, LIST)	Formats the list using the format string, and sends the resulting list to the file specified by the file handle and returns true if successful. Note that there is no comma after the file handle.	12	
printf (FORMAT, LIST)	Formats the list using the format string, sends the resulting list to the standard file output, and returns true if successful.	12	
push(LISTNAME, LIST)	Adds the items of the list in the second argument to the end of the list named in the first argument.	7	
q/STRING/	Returns the string with no interpretation of the string's contents. This is similar to using single quotes ("), except that you can choose the quoting character.	5	
qq/STRING/	Quotes the string, with interpretation of the string's contents. This is similar to using double quotes (""), except that you can choose the quoting character.	5	
quotemeta(STRING)	Returns the value of the argument with all regular expressions' metacharacters appropriately backslashed.	14	New

Name	Brief Description	Chapter	New in Perl 5
qw/STRING/	Returns the words in the string with no interpretation. This ignores differences in whitespace between the words.	14	New
qx/COMMAND/	Returns the output of running the command. This is like using the backtick character (") except that you can choose the quoting character.	18	New
rand(NUMBER)	Returns a random number between 0 and the specified number (including 0 but not including the specified number). If no argument is given, it returns a random number between 0 and 1. The seed used for the random number is set with the srand function.	9	
read(FILEHANDLE, VARIABLE, LENGTH, OFFSET)	Reads the number of bytes from the file into the scalar variable. The function starts writing into the variable at the given offset, which is optional. The function returns the actual number of bytes read; this may be less than the desired number if the function read off the end of the file or 0 if you are already at the end of the file.	13	
readdir(DIRHANDLE)	Reads the next entry from the directory. In scalar context, the function returns the next file name in the directory; in scalar context, the function returns the rest of the file names.	13	
readlink (FILENAME)	Returns the name of the file pointed to by the symbolic link in the file name given in the argument. If the named file is not a symbolic link or there is some other error, the function returns the undefined value.	13	
recv(SOCKET, VARIABLE, LENGTH, FLAGS)	Receives a message on the socket and puts it in the variable.	21	
redo	Restarts the innermost loop without reevaluating the conditional test for the loop. You can also give an argument of a label, which causes Perl to restart the loop with that label.	8	
ref(VARIABLE)	Returns true if the variable is a reference, otherwise returns the null string. The value returned is a string indicating the kind of reference.	21	

Name	Brief Description	Chapter	New in Perl 5
rename(FILENAME, NEWNAME)	Renames a file and returns true if successful. This will not work across filesystems on Unix systems.	13	
require(FILENAME)	Executes the named Perl program as long as that program has not already been executed.	10	
require(NUMBER)	Stops the program if the version number of Perl is less than the argument.	10	New
require (PACKAGENAME)	Loads the package like the use function, except that the package is loaded while the program is running, not when it is compiled.	21	New
reset	Resets variables and single-match searches performed with the ?? operator.	8	
reset(STRING)	Resets all variables whose name starts with the letter in the string. If the string is more than one character, it should be a range expressed with a hyphen, in which case all variables whose first letter starts with those letters are reset. You should not use this function.	8	
return(LIST)	Returns from a subroutine with the specified value. If the subroutine is in the scalar context, the first item in the list is returned; if the subroutine is in the list context, the whole list is returned.	10	
reverse(LIST)	Returns a list in the reverse order of the argument.	9	
rewinddir (DIRHANDLE)	Sets the position of the next readdir function to the beginning of the directory.	13	
rindex(STRING, SUBSTRING, POSITION)	Returns the position of the last occurrence of the substring in the string, or -1 if the substring isn't found. If the position is specified, Perl starts looking from that position instead of from the beginning of the string.	9	
rmdir (DIRECTORYNAME)	Removes the directory as long as the directory is empty.	13	
scalar(EXPRESSION)	Forces the argument to be evaluated in scalar context. This is useful if the expression might be a list and you don't want it to be evaluated in list context.	7	

Name	*Brief Description*	*Chapter*	*New in Perl 5*
`seek(FILEHANDLE, POSITION, RELATIVE`	Sets the position of the file pointer for the file. The value of the third argument specifies where the position is relative to: 0 means relative to the beginning of the file; 1 means relative to the current position; and 2 means relative to the end of the file. The function returns true if successful.	13	
`seekdir(DIRHANDLE, POSITION)`	Sets the position for the `readdir` function.	13	
`select(FILEHANDLE)`	Selects the file handle that will be used by the `print` and `write` functions if no file handle is specified in them. The function returns the file handle that was being used before the function was called. If you do not give an argument to the function, it simply returns the file handle being used.	12	
`select(READBITS, WRITEBITS, EXCEPTIONALBITS, TIMEOUT)`	Tells you which of your file descriptors are ready to do reads or writes, or are reporting an exceptional condition.	21	
`semctl(ID, SEMNUM, COMMAND, ARGUMENT)`	Controls semaphore messages on systems that support semaphores.	21	
`semget(KEY, NSEMS, FLAGS)`	Returns a semaphore ID on systems that support semaphores.	21	
`semop(KEY, OPSTRING)`	Performs semaphore operations on systems that support semaphores.	21	
`send(SOCKET, MESSAGE, FLAGS,TO)`	Sends a message to the socket.	21	
`setgrent`	Causes the next call to `getgrent` to start reading from the top of the /etc/groups file.	18	
`sethostent`	Causes the next call to `gethostent` to start reading from the top of the /etc/hosts file.	21	
`setnetent`	Causes the next call to `getnetent` to start reading from the top of the /etc/networks file.	21	
`setpgrp(PROCESSID, PROCESSGROUP)`	Sets the process group for the process specified in the first argument.	21	
`setpriority (PROCESSKIND, WHO, PRIORITY)`	Sets the priority for a process, a process group, or a user.	18	

Name	Brief Description	Chapter	New in Perl 5
setprotoent	Causes the next call to getprotoent to start reading from the top of the /etc/protocols file.	21	
setpwent	Causes the next call to getpwent to start reading from the top of the /etc/passwd file.	18	
setservent	Causes the next call to getservent to start reading from the top of the /etc/services file.	21	
setsockopt(SOCKET, LEVEL, OPTIONNAME, OPTIONVAL)	Sets an option on the socket.	21	
shift(LISTNAME)	Shortens the list by removing the first item, and returns that item. If the list is empty, it returns the undefined value. Note that the argument must be the name of a list, not an actual list.	7	
shmctl(ID, COMMAND, ARGUMENT)	Controls shared memory on systems that support shared memory.	21	
shmget(KEY, SIZE, FLAGS)	Returns the shared memory ID on systems that support shared memory.	21	
shmread(ID, VARIABLE, POSITION, SIZE)	Reads from shared memory on systems that support shared memory.	21	
shmwrite(ID, STRING, POSITION, SIZE)	Writes to shared memory on systems that support shared memory.	21	
shutdown (SOCKET, HOW)	Closes the socket.	21	
sin(NUMBER)	Returns the sine of the number, expressed in radians.	6	
sleep(NUMBER)	Causes the program to sleep for a specified number of seconds. If no argument is given, the program sleeps until it receives a SIGALRM signal from some other program. The function returns the actual number of seconds slept.	9	
socket(SOCKET, DOMAIN, TYPE, PROTOCOL)	Opens a socket and returns true if successful.	21	
socketpair (SOCKET1, SOCKET2, DOMAIN, TYPE, PROTOCOL)	Creates a pair of sockets and returns true if successful.	21	

Name	*Brief Description*	*Chapter*	*New in Perl 5*
sort { BLOCK } LIST	Returns a list of the items in the list argument sorted using the comparison specified in the block. The block compares two variables, $a and $b, and the comparison determines how sorting is done.	9	
sort(LIST)	Returns a list of the items in the argument sorted in ascending string order.	9	
sort SUBROUTINE-NAME LIST	Returns a list of the items in the list argument sorted using the comparison specified in the subroutine. The subroutine compares two variables, $a and $b, and the comparison determines how sorting is done.	9	
splice(LISTNAME, REMOVEOFFSET, REMOVENUMBER, ADDLIST)	Returns a list that is the named list with the specified number of items removed from the specified offset, with the list in the fourth argument added at this offset. Note that the first argument must be the name of a list, not an actual list.	7	
split(/PATTERN/, STRING, LIMIT)	Returns a list that is the string split apart where the pattern matches a substring of the full string. If a limit is specified, only that many items will be returned, with the last item being the remainder of the string after the first parts were split out; if no limit is specified, any number of items might be returned. In scalar context, the function only returns the number of items that would have been returned in list context. If the pattern contains parentheses, the delimiter matched in each set of parentheses is returned interspersed with the other list items.	14	
sprintf(FORMAT, LIST)	Formats the list using the format string and returns the resulting list.	12	
sqrt(NUMBER)	Returns the square root of the argument.	6	
srand(NUMBER)	Sets the seed value for the rand function to the number specified. If you do not specify an argument, Perl uses the time function as the argument.	9	
stat(FILE)	Returns information about the file. The argument can be either a file handle or a string with the file's name. If the file is a symbolic link, the information is about the link itself, not the file that is linked to. These items	13	

Name	Brief Description	Chapter	New in Perl 5
	in the list are returned: device number of the filesystem, inode number, file permissions (number), number of hard links to the file, user number of file's owner, group number of the file's owner, device identifier for special files, size of file, last access time, last modify time, last inode change time, preferred block size, number of blocks allocated.		
study(SCALAR)	Looks carefully at a string in order to speed up later searches on it.	21	
sub NAME { BLOCK }	Defines a subroutine. You also include a prototype for calling the subroutine between the name and the block. If you do not specify a block, Perl will note that the name exists when it is interpreting your program.	10	
substr(STRING, OFFSET, LENGTH)	Returns a string that is a substring of the first argument. The substring starts at the specified offset and is of the specified length, if possible. If the offset is negative, the offset is from the end of the string instead of from the beginning. If you do not specify a length, everything from the offset to the end of the string is returned. This function can also be used on the left side of an assignment, in which case the string must be a string name, and the contents of the string will change.	9	
symlink(OLDFILE, NEWFILE)	Creates a new file that has a symbolic link to the old file. Returns true if successful.	13	
syscall (CALLNAME, LIST)	Executes the specified system call, using the list as arguments.	21	
sysopen(FILEHANDLE, FILENAME, MODE)	Opens the file using low-level system calls.	21	
sysread(FILEHANDLE, VARIABLE, LENGTH, OFFSET)	Reads from the file using low-level system calls.	21	
system(COMMAND)	Runs the command and waits for it to finish. The function returns the exit status of the program multiplied by 256.	18	
syswrite(FILEHANDLE, VARIABLE, LENGTH, OFFSET)	Writes to the file using low-level system calls.	21	

Name	Brief Description	Chapter	New in Perl 5
tell(FILEHANDLE)	Returns the file position keeper of the specified file.	13	
telldir(DIRHANDLE)	Returns the directory position keeper of the file.	13	
tie(VARIABLE, PACKAGENAME, LIST)	Associates the variable with a particular package so that calls to the package are reflected in the variable.	21	New
tied(VARIABLE)	Returns a reference to the object that is tied to the variable.	21	New
time	Returns the current time, which is the number of nonleap seconds since the time specified as the "beginning of time" for the operating system.	9	
times	Returns a list of the amount of CPU seconds used. The items in the list are the number of seconds for user instructions for this process, system instructions for this process, user instructions for child processes, and system instructions for child processes.	21	
truncate(FILEHANDLE, LENGTH)	Shortens the file to the specified length.	13	
uc(STRING)	Returns the string in all uppercase.	5	New
ucfirst(STRING)	Returns the string with the first character changed to uppercase.	5	New
umask(MODE)	Sets the Unix umask value for the current process.	21	
undef(VARIABLE)	Undefines the value of the variable or sets the value of the variable to the undefined value.	21	
unless(TEST) { BLOCK1 }	Executes the block if the test is false. The first block may be followed by else { BLOCK2 }. In this case, if the test is true, the second block is executed. The first block may also be followed by one or more instances of elsif { BLOCKn }, which acts the same as else if.	8	
unlink(FILENAMES)	Deletes the files in the list and returns the number of files deleted.	13	
unpack(TEMPLATE, STRING)	Returns a list of items that is the string examined using the template.	21	
unshift(LISTNAME, LIST)	Adds the items of the list in the second argument to the beginning of the list named in the first argument.	7	

Name	Brief Description	Chapter	New in Perl 5
untie(VARIABLE)	Unbinds a variable from a package.	21	New
until(TEST) { BLOCK }	If the test returns false, Perl executes the block and redoes the test to determine whether or not to execute the block again.	8	
use MODULE	Imports semantics from the module into the current package. You can also specify a list of arguments for the module. Perl's pragmas are also implemented with this function.	19	New
utime(ACCESSTIME, MODTIME, FILENAMES)	Changes the access time and modification time on the named files. The function returns the number of files successfully changed.	13	
values(ARRAY)	Returns a list of the values in the associative array.	16	
vec(STRING, OFFSET, NUMBITS)	Returns the value of the element of the string that is the number of bits wide, starting at the specified offset.	21	
wait	Waits for a child process to terminate.	21	
waitpid(PID, FLAGS)	Waits for the specified child process to terminate and returns true when the process is dead.	21	
wantarray	Returns true if the current subroutine is looking for a list value or false if it is looking for a scalar.	21	
warn(LIST)	Sends the list to the standard error output.	10	
while(TEST) { BLOCK }	If the test returns true, Perl executes the block and redoes the test to determine whether or not to execute the block again.	8	
write(FILEHANDLE)	Writes text formatted with the format function to the specified file.	21	

Operators, Functions, and Statements, Listed by Chapter

Because the chapters of this book are grouped by topic, this chart should help you see the relationships between various operators, functions, and statements.

Chapter	Perl Feature
5	.
5	chomp(STRINGVAR)
5	chop(STRINGVAR)
5	chr(NUMBER)
5	lc(STRING)
5	lcfirst(STRING)
5	length(STRING)
5	ord(STRING)
5	q/STRING/
5	qq/STRING/
5	uc(STRING)
5	ucfirst(STRING)
5	x
6	++
6	**
6	-
6	*
6	+
6	=
6	--
6	/
6	%
6	-
6	+
6	abs(NUMBER)
6	atan2(Y, X)
6	cos(NUMBER)
6	+= -= *= etc.
6	exp(NUMBER)
6	hex(STRING)
6	int(NUMBER)
6	log(NUMBER)

Chapter	Perl Feature
6	oct(STRING)
6	sin(NUMBER)
6	sqrt(NUMBER)
7	,
7	..
7	pop(LISTNAME)
7	push(LISTNAME, LIST)
7	scalar(EXPRESSION)
7	shift(LISTNAME)
7	splice(LISTNAME, REMOVEOFFSET, REMOVENUMBER, ADDLIST)
7	unshift(LISTNAME, LIST)
8	< > <= >= == != <=>
8	?:
8	and
8	continue { BLOCK }
8	eq ne cmp lt gt le ge
8	for (INITEXPR; TESTEXPR; ENDEXPR) { BLOCK }
8	foreach VARIABLE (LIST) { BLOCK }
8	goto LABEL
8	if(TEST) { BLOCK1 }
8	last
8	map { BLOCK } LIST
8	map(EXPRESSION, LIST)
8	next
8	not
8	or
8	redo
8	reset
8	reset(STRING)
8	unless(TEST) { BLOCK1 }
8	until(TEST) { BLOCK }

Chapter	Perl Feature
8	while(TEST) { BLOCK }
8	xor
9	<< >>
9	~
9	&
9	|
9	^
9	defined(VARIABLE)
9	gmtime(TIME)
9	index(STRING, SUBSTRING, POSITION)
9	join(SEPARATOR, LIST)
9	localtime(TIME)
9	rand(NUMBER)
9	reverse(LIST)
9	rindex(STRING, SUBSTRING, POSITION)
9	sleep(NUMBER)
9	sort { BLOCK } LIST
9	sort(LIST)
9	sort SUBROUTINENAME LIST
9	srand(NUMBER)
9	substr(STRING, OFFSET, LENGTH)
9	time
10	caller(NUMBEROFSTACKS)
10	die(TEXT)
10	eval(EXPRESSION)
10	exit(NUMBER)
10	local(VARIABLES)
10	my(VARIABLES)
10	package NAME
10	require(FILENAME)
10	require(NUMBER)
10	return(LIST)

Chapter	Perl Feature
10	sub NAME { BLOCK }
10	warn(LIST)
12	< >
12	chdir(DIRNAME)
12	close(FILEHANDLE)
12	File tests: -X FILENAME
12	open(FILEHANDLE, NAME)
12	print(FILEHANDLE, LIST)
12	print(LIST)
12	printf(FILEHANDLE FORMAT, LIST)
12	printf(FORMAT, LIST)
12	select(FILEHANDLE)
12	sprintf(FORMAT, LIST)
13	binmode(FILEHANDLE)
13	chmod(NUMMODE, LISTOFFILES)
13	chown(USERID, GROUPID, LISTOFFILES)
13	closedir(DIRHANDLE)
13	eof(FILEHANDLE)
13	getc(FILEHANDLE)
13	glob(STRING)
13	link(OLDFILE, NEWFILE)
13	lstat(FILE)
13	mkdir(DIRNAME, PERMISSION)
13	opendir(DIRHANDLE, DIRNAME)
13	read(FILEHANDLE, VARIABLE, LENGTH, OFFSET)
13	readdir(DIRHANDLE)
13	readlink(FILENAME)
13	rename(FILENAME, NEWNAME)
13	rewinddir(DIRHANDLE)
13	rmdir(DIRECTORYNAME)
13	seek(FILEHANDLE, POSITION, RELATIVE)
13	seekdir(DIRHANDLE, POSITION)

Chapter	Perl Feature
13	stat(FILE)
13	symlink(OLDFILE, NEWFILE)
13	tell(FILEHANDLE)
13	telldir(DIRHANDLE)
13	truncate(FILEHANDLE, LENGTH)
13	unlink(FILENAMES)
13	utime(ACCESSTIME, MODTIME, FILENAMES)
14	=~ !~
14	grep(BLOCK, LIST)
14	grep(REGEXP, LIST)
14	m/PATTERN/MODIFIERS
14	pos(VARIABLE)
14	quotemeta(STRING)
14	qw/STRING/
14	s/PATTERN/REPLACEMENT/MODIFIERS
14	split(/PATTERN/, STRING, LIMIT)
14	tr/FROMRANGE/TORANGE/
16	=>
16	delete($ARRAY{KEY})
16	each(ARRAY)
16	exists($ARRAY{$KEY})
16	keys(ARRAY)
16	values(ARRAY)
17	dbmclose(ARRAY)
17	dbmopen(ARRAY, FILENAME, MODE)
18	` (Backtick)
18	chroot(DIRECTORY)
18	endgrent
18	endpwent
18	exec(PROGRAM)
18	getgrent
18	getgrgid(GROUPID)

Chapter	Perl Feature
18	getgrnam(GROUPNAME)
18	getlogin
18	getpgrp(PROCESSID)
18	getppid
18	getpriority(PROCESSKIND, WHO)
18	getpwent
18	getpwnam(USERNAME)
18	getpwuid(USERID)
18	qx/COMMAND/
18	setgrent
18	setpriority(PROCESSKIND, WHO, PRIORITY)
18	setpwent
18	system(COMMAND)
19	->
19	no MODULE
19	use MODULE
21	\
21	accept(NEWSOCKETHANDLE, GENERICSOCKETHANDLE)
21	alarm(TIME)
21	bind(SOCKET, NAME)
21	bless(REFERENCE, PACKAGE)
21	connect(SOCKET, NETADDRESS)
21	crypt(PLAINTEXT, SALT)
21	do { BLOCK }
21	do(FILENAME)
21	dump
21	endhostent
21	endnetent
21	endprotoent
21	endservent
21	fcntl(FILEHANDLE, FUNCTION, SCALAR)

Chapter	Perl Feature
21	fileno(FILEHANDLE)
21	flock(FILEHANDLE, OPERATION)
21	fork
21	format NAME= FORMATLIST
21	formline(PICTURE, LIST)
21	gethostbyaddr(PACKEDADDR, ADDRTYPE)
21	gethostbyname(DOMAINNAME)
21	gethostent
21	getnetbyaddr(PACKEDADDR, ADDRTYPE)
21	getnetbyname(DOMAINNAME)
21	getnetent
21	getpeername(SOCKET)
21	getprotobyname(PROTONAME)
21	getprotobynumber(PROTONUMBER)
21	getprotoent
21	getservbyname(SERVICENAME, PROTO)
21	getservbyport(PORT, PROTO)
21	getservent
21	getsockname(SOCKET)
21	getsockopt(SOCKET, LEVEL, OPTIONNAME)
21	import(CLASSNAME)
21	ioctl(FILEHANDLE, FUNCTION, SCALAR)
21	kill(SIGNAL, LIST)
21	listen(SOCKET, MAXCONN)
21	msgctl(ID, COMMAND, ARGUMENT)
21	msgget(KEY, FLAGS)
21	msgrcv(ID, VARIABLE, SIZE, TYPE, FLAGS)
21	msgsnd(ID, MESSAGE, FLAGS)
21	new(CLASSNAME)
21	pack(TEMPLATE, LIST)
21	pipe(READHANDLE, WRITEHANDLE)
21	recv(SOCKET, VARIABLE, LENGTH, FLAGS)

Chapter	Perl Feature
21	ref(VARIABLE)
21	require(PACKAGENAME)
21	select(READBITS, WRITEBITS, EXCEPTIONALBITS, TIMEOUT)
21	semctl(ID, SEMNUM, COMMAND, ARGUMENT)
21	semget(KEY, NSEMS, FLAGS)
21	semop(KEY, OPSTRING)
21	send(SOCKET, MESSAGE, FLAGS, TO)
21	sethostent
21	setnetent
21	setpgrp(PROCESSID, PROCESSGROUP)
21	setprotoent
21	setservent
21	setsockopt(SOCKET, LEVEL, OPTIONNAME, OPTIONVAL)
21	shmctl(ID, COMMAND, ARGUMENT)
21	shmget(KEY, SIZE, FLAGS)
21	shmread(ID, VARIABLE, POSITION, SIZE)
21	shmwrite(ID, STRING, POSITION, SIZE)
21	shutdown(SOCKET, HOW)
21	socket(SOCKET, DOMAIN, TYPE, PROTOCOL)
21	socketpair(SOCKET1, SOCKET2, DOMAIN, TYPE, PROTOCOL)
21	study(SCALAR)
21	syscall(CALLNAME, LIST)
21	sysopen(FILEHANDLE, FILENAME, MODE)
21	sysread(FILEHANDLE, VARIABLE, LENGTH, OFFSET)
21	syswrite(FILEHANDLE, VARIABLE, LENGTH, OFFSET)
21	tie(VARIABLE, PACKAGENAME, LIST)
21	tied(VARIABLE)
21	times
21	umask(MODE)
21	undef(VARIABLE)

Chapter	Perl Feature
21	unpack(TEMPLATE, STRING)
21	untie(VARIABLE)
21	vec(STRING, OFFSET, NUMBITS)
21	wait
21	waitpid(PID, FLAGS)
21	wantarray
21	write(FILEHANDLE)

Perl's Special Variables

This section gives brief descriptions of Perl's special variables. Because most of these aren't covered in the book, don't be surprised if the descriptions don't make much sense. Only a few of the special variables are useful for novice and intermediate Perl programmers.

General-purpose variables

This is a catch-all category, but some of the variables are quite useful.

Variable	Description
$_	The default input to many functions and operations. Most useful with while(<FILEHANDLE>).
$/	The input record separator. The default depends on the operating system.
$[	Index of the first element in a list. This is normally 0 (and you really shouldn't change it), but some people insist that the first item of a list is numbered "1."
$|	Forces automatic flushing to the selected file handle if set to true. If false (the default), output to the selected file handle will only be done when the operating system feels like it or when the file is closed.
$]	Version of Perl.
$0	The name of the file containing the Perl program being run.
$^T	Time at which this program started running.
$.	The input line number of the last file handle read.

Variable	Description
$ARGV	Name of the current file, when using <ARGV>.
@ARGV	Command-line arguments for the program.
@INC	List of directories in which Perl will look for programs named in do, require, and use.
%INC	The files that have already been used by do and require. The keys are the filename specified, and the values are the full path to the found file.
%ENV	Operating system environment variables.

Variables that relate to errors and return values

Variable	Description
$!	The current system error number or string.
$?	Status returned by the last system function, " (backtick) command, or pipe. This value is actually 256 times the number returned from the process.
$@	Error message returned by the last eval function.

Special variables for regular expressions

These special variables let you see what was and wasn't found in a regular expression.

Variable	Description
$&	The text matched by the last successful pattern match in a regular expression.
$'	The text preceding the last successful pattern match in a regular expression.
$'	The text following the last successful pattern match in a regular expression.
$+	The text that matched the last successful bracketed pattern in the regular expression.
$digit	The text matched by the set of parentheses in a regular expression. The digit corresponds to the number of the matched set.

Variables that relate to processes

These variables let you look at information that is specific to the process, such as the process number.

Variable	Description
$$	The Perl program's process number.
$<	The real userid of this process.
$>	The effective userid of this process.
$(	The real groupid of this process.
$)	The effective groupid of this process.

Variables for formats

These special variables pertain to formats, which are covered only briefly in Chapter 21.

Variable	Description
$%	Current page number.
$-	Number of lines left on the current page.
$=	Page length.
$~	Name of the report format.
$^	Name of the top-of-page format.
^L	Text that a format puts out when doing a formfeed.
$:	Text after which a string may be broken for format continuation fields.
$^A	Contents of the accumulator of format lines.

Obscure variables

This is a hodgepodge of Perl special variables that don't fit into any other categories.

Variable	Description
$,	Output field separator, which is printed between each item in the list that is output by print.
$\	Output record separator, which is printed at the end of the list that is output by print.

Variable	Description
$"	List separator, which is put between each item in a list if that list is interpreted in double-quotes, such as "@a".
$;	Separator that is put between subscripts of multidimensional arrays.
$^D	Debugging flags.
$^F	Maximum system file descriptor.
$^H	Internal compiler hints.
$^I	In-place edit extension.
$^O	Name of the operating system that Perl was compiled for.
$^P	Internal flag for the debugger.
$^W	Value of the warning switch.
$^X	Name that the Perl binary was compiled as.
@F	Holds the results of the -a command-line option.
%SIG	Signal handlers.

Perl's Special File Handles

The following file handles are predefined by Perl.

File Handle	Description
ARGV	Iterates over the filenames in @ARGV.
STDERR	Standard error output.
STDIN	Standard file input.
STDOUT	Standard file output.
DATA	Anything that follows a token __DATA__ in your program.
_	Cache for the stat and lstat functions, and the file test operators.

Index

• *G* •

word count, 54
WordPad, 33
World Wide Web
  getting documents from,
      243–244
  Perl and, 167
  See also Web sites
write function, 298

• X •

x modifier, 229, 230
x operator, 107
xor operator, 116–117
  defined, 116
  results of, 117

• Y •

y/// operator, 237

IDG BOOKS WORLDWIDE, INC.

END-USER LICENSE AGREEMENT

Read This. **You should carefully read these terms and conditions before opening the software packet(s) included with this book ("Book"). This is a license agreement ("Agreement") between you and IDG Books Worldwide, Inc. ("IDGB"). By opening the accompanying software packet(s), you acknowledge that you have read and accept the following terms and conditions. If you do not agree and do not want to be bound by such terms and conditions, promptly return the Book and the unopened software packet(s) to the place you obtained them for a full refund.**

1. **License Grant.** IDGB grants to you (either an individual or entity) a nonexclusive license to use one copy of the enclosed software program(s) (collectively, the "Software") solely for your own personal or business purposes on a single computer (whether a standard computer or a workstation component of a multiuser network). The Software is in use on a computer when it is loaded into temporary memory (i.e., RAM) or installed into permanent memory (e.g., hard disk, CD-ROM, or other storage device). IDGB reserves all rights not expressly granted herein.

2. **Ownership.** IDGB is the owner of all right, title, and interest, including copyright, in and to the compilation of the Software recorded on the disk(s)/CD-ROM. Copyright to the individual programs on the disk(s)/ CD-ROM is owned by the author or other authorized copyright owner of each program. Ownership of the Software and all proprietary rights relating thereto remain with IDGB and its licensors.

3. **Restrictions on Use and Transfer.**

   (a) You may only (i) make one copy of the Software for backup or archival purposes, or (ii) transfer the Software to a single hard disk, provided that you keep the original for backup or archival purposes. You may not (i) rent or lease the Software, (ii) copy or reproduce the Software through a LAN or other network system or through any computer subscriber system or bulletin-board system, or (iii) modify, adapt, or create derivative works based on the Software.

   (b) You may not reverse engineer, decompile, or disassemble the Software. You may transfer the Software and user documentation on a permanent basis, provided that the transferee agrees to accept the terms and conditions of this Agreement and you retain no copies. If the Software is an update or has been updated, any transfer must include the most recent update and all prior versions.

4. <u>Restrictions on Use of Individual Programs</u>. You must follow the individual requirements and restrictions detailed for each individual program in Appendix A of this Book. These limitations are contained in the individual license agreements recorded on the disk(s)/CD-ROM. These restrictions may include a requirement that after using the program for the period of time specified in its text, the user must pay a registration fee or discontinue use. By opening the Software packet(s), you will be agreeing to abide by the licenses and restrictions for these individual programs. None of the material on this disk(s) or listed in this Book may ever be distributed, in original or modified form, for commercial purposes.

5. <u>Limited Warranty</u>.

(a) IDGB warrants that the Software and disk(s)/CD-ROM are free from defects in materials and workmanship under normal use for a period of sixty (60) days from the date of purchase of this Book. If IDGB receives notification within the warranty period of defects in materials or workmanship, IDGB will replace the defective disk(s)/CD-ROM.

(b) IDGB AND THE AUTHOR OF THE BOOK DISCLAIM ALL OTHER WARRANTIES, EXPRESS OR IMPLIED, INCLUDING WITHOUT LIMITATION IMPLIED WARRANTIES OF MERCHANTABILITY AND FITNESS FOR A PARTICULAR PURPOSE, WITH RESPECT TO THE SOFTWARE, THE PROGRAMS, THE SOURCE CODE CONTAINED THEREIN, AND/OR THE TECHNIQUES DESCRIBED IN THIS BOOK. IDGB DOES NOT WARRANT THAT THE FUNC-TIONS CONTAINED IN THE SOFTWARE WILL MEET YOUR REQUIREMENTS OR THAT THE OPERATION OF THE SOFTWARE WILL BE ERROR FREE.

(c) This limited warranty gives you specific legal rights, and you may have other rights which vary from jurisdiction to jurisdiction.

6. <u>Remedies</u>.

(a) IDGB's entire liability and your exclusive remedy for defects in materials and workmanship shall be limited to replacement of the Software, which may be returned to IDGB with a copy of your receipt at the following address: Disk Fulfillment Department, Attn: Perl 5 For Dummies, IDG Books Worldwide, Inc., 7260 Shadeland Station, Ste. 100, Indianapolis, IN 46256, or call 1-800-762-2974. Please allow 3–4 weeks for delivery. This Limited Warranty is void if failure of the Software has resulted from accident, abuse, or misapplication. Any replacement Software will be warranted for the remainder of the original warranty period or thirty (30) days, whichever is longer.